THE DOORS

When the Music's Over

THE STORIES BEHIND EVERY SONG

THIS IS A CARLTON BOOK

Published in the United States by
THUNDER'S MOUTH PRESS
841 Broadway, Forth Floor, New York, NY 10003

ISBN 1 56025 266 9

Library of Congress Catalog Card Number: 99-69542

Distributed by Publishers Group West, 1700 Fourth Street,
Berkeley, CA 94710

Printed and bound in Dubai

Executive Editor: Lorraine Dickey
Art Direction: Rob Fairclough
Design: Carol Wright, Sallie Collin
Project Editors: Nigel Matheson, Lol Henderson
Picture Research: Charlotte Bush
Production: Garry Lewis

10 9 8 7 6 5 4 3 2 1

THE DOORS

When the Music's Over

THE STORIES BEHIND EVERY SONG

Chuck Crisafulli

Consultant Editor Dave DiMartino

Contents

7 paul rothchild remembered

8 preface

10 introduction

22 the doors
soul kitchen; break on through; the crystal ship; twentieth century fox; light my fire; i looked at you; end of the night; take it as it comes; the end

40 strange days
strange days; you're lost little girl; love me two times; unhappy girl; horse latitudes; moonlight drive; people are strange; my eyes have seen you; i can't see your face; when the music's over

58 waiting for the sun
hello, i love you; love street; not to touch the earth; summer's almost gone; wintertime love; the unknown soldier; spanish caravan; my wild love; we could be so good together; yes, the river knows; five to one

74 the soft parade
tell the people; touch me; shaman's blues; do it; easy ride; wild child; runnin' blue; wishful sinful; the soft parade

90 morrison hotel
roadhouse blues; waiting for the sun; you make me real; peace frog; blue sunday; ship of fools; land ho!; the spy; queen of the highway; indian summer; maggie m'gill

110 absolutely live
love hides; build me a woman; universal mind; break on through 2; the celebration of the lizard

120 l.a. woman
the changeling; love her madly; been down so long; cars hiss by my window; l.a.woman; l'america; hyacinth house; the wasp (texas radio & the big beat); riders on the storm

138 other voices
in the eye of the sun; variety is the spice of love; ships w/sails; tightrope ride; down on the farm; i'm horny i'm stoned; wandering musician; hang on to your life

146 full circle
get up and dance; 4 billion souls; verdilac; hardwood floor; the mosquito; the piano bird; it slipped my mind; the peking king and new york queen

154 an american prayer
awake ('ghost song', 'dawn's highway', 'newborn awakening'); to come of age ('black polished chrome/latino chrome', 'angels and sailors', 'stoned immaculate'); the poet's dreams ('the movie', 'curses, invocations'); world on fire ('american night', 'roadhouse blues', 'lament', 'the hitchhiker'); an american prayer

170 chronology

172 discography

174 index

DEDICATION

For Kyra, who will always light my fire.

ACKNOWLEDGEMENTS

The author gratefully acknowledges the following persons, who granted interviews specifically for this book: Linda Albertano, Arthur Barrow, Paul Body, Rodney Bingenheimer, Chris Darrow, Henry Diltz, Len Fagan, Michael C. Ford, Kim Fowley, Bruce Gary, Jimmy Greenspoon, Heather Harris, Billy James, Harvey Kubernick, John Lodge, Patricia Kennealy Morrison, Michael Nesmith, Judy Raphael, Bill Siddons, Lewis Shiner, Dallas Taylor.

For their aid and assistance, the author thanks the following persons: Joel Amsterdam of Elektra Records, Len Fagan, Art Fein, Robert Hilburn, Bill Holdship, Steve Hochman, Bobby Klein, Harvey Kubernick, Elliot Mintz, Dr. Frank Thompson.

The author also respectfully acknowledges the following writers and journalists, whose works proved to be an invaluable inspiration and reference: John Carpenter, Bob Chorush, John Densmore, Ben Fong-Torres, Pete Fornatale Wallace Fowlie, Richard Goldstein, Jerry Hopkins, Blair Jackson, Lizze James, Paul Laurence, Frank Lisciandro, Robert Matheu, Patricia Kennealy Morrison, Jerry Prochnicky, James Riordan, Salli Stevenson, Danny Sugerman, John Tobler, Paul Williams.

And finally, thanks to Ray, Robby, John and Jim for taking us all on a moonlight drive.

paul rothchild remembered

Doors producer Paul Rothchild died at his beloved Los Angeles home on 30 March 1995, after a five-year battle with lung cancer. He was 59 years old. It is almost impossible to overstate the significance of Rothchild's contributions to the music of the Doors. He was the sure-handed pilot who steered the group in their attempts to break on through and, with as explosive a talent as Jim Morrison in the studio, Rothchild's calming presence and keen intuition were indispensable in the creation of their music. His piercing intelligence, fervent musicianship, irreverent sense of humour and impeccable studio-craft were essential elements of the Doors' sound and without Rothchild's talents the music created on the Doors' albums, from their debut through to *Morrison Hotel,* would not have been possible.

Rothchild will probably be best remembered for his part in the Doors' history – he was often referred to as "the fifth Door" – but in his long and fruitful career he consistently drew stunning music from a wide variety of artists. As director of recording for Jac Holzman's budding Elektra Records in the early Sixties, Rothchild produced great folk artists such as Phil Ochs, Tim Buckley, Tom Rush and Fred Neil. As Rothchild guided the label towards more electric sounds in the mid-Sixties, he worked with such acts as the Paul Butterfield Blues Band and Love. He helped bring Crosby, Stills & Nash together, produced Janis Joplin's finest songs and later worked with the Everly Brothers, the Outlaws and Bonnie Raitt.

At the end of Rothchild's life, when it became clear that death was imminent, he and his trusted, long-time friend Bobby Klein began to make preparations for a memorial service that would bring Rothchild's closest friends and associates together after he passed on. Ever the producer, Rothchild planned out every detail of his own service, from the photographs that would be displayed to the incense that would be burned and the music that would be played by a string quartet.

On 8 April, a beautiful spring day in Los Angeles, the service that Klein and Rothchild planned was held at his home on Lookout Mountain Drive. In addition to the producer's family, Ray Manzarek, John Densmore and Robby Krieger were all in attendance, as were Graham Nash, Dallas Taylor, Bruce Gary, Billy James, Henry Diltz, Mark James, Bobby Neuwirth and many others who'd known and worked with Rothchild over the years.

Bobby Klein and Paul's son Dan, a producer in his own right, both spoke beautifully about their relationships with Rothchild as friend and father, respectively. When guests were encouraged to remember Rothchild with a few thoughts or stories, John Densmore rose and said he had a feeling that Paul was already working on getting Jim and Janis to sing some duets. He also pointed out that, while he often thought he hated Paul at take 99 in the studio, by take 102 he'd always realize that the producer had pulled great music out of him that he hadn't thought he was capable of. Ray Manzarek then stood up and explained that he couldn't imagine a smarter producer than Paul Rothchild or one who was more of a pleasure to work with. Finally, Robby Krieger told the group that Paul Rothchild's lust for life had balanced Jim Morrison's lust for death and, for the Doors, being in between the two was an amazing place to be.

Paul Rothchild's love of music and the depth of his talents were probably best captured in an anecdote that Bobby Klein told at the end of the service. He explained that when Rothchild finally admitted to himself and to his friends that his final hours were nearing, Klein asked him who he would most like to hang out with when he "crossed over to the other side". Without hesitation, the producer who had brought the world so much great rock'n'roll smiled and said, "Mozart, man, Mozart!"

preface

It dawned on me sometime in the mid-Eighties that the Doors aren't ever going to fade away.

That seems obvious now, 10 years later, after director Oliver Stone has seen fit to snuggle Jim Morrison between John F. Kennedy and the Vietnam War in his filmed version of 1960s America. It's even more obvious after the recent announcement of the inevitable Doors CD boxed set — much-anticipated and slated to arrive in stores nearly 30 full years after 'Break On Through' signalled what was to come and apparently never leave. And obvious, finally, via the continuous barrage of new Doors-related product — books, videos, and soon CD-ROMS — aiming to quench an insatiable consumer thirst.

Pop writers and film directors alike can and do oversimplify matters too complex to digest in one sitting: another name for that is "earning a living". As painful as it may be to mention, therefore, let it be said again: the Doors were much more than a rock'n'roll band. That they have come to represent sixties popular culture in the States is evidenced not only in Stone's biopic, but in the soundtracks of film masterworks such as Francis Ford Coppola's *Apocalypse Now* and Robert Zemeckis' *Forrest Gump*. The sonic shorthand their music now carries is an indelible stamp of time - the turbulent Sixties - and of place - America, specifically Los Angeles.

To anyone my own age — I'm 41 as I write this — the Doors were very much the right band at the right time. All you need is love? Tell that to the 14-year-old boy whose first encounter with Oedipus came in 1967, courtesy of Jim Morrison and his sublimely mystic walk down the hall in 'The End'. I remain astounded that my very first favorite band in the world continues to mean anything to anyone three decades later.

Chuck Crisafulli's well-researched account of the Doors' many songs is, by design, episodic; so too are our own lives. One of the embarrassing side effects of spending your professional life writing about pop music is that your audience naturally gets younger as you yourself get older. Among my adolescent friends I was not alone in enjoying the Doors' first album in 1967, but I'm probably one of the very few still called upon to think about it, in print, every three years or so.

Perhaps the reason I still write about pop music is that, as fate would have it, I spent my adolescent years in Miami, Florida, and I spent one very memorable night in 1969 in the audience at Dinner Key Auditorium. There I see the Doors for the very first time; there I would see Jim Morrison expose himself in more ways than one on-stage; and there I see how the power of one man - and the power of rock music - could very nearly start a riot. Experienced first hand, it was a powerful perception, Aldous Huxley reference duly noted.

The night I first saw Sam Peckinpah's classic cinematic bloodbath *The Wild Bunch* was yet another memorable episode: It came two years later and, on the way home, the film's gut-level violence still riding in the car with us, the radio announced that Jim Morrison had died, mysteriously, in Paris. College would come soon after, and some of us in that car would see what was left of the Doors in Philadelphia, on their brief tour without Jim Morrison. It was sad, it was pitiable, it was a life lesson for any college freshman, myself included - and it was, I thought, the last many of us would think much of anything about the Doors. Wrong. Within a year, in a small club in East Lansing, Michigan, I saw Iggy Pop and his Stooges for the first time. I was a writer, I was astonished by what I had seen - and backstage with the man, all I could think to ask was if he had ever seen Jim Morrison perform live. "Sure," he told me, 21 years ago. "*Why?*"

The Doors were gone, but they weren't. In 1978, I would recount my recollections of the Miami concert in a review of the newly-released *American Prayer* album; hearing Jim Morrison's voice again - for the first time, in many ways - brought back memories I'd thought were long gone. By 1981, mine wasn't the only memory stirred. Here in the States, the music of the Doors enjoyed a stunning resurgence of popularity; at *Creem* magazine, where I worked, we put together a "special ten year commemorative issue" which bore the admittedly cheesy headline "The Legend Lives On!" but sold like wildfire.

Had I been asked then whether the Doors would matter nearly 15 years later, I might have said no. Wrong again. There would be the Oliver Stone movie, the numerous newly-discovered concert videos - and that night in 1993, when the Doors were inducted into the Rock 'N' Roll Hall of Fame. Jim Morrison was long gone, but on-stage singing 'Roadhouse Blues', 'Break On Through', and 'Light My Fire' with the surviving trio was no less a contemporary figure than Pearl Jam's Eddie Vedder - a testimony to the timelessness and relevance of the Doors' remarkable music.

View life as a series of fragmented episodes and you'll construct your own meaning wherever you find it. Last year I drove past my old neighborhood in Hollywood and saw a fleet of firetrucks. My former house was burning. Firemen were aiming gushing hoses of water at it. And my car radio was playing 'Light My Fire' at that very moment.

Looking over Chuck Crisafulli's faithful account of the Doors' many wonderful songs, I am listening to a new CD I received in the mail today from Elektra Records. It is a newly-revamped edition of Jim Morrison's *An American Prayer* and it boasts three bonus tracks. I have a wife and two small children now, and I look forward more often than I look backward. But American Prayer is playing and I am sitting in Dinner Key Auditorium waiting to watch a man scream "WAKE UP!" at the top of his lungs. The Doors won't go away, but we will. To me, the older I get, the more OK that sounds.

Dave DiMartino • Los Angeles 1995

introduction

introduction

Local sensations – it
didn't take long for
the Doors to become
worldwide rock'n'roll
stars, but their sound,
look and message
was very much a
local export of
Southern California –
specifically Venice,
where the feast
of friends first
took place.

The music isn't over. Almost 25 years since the death of Jim Morrison and the subsequent demise of the Doors, the music the band created is still vital, powerful and, ultimately, disturbing.

For some 30 years, the band has been loved and hated, and Jim Morrison in particular has been mythologized as well as mocked – but the enduring fact of the matter is that the music of the Doors continues to be heard: the time to "turn out the light" hasn't yet arrived.

In fact, the songs of the Doors have become familiar without fading – showing up now and again like recurring scenes from an old, enjoyably frightening nightmare. It's still hard to imagine a better song to blast while pushing the speed limit than 'LA Woman'. And listeners are still getting chills from the killer on the road in 'Riders On The Storm' and that walk down the hall in 'The End'. Doors music continues to capture the chaos that's out there: people remain strange and there's still blood on the streets.

Even 'Light My Fire', that hit heard a thousand times, will still occasionally catch listeners by surprise and, with its blend of pop-smarts and baroque grandeur, leave them mystified once more.

While the work of most bands from the mid-Sixties has either been dismissed, forgotten or wrapped in the comforting swaddle of nostalgia and consigned to "classic rock" radio formats, Doors music is still starting arguments: was Morrison shaman or charlatan/rock visionary or class clown?; what's with the "Lizard King" thing?; and what's so important about the Doors anyway?

The merits and demerits of Mr Morrison can be debated endlessly – but it's a warming thought that Jim would probably have liked it that way. For, in his brief life and meteoric career, Morrison was capable of, and accomplished at, almost all of the things he is customarily applauded for and/or accused of.

Firstly, he was indeed capable of producing a certain kind of magic: we at least have the records and the film footage to bear witness to that. And the gifts Jim Morrison put to use with the Doors were honest ones. At the same time, he also loved a put-on and, with a perfectly straight face, enjoyed feeding wide-eyed members of the press with the oft-quoted declaration that the Doors were "erotic politicians", only to shrug that phrase off later as he explained that he thought his greatest talent lay in his ability to manipulate the media.

Morrison as visionary? While fronting the Doors, Jim saw rock'n'roll as a medium well suited for conveying nightmares and rock'n'roll has been dancing with demons ever since. For better or worse, rock'n'rollers of every conceivable sub-genre have been copying Jim's facial expressions, his moves, voice, attitude and even trousers, ever since he let it all rip at the Whisky A Go Go.

Jim saw where the music could go, did what came naturally – what came unnaturally too – and unwittingly became rock-'n'roll's most arousing archetype.

It doesn't hurt to point out that the iconic side of Jim Morrison has often been taken a little too seriously: a lot of the time he was just playing the fool. For all the riveting command he exerted over his audiences, he'd also engage them with a gentle sense of playfulness and moments of conspiratorial humour could pop up during the most solemn sections of Doors sets.

And while there aren't any jokes *per se* in the album versions of Doors songs, in Morrison's words there is laughter that can be shared. Dark laughter to be sure, but laughter nonetheless. Listen again to 'People Are Strange', 'The Soft Parade' and 'Maggie M'Gill'.

But what was Morrison really like? The Lizard King, that creation of his, an oddly triumphant monster who rises to address an audience at the end of an epic tale, was only a fragment of his complex personality. It has always been tempting to consider that those lines at the end of 'The Celebration Of The Lizard' represented the deepest of confessions on Morrison's part, an indication of his true identity and his purpose before us.

The truth is that the Lizard King is just as fanciful as the "Twentieth Century Fox" or the "Back Door Man". Reptilian *mythos* notwithstanding, Morrison proved all too human. Flawed, frayed and ultimately forlorn enough to drink himself out of the public's good graces and, with one final, careless loss of footing, to slip himself into an early, Parisian grave. But he was a human of amazing talents.

As the legend of the Doors has grown, those talents have become partially obscured. That's why it's necessary to remind ourselves every so often that, above all, Morrison was a writer and a poet. And it's his writing that needs to be celebrated.

The purpose of this book then is to get that celebration started. It can't claim to present a comprehensive history of the band

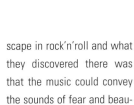

The Doors pushed rock'n'roll songwriting forward, but the Doors' songwriters were pulling from some classic rock 'n'roll influences. Jim Morrison was a big-fan of Elvis Presley. and Robby Krieger had grown up listening to Fats Domino records.

– others have already done that job exceptionally well. Nor is it a technical manual on how the Doors music was pieced together in the studio, though occasionally events there are described in detail.

What this book hopes to do is to convey a sense of the intellectual energy and unique inspirations behind the songs of the Doors and the writing of Jim Morrison. (Although let's point out here and now that Robby Krieger was a major song writing force for the Doors too and he will also get his due.)

The songs of the Doors created a dark and frightening world: sometimes, by looking into the genesis of a song, that world can be illuminated. Again and again, the stories behind the songs serve to reveal the one great secret of the Doors: far from being a wild-eyed, non-stop lush and Lothario, Jim Morrison was actually an extremely intelligent, amazingly well-read man who loved his·craft.

The Doors brought heavyweight literature to the world of rock'n'roll and the works that inspired Jim were often given a kind of second life in his songs. It's illuminating to learn why Jim chose to take the highway to the end of the night, or what induced him to become a spy in the house of love. The explanations certainly don't make the songs any better or worse, but they do offer a fresh perspective on the creative process.

Finally, even if the Doors' music now seems to exist in a kind of timeless, universal rock'n'roll realm, the songs were actually the inspired products of a specific place and time – Southern California in the Sixties. Doors songs can be better appreciated when they are heard firmly anchored in context.

To establish that context, many witnesses to the Doors' history have been interviewed. They include college friends, professional acquaintances and musical contemporaries. There are others who have been interviewed because they simply had the good fortune to be open to what the Doors were doing way back in the Sixties.

So, not every voice that appears in these stories belongs to an official Doors insider, but all the voices belong to people who were there and who can shed greater or lesser insight on the band's music.

But the crucial question remains: what's so important about the Doors? The answer is easy: they were the first band to scare the hell out of us.

The Doors mapped out a previously uncharted psychic land-scape in rock'n'roll and what they discovered there was that the music could convey the sounds of fear and beauty, passion and paranoia, liberation, triumph, dementia and dread all at once.

The Doors made rock'n'roll scary. They also made rock'n'roll think.

" *They were the first evil band, just like the Beatles were the first long-hair band."*
Kim Fowley, producer, songwriter, performer and denizen of the Sunset Strip circa 1966

The roots of the Doors – their frame, if you will – could be seen early on in all four players' histories: by the time he was in elementary school, Jim Morrison had developed a love of word-play and a hunger for knowledge of the obscure; the pre-teen Ray Manzarek was spending his days mastering classical etudes on the piano and his nights listening to raucous Chicago blues on a transistor radio; Robby Krieger picked up his earliest musical influences through a mix of Fats Domino and *Peter And The Wolf*, then he learnt to express himself on flamenco guitar; and John Densmore practised his way up to becoming an ace snare drummer in the University High School marching band, later working the wedding and *bar mitzvah* circuit in dance bands and using a fake ID to catch beloved jazz acts at Shelley Manne's Manne Hole.

" *They had an LA sound, but it wasn't a Sunset Strip sound. Three Dog Night, the Daily Flash, Rhinoceros – all these Strip bands seemed to have at least a little something in common. The Doors were unique."*
Jimmy Greenspoon, keyboardist with Three Dog Night

" *The fact that the music wasn't guitar-oriented – that it was keyboard-driven – that made it different. And the words had drama. Morrison was a great creator of images. A lot was said by the collision and impact of his strings of words. And some of it actually scared me – it was insight pulled from dark terror."*
Harvey Kubernick, record producer, journalist and Los Angeles native

It took a charmed series of events to get the Doors up and running and that began with a Kerouac-style trek across the country for Jim Morrison. In February 1964, 20-year-old Morrison transferred from Florida State University in Tallahassee to the University of California in Los Angeles, where he enrolled in the theatre arts department and began studies in film production.

The move wasn't just about Morrison refocusing his academic priorities – it was a clean break from his parents and his past, as well as surrender to an adventurous, uncertain future. In 1964, when even the winsome Beatles were perceived by many as long-haired threats to society, the idea of a fine young son moving to Los Angeles, that garish Gomorrah, to study, of all things, the decadent medium of film, was a parent's worst nightmare.

Jim's parents forbade him to move. He responded by hitch-hiking to California and diving in to the active arts scene he found there. In effect, this move was Jim's notice that he was severing all further contact with his family, and his father's response was to disown him. Once Jim arrived at UCLA, his family days were over, but the "feast of friends" was just beginning.

For Jim, the past could not be too soon forgotten. He was the oldest son of Steve Morrison, a career Navy man and his wife Clara. The Morrison family moved often during Jim's childhood – by the time he was a high school student, he'd lived in California, Florida, New Mexico, Washington DC and Virginia. The constant moves were hard on Jim and, while sometimes he expressed his frustrations by being a little terror around the house, he was often shy and withdrawn among classmates at the ever-changing schools he attended.

Early on, Jim felt a cold, gaping distance between himself and his father. Steve Morrison was often away from home on naval missions, leaving Clara to run the house and, when he was at home, he was more a figure to be respected and tip-toed around rather than a dad to be bonded with. It's a rather chilling indication of how things stood within the Morrison family that

at early Doors press conferences Jim told the world that his parents were dead.

It would seem significant too that Steve Morrison was not just a father, but a father in uniform – he was the first of many authority figures that Jim would have tremendous difficulty dealing with.

"*A large part of what Jim was about was that he provoked you to the point that your natural defence mechanisms came into play. He was always trying to cut through the pretences and personas that we all build up around ourselves. He'd actually get you using your survival instincts – because he wanted to make you more real. The moment he made somebody scream and yell and jump up and down, he'd laugh hysterically. Because he'd won.*"
Bill Siddons, Doors manager

Young Jim discovered a way of escaping the tensions at home and the awkwardness of being "the new kid" at every school he attended and that was by immersing himself in the world of literature. The "wild man" reputation that grew around the adult Jim may lead some fans to suspect that he slouched through his school years as a budding delinquent, but in fact his eager mind was fascinated by the world that opened up to him inside books.

As a young boy, Morrison also began to explore the pleasures of putting his thoughts down on paper. The results were sometimes more scatological hijinks than soulful expression, but with every movement of his pen Jim's imagination was further unleashed and he began to develop a keen writer's eye, mind and voice. He must have recognized that some of the creative imagery in his early writing was worth hanging on to, because he'd rework a favourite phrase or idea in his notebooks until he felt he'd finally perfected it. In a few cases, that editing process stretched from elementary school all the way to Doors albums – one poem that he spent a good deal of effort on while in grade school, 'The Pony Express', served as a humble precursor to the active imagery later used in a high school poem, 'Horse Latitudes', which eventually became one of the Doors' most potent chunks of psycho-drama.

By the time he was attending George Washington High School in Alexandria, Virginia, Morrison's status among his

The other end of the Strip. Compared to the work of Jim Morrison and the Doors, bands like Three Dog Night sounded positively fluffy. But their guitarist Jimmy Greenspoon was one of Morrison's hell-raising drinking buddies.

Jim Morrison was no natural ham – he was paralyzed with stage-fright at most of the early Doors gigs. But as he became more comfortable he left his inhibitions behind and practically reinvented himself.

schoolmates had shifted somewhat. He was no longer the barely noticed, painfully polite shy kid, but had blossomed into an often gleeful troublemaker – the kind of student flustered teachers invariably described as "a character".

And the penchant for mischief that developed in Morrison during these years never disappeared.

" *I* first saw them at Ciro's in 1966 – I think I'd first heard about them from Billy James. I got to Ciro's before the Doors set began, and the musicians were up on stage setting up. A heckler started yelling at the band: 'You guys are horrible. You can't play. You're crap. You can't drink, you can't think, you can't fight, you can't fuck.' He was in dirty clothes and looked dangerous. The band looked nervous and started playing – and this guy hopped up on stage and started singing. It was Morrison, who'd been heckling his own band. That was one of the best things I'd ever seen in a club. No introduction – just the singer yelling at the band and then the music. I thought, 'My god, these guys are going to be interesting to watch.'"
Kim Fowley

Poet Michael C. Ford was an early musical associate of Jim and Ray's and later became a key supporter when Morrison wanted to get serious about his writing.

" *O* ne night they were at the studio at Elektra. Jim was supposed to show up at seven pm, so of course he shows up at 10. There are all sorts of drugs laying out along the console. The door opens and Jim walks in, clearly pretty drunk, and he's with a couple of guys in suits and ties. Paul Rothchild looks stunned as Jim proceeds to introduce everybody to Tom and Larry – his newest drinking buddies that he's just had a great talk with at a nearby bar. 'Larry' was Laurence Olivier and 'Tom' was Tom Reddin, the police chief of Los Angeles. They stood behind this drug-laden console and watched Jim sing a track, then said their good-byes and took off. Jim loved that kind of situation. He was a sweet guy, and there was even a certain innocence to him. But he was also impish and mischievous. If

you spent any time with him, he'd manage to surprise you in some way."
Bill Siddons

At the age of 17, while classmates were idolizing pop stars, movie stars and athletes, Jim's heroes were to be found on library shelves – William Blake, Charles Baudelaire, Arthur Rimbaud, Jack Kerouac, Friedrich Nietzsche and Franz Kafka. Together, these writers fanned the creative flame in Morrison that would blaze so fiercely with the Doors.

The aphorisms of Nietzsche and the journals of Kafka were particularly influential and, by the time Jim graduated from high school in June 1961, he had notebooks full of daily journal entries, poetic observations and his own brand of Morrisonian aphorisms. The heady stew of poetry and philosophy that he consumed during his high school years was crucial nourishment for the future writer. The expansive, extensive literary frame of reference Jim Morrison established for himself early on would shape all the work that was to come.

" *W* hen he did the bridge to 'End Of The Night', he said 'Realms of bliss Realms of light' – I said 'Jim, that's William Blake's 'Songs Of Innocence'.' He said, 'I know, but nobody's busted me yet.' The Doors really represented the first time a rock band really tapped into literature, and it worked."
Michael C. Ford, Los Angeles poet

By the end of high school, Jim would have been comfortable leaving the furthering of his education up to experience, happenstance and his own reading lists, but his parents expected his education to continue more formally. They enrolled him in St Petersburg Junior College in Florida, where Jim could attend classes while living nearby with his grandparents.

Having his immediate future mapped out for him by his folks may have rankled, but Jim was also excited at the prospect of getting away from home. He spent a year at St Petersburg and then transferred to Florida State. He was interested by a few of the psychology courses he took, but developed an even deeper interest in the records of Elvis Presley.

After a couple of years, Jim grew tired of his Florida sur-roundings and junior college studies. Film seemed to be the medium of the moment, where the greatest artistic leaps were being taken and that's what Jim wanted to study. To pursue those studies, he wanted to get as far away from where he was as he possibly could. He'd taken to heart the adventuresome spirit of Kerouac's *On The Road*. California was beckoning.

"*I was hanging out on the Strip one day when he came up to me. I knew who he was but we hadn't met yet. I was eating a moonpie, and he just strolled up and said, 'Hey, Rodney, give me a bite of that pie.' He was a friendly very, nice guy. We talked about moonpies and that led us into talking about Elvis. He was a huge Elvis fan, and from then on we'd talk about Elvis every time we ran into each other.*"

Rodney Bingenheimer, Los Angeles deejay and "scen-ester extraordinaire"

At UCLA in the early Sixties, there were some students who treated film school as a technical training ground that would lead straight to a lucrative job in Hollywood, but there was also a contingent of aspiring film-makers who were already begin-ning to express some of the revolutionary spirit that would shortly define the increasingly free-spirited decade.

Morrison quickly fell in with this crowd of wily, rebellious intellectuals, a group that included one figure who would play a pivotal role in shaping Jim's future – a talented, slightly older film student named Ray Manzarek.

Jim and Ray became part of a circle of friends that included several people who remained close as the Doors took shape – Alan Ronay, John Debella, Philip Oleno, Paul Ferrara and Frank Lisciandro. Michael C Ford was also a part of that group. Ford was also a little older than most of the students and he was auditing film classes when he met Ray and then Jim.

Originally, Ford had started showing up at UCLA simply to watch some interesting films, but he was excited to find on campus an energetic, kindred spirit in Manzarek and it wasn't long before the two cemented a friendship by working together as a piano/upright bass backing duet for a campus theatre pro-duction. Ford recalls that in an era of frenetic experimentation and exploration, it was hard to tell if artistic sparks were des-tined to fly between his two new friends.

"You didn't think of it in terms of that," he explains. "You did-n't think, 'Wow – those two guys are into William Blake and the Beat Generation.' You just thought, 'Well there's a normal con-nection. Of course they're listening to Beat poetry and Charlie Parker albums.' That was what we all did. That scene at that place was just bursting with creative energy, which we all thought was business as usual. It may seem sappy to talk about the past that way, but there really was a volcanic kind of power there. I still carry that time around with me like a backpack of magic supercharged batteries."

Around UCLA, Ford continued to be involved in musical projects with Manzarek, including the White Trash Quintet. Things used to get pretty loose on-stage and it was with that band that Morrison was finally coaxed into performing in front of an audience.

"The White Trash Quintet was me on bass, Ray on piano, Ed Cassidy – later of Spirit – on drums and two horn players who went on to play in Frank Zappa's bands," Ford explains. "Morrison would come play with us and just turn his back to the audience and bang on a tambourine. I said 'Who do you think you are – the Miles Davis of the tambourine?' But he was just shy. He could not face the audience. That didn't last too long – pretty soon he was the lead singer who would say all the things that lead singers weren't supposed to say. But I think that shy kid who got bullied by a military father was always inside Jim somewhere."

Inspired by the environment he found at UCLA, Morrison was indeed undergoing a transformation and a significant part of that change was physical. Boyish and plump when he arrived, Morrison was a changed man by the time he graduated – he'd become lean, long-haired and remarkably handsome. Film student Judy Raphael had a first-hand look at those changes.

"Ray and I were roughly in the same crowd," she explains. "It seemed like there were only about 10 of us in the early Sixties that liked rock music and got high. Film school was still for a lot of the very straight kids. I naturally fell in with Ray, and Ray kind of brought Jim into the crowd. I'd first seen Jim work-ing in the theatre arts library. We thought he was kind of a nerd. He had a buzz cut and was a little plump. I liked guys with long hair and moustaches, so I didn't think much of Jim. But he changed pretty quickly. A little later I was working as an artist's model for some college art classes, and I remember Jim dating a couple of the other girls who were doing that. I don't think he

A common love of moonpies and Elvis Presley first brought Jim Morrison together with famed L.A. columnist, deejay, club owner and bon-vivant Rodney Bingenheimer.

turned too many heads when he first came to UCLA, but it wasn't long before he was breaking hearts left and right."

" *I just missed Jim and Ray at UCLA, but the stories were still fresh. When the 'Break On Through' single came out, I went and saw them play at the Valley Music Centre on a bill with the Byrds, Buffalo Springfield, Peter, Paul & Mary and Hugh Masakela. Then I went to see them at the Shrine Auditorium show with Iron Butterfly, Sweetwater and Bluesberry Jam. I got very close to the stage to take a photo – this was when you were still allowed to bring a camera to shows. Jim fell off the stage near me, and I remember he didn't smell too good – the leathers smelled a little rank. But it was a great show. A typical Doors show."*
Heather Harris, former arts editor of the *UCLA Bruin*

As UCLA days drew to a close, Ray Manzarek used to regularly belt out rock'n'roll standards as "Screaming Ray Daniels", the *nom de blues* he'd adopted as piano player and lead singer of a band called Rick & The Ravens. Rick was Rick Manzarek, Ray's guitar-playing brother and the band also featured brother Jim Manzarek on harmonica. Throughout the spring of 1965, the Ravens cranked out good-time music at the Turkey Joint West in Santa Monica. The band got by on sloppy energy and raunchy humour and attracted a steady following. ("I used to love watching 'Screaming Ray Daniels' work," laughs Michael C Ford. "'Screaming Ray' was basically regular Ray in a blue velvet tuxedo.") Many of the Ravens' friends were called up on stage to add to the entertainment and one of those coaxed into background vocals was Jim Morrison. As Jim uneasily hollered out some dirtied-up lyrics to 'Louie Louie', it's doubtful that anybody, "Screaming Ray" included, realized that in a year-and-a-half he'd be rock'n'roll's biggest sensation.

" *There were singers who were handsome who couldn't sing. And singers who sounded handsome who looked like twerps. Morrison was a handsome man who sounded handsome and could think too. That was a surprising package."*
Kim Fowley

" *At first it didn't seem to matter that we boys listened to the Doors. The girls in the high school homeroom*

couldn't care less. But within a matter of weeks after the band's Ed Sullivan appearance, when Jim was forbidden to sing the 'higher' in 'Light My Fire' and did it anyway, it got to the point where we guys couldn't possibly compete with Jim Morrison. He was all over girls' lockers. All of a sudden, there were no Beatles or Stones or Dave Clark Five. People started parading the image of Morrison. He was the ultimate beautiful bad boy."
Harvey Kubernick

By the time Jim received his bachelor's degree from UCLA in June 1965, he had achieved a kind of creative critical mass. He had finally managed to fill his mind with just about all the raw knowledge it had craved and now he was beginning to generate creative insights at a new level. His imagination had been stimulated by his film studies, particularly by his exposure to experimental films and surrealistic imagery. Among the notebooks he kept at UCLA was a self-styled "thesis on film esthetics", which would later be published as *The Lords: Notes On Vision*.

Jim was equally passionate about the study of Greek and Roman drama, which he'd taken up on his own. His mild obsession with quintessential rocker Elvis Presley had given way to a respectful infatuation with consummate military man Alexander the Great, as described by the Greek historian Plutarch. He also remained fascinated by legends, folklore and the religious rituals of ancient cultures, all of which he'd researched for himself at the UCLA library.

The store of knowledge he'd found for himself in Los Angeles proved vital in the development of Jim Morrison as a writer and he was soon ready to take all that he'd learned and use it to create something powerful.

It was during the summer of 1965 that Morrison first began to half-seriously imagine a band called "the Doors". He still considered William Blake to be an unparalleled thinker and poet, and one of Blake's lines had stuck with Morrison for many years: "If the doors of perception were cleansed, every thing would appear as it is, infinite." Morrison had also read Aldous Huxley's philosophical description of his experiences with mescaline, which was titled with a phrase borrowed from Blake, *The Doors Of Perception*. To Morrison, the Blake line and the Huxley book suggested a perfectly simple, allusive, subtextually rich name for a band – the Doors. A perfect in-joke for high-minded rock-'n'rollers.

Some bands on the Sunset Strip could make music as heavy as the Doors – Iron Butterfly of "In A Gadda Da Vida" fame, for example. But Jim Morrison's showmanship and his band's jazzy innovations made the Doors a unique attraction.

"*I saw the Doors at the Whisky all summer long in 1966. I was a big fan of Van Morrison and Them, and the Doors opened when Them came to the Whisky. Love had always been my favourite LA band, and I thought the Doors were very strange. But their sound grabbed me. They were covering 'Gloria' and playing 'Moonlight Drive' and it was a whole new sound.*"
Paul Body, witness to the Doors' ascent on the Sunset Strip

As Morrison worked up on his rooftop, he found that the poetry he was writing flowed most freely when he thought of his words as lyrics. He had no way of expressing the music he heard in his head behind these poems, but found that, when he allowed that cerebral music to flow, his words picked up a rhythm, depth and intensity that he'd never attained before.

This rich writing was taking place in some very humble places – mostly on the rooftop overlooking Venice Beach. Morrison had made plans to travel to New York after graduation to pursue a proper film career and had told most of his UCLA friends, including Ray, that he was leaving town. But as Morrison's mind began to soar, he quickly found he wasn't interested in a proper career anymore. Simply pursuing his muse was of much more interest – a pursuit which that summer entailed gobbling enough acid to keep his consciousness elevated while keeping fresh notebooks handy at all times.

The rooftop of the decrepit Venice office building was a rent-free crash pad where Morrison could work in solitude as he perfected his craft. The writing accomplished on that roof in the space of a few weeks would prove to be immeasurably important for the Doors – the Venice notebooks spawned most of the first two Doors albums and provided lyrics and inspiration all the way through to *LA Woman*.

"*He said he'd be happy if people remembered him five years after he was dead – and he really meant that. He wanted to be cremated and scattered over Venice Beach. That's where the whole thing had started, and he liked the idea of ending up there as flotsam.*"
Patricia Kennealy Morrison, who was unofficially married to Jim in a 1970 pagan handfasting ceremony

In the summer of 1965, Morrison had a perfect band name, notebooks full of material and a mind abuzz with creative possi-

bilities – but it was a fortuitous meeting with buddy Ray Manzarek on the beach at Venice that made the Doors a reality.

Ray was surprised to see that Jim was still in town and was even more surprised when Jim told him that he'd been working on some songs. When, at Ray's insistence, Jim softly sang the lyrics to 'Moonlight Drive', Ray was ecstatic. He told Jim that together they would bring this concept – "The Doors" – to life. Ray felt that if Jim was walking around with musical ideas this strong and was capable of words this powerful, there was a fair chance that he also had the ability to be a captivating frontman.

Morrison moved off the rooftop and into the tiny apartment shared by Ray and his long-time girlfriend Dorothy Fujikawa. He kept up his prolific writing and both he and Ray began to work up some music in a post-Ravens/pre-Doors line-up with Rick and Jim Manzarek.

On the strength of their live performances, Rick & The Ravens had secured a contract with Aura Records and released a single that didn't sell well. Aura was obligated to put out a second single, but offered instead to give the Ravens free studio time as a way of satisfying their contract. With Morrison bringing fresh energy and material to the Manzareks, the revamped group began preparing for their first recording session at Dick Bock's World Pacific Studios on Third Street in Los Angeles.

One enduring problem for the Ravens had been finding drummers and bassists who would stay with the group more than a gig or two. When Jim started working with the Manzareks, they still hadn't found a steady rhythm section but half of that problem was solved when Ray encountered Los Angeles native John Densmore at Maharishi Mahesh Yogi's brand new Meditation Center, also on Third Street.

At one of the sessions, a mutual friend pointed out Densmore to Ray as a promising drummer. Ray promptly introduced himself. Soon afterwards, Ray invited John to a rehearsal with Jim and his brothers. John was blown away by the cryptic Morrison-

Jim Morrison had a troubled relationship with his military father, but he was a fervent admirer of the quintessential military man, Alexander the Great. The first high-fashion haircut Morrison received after the Doors were signed to Elektra was patterned after a bust of the Macedonian king.

When the Doors first began to make it on Sunset Strip, their goal was to be as big as Arthur Lee's Love. In the summer of 1966 they were opening shows for Love at the Whisky A Go Go –in the space of a year they were bigger than they had ever imagined.

penned lyrics he was shown on some crumpled sheets of paper.

John couldn't tell where this group was headed, but it looked like it was going to be an interesting ride. He told Ray to count him in.

"John's drum parts were outrageously unique. A lot of people were influencing my playing back then, but I picked up some very serious influence from John's very unusual way of pushing the music. He had a conceptual approach to the material and came up with some very interesting formulas. He wrote great drum parts."
Bruce Gary, drummer with The Knack

With Densmore adding a steadying presence and rhythmic flair to the prototype Doors line-up, the group was ready to use its studio time to record a demo tape. In September 1965, Ray, Jim, John, Ray's brothers and an unnamed female bassist spent several hours working on six songs that had come together particularly well during rehearsals – 'Moonlight Drive', 'End Of The Night', 'My Eyes Have Seen You', 'Hello, I Love You', 'Summer's Almost Gone' and 'A Little Game'. The sound was raw and unpolished – it was not what would later be instantly recognizable as "the Doors sound". But there was no filler material here; all of these songs would later appear on Doors albums. ('A Little Game', alternatively referred to as 'Go Insane', would later surface as a section of 'The Celebration Of The Lizard'.)

"It's incredible they got a deal off that first demo, because they almost sounded incompetent. The female bass player is like a full beat behind on everything."
Bill Siddons

The demo may have been crude, but it was also shockingly original. The pop sound of Southern California at that time was epitomized by the Beach Boys with their harmonious anthems to surf and sand, sun and fun. The sound that Jim and Ray were shaping was just as much a product of Southern California, but it represented the other side of the sunny coin.

'Moonlight Drive' had surf in it, but it was surf to be drowned in, not frolicked in. The popular Southern California sound had succeeded in bouncing beachy teen dreams back to the kids

across the country – now the proto-Doors were beginning to articulate the notion that teen dreams could be accompanied by ancient nightmares. Bikinis and burgers, surfboards and woodies were about to surrender to sex and dread, fear and loathing.

"The fun was getting their wildest thoughts on the radio and being rewarded for it one way or the other. A lot of bands didn't want to try for the brass ring."
Kim Fowley

Victory was a record deal away though and, in order for a deal to be made, the demo had to be heard.

Luckily, Billy James had ears that were ready to listen. James was a hustling record company exec who was working at Columbia, where he had created the job title "Director of Talent, Acquisition & Development".

In the Doors' history, James is something of an unsung hero – if he hadn't been open-minded enough to dig the demo, it's quite possible that the Doors would have been shut down six songs into their career. But he gives them credit for making sure they got heard.

"It was a two-way street," says James. "I didn't always discover artists – they discovered me too. And the Doors discovered me. I spotted them around my secretary's desk when I came back from lunch one day. We talked and I ended up being very intrigued by them. I later asked Morrison how come they chose me as someone to bring their demo to. He said he'd seen a picture of me in one of the trade magazines and liked the fact that I had a beard. He said he figured I was into 'something'."

Morrison's intuition paid off, because Billy James liked the demo enough to offer the band a five-and-half-year contract, with the half year being the period in which to get a first single out.

"'Moonlight Drive', 'Go Insane' – they really jumped out at me," James says. "It was rough, but there was a completely unique energy in the music. What a great band," he laughs. "I thought I got it. I thought I knew what they were about."

James had a hard time convincing anybody else at Columbia that he had found the Next Big Thing. The Doors got some free equipment from the label, including the Vox organ that was to produce Ray's trademark sound, but when the first six months of the contract were up, the single hadn't happened. This meant that the rest of the contract was void and that the Doors had thus been signed to, then dropped by, Columbia without recording a note. (They were in good company – other acts that Billy James unsuccessfully tried to bring to Columbia included Frank Zappa, Jefferson Airplane, Tim Hardin and Lenny Bruce.)

"Very few people in the industry were hanging out in clubs, and a stylistic change took place among the musicians well before it came to the industry," says James. "I kept bringing these acts to Columbia and I got the feeling that the higher-ups were thinking 'What is this shit this kid keeps bringing us?'"

"It was an amazing time on the Strip. Love would be at Ciro's, Iron Butterfly at the Galaxy, the Doors at the London Fog. Groups that didn't play the Whisky or the Trip were at Stratford on Sunset, which is where I played with a lot of bands. I remember backing up a duo called Caesar and Cleo – she was striking, he was 'eh'. They became Sonny and Cher.

"We'd all hang out after hours at Canter's Deli on Fairfax. Every freak in town and every band in town. All Zappa's people and all the Doors. All the Byrds, Arthur Lee with his scarves, Buffalo Springfield, the Daily Flash, Sons of Adam. We'd exchange acid, stories, girlfriends and sandwiches. Morrison stood out because he was incredibly handsome and, if he wanted to, he could get very loud. Everybody attracted a different kind of hanger-on, and even then Jim was already attracting the budding little dark poets and little lost waifs."
Jimmy Greenspoon

As became clear, Columbia weren't particularly interested in making anything happen for the group right away and Ray's brothers grew so discouraged they decided to call it quits, leaving Ray, Jim and John to reconsider what the Doors line-up was going to be.

They were still having trouble finding a bass player who would fit in with the sound they were developing: the problem was that standard rock'n'roll basslines tended to make the Doors sound like a standard rock'n'roll band. Even more problematic was the search for a guitar sound.

Ray was achieving tremendous breakthroughs in adapting his old piano techniques to the organ and was in the process of discovering his own gracefully meaty approach to the keyboard.

His sense of rhythm was well supported by Densmore – the love of jazz that the two shared was not always obvious in the songs they fashioned around Morrison's words and melodies, but it was strongly evident in the feel of the elegant grooves they played.

As the band rehearsed, Morrison was slowly building up confidence in himself as a performer. But where were these three Doors going to find a guitar player who could complement the sound they were slowly but surely crafting?

It turned out that they didn't have far to look – one of John Densmore's old Uni High buddies played guitar and was always looking for new people to play with. Densmore had worked with him before in a band and in fact had brought him along to the Meditation Center where John and Ray first hooked up. John was sure that this friend would be interested in the music the fledgling Doors were coming up with. Densmore's guitar-playing friend was, of course, Robby Krieger.

Unlike Densmore, Krieger wasn't immediately convinced that he'd found a group he wanted to be part of, but, at his very first rehearsal with the Doors when he came up with some spine-tingling bottleneck parts for 'Moonlight Drive', the band knew they wanted him. After a few more rehearsals, when Densmore asked him to forget about playing with other bands, Krieger agreed.

Throughout the Doors' ensuing years of craziness, Robby Krieger remained the band's gentlest spirit, quietly focused on his steady artistry. You'd almost forget he was there until, with a few unassuming fingerplucks on his Gibson SG, he would astonish you.

Ray, Jim and John may have realized immediately that they'd recruited a uniquely talented guitar player, but they had no inkling that they had just added a second formidable songwriter to the band – even Krieger wasn't aware of his song writing abilities at that point. But all it took at one of the foursome's early rehearsals was a suggestion that everybody come up with some new song ideas and Krieger brought 'Light My Fire' and 'Love Me Two Times' with him to the next rehearsal.

By the end of 1965, Morrison, Manzarek, Krieger and Densmore were well on their way to becoming a four-headed monster. Rehearsing almost every day at Ray's beachside apartment, they quickly learned how to fit their individual music-making abilities together to achieve the greatest effect. In many ways, they were the perfect collection of musical oddballs – four idiosyncratic performers who might have had a hard time shining as part of any other ensemble but together they made each other sound stronger, until what they created was not four sounds but one.

And, even in their cramped rehearsal space, they began to develop the sense of theatre-through-music that they'd eventually perfect. The extended breaks in 'Light My Fire', 'The End' and 'When The Music's Over' gave Ray, Robby and John the chance to engage in collective improvisation, while Jim was free to cut loose with whatever lyrical inspirations came to mind.

But the Doors were not prepared to change the way they played just to get gigs and, as the band took their first timid steps round the Los Angeles club circuit, they were treated to some very swift rejections: the phrase that seemed to echo after each unsuccessful audition was "too weird".

But one specific lousy audition offered up an important consolation prize. Ray noticed that the keyboardist in the house band for a club they were in the process of being rejected by used an odd short-scale instrument to get extra oomph out of his bass notes.

It was a Fender Rhodes piano bass and, once Ray saw it and heard it, he had to have one. The bass troubles of the Doors were now solved and their distinctive sound was complete.

" *They didn't need a bass player – that was an amazing thing. Ray was able to handle the basslines so expertly with his left hand and create such rich arrangements with his right hand. Even though Jim was a dynamic performer, he was a part of the band, and they had a strong identity as a band. It wasn't Jim Morrison and the Doors – it was 'the Doors'."*
Bruce Gary

" *They were rock stars, but they were never a rock'n'roll band. The music was Kurt Weill meets Chess Records."*
Kim Fowley

The Doors finally got themselves a steady Sunset Strip gig in January 1966. Granted it was at the London Fog, a tiny, dingy, disreputable watering hole where down-and-outers drowned their sorrows. But it was work, and it was the Strip. The Doors had finally been granted an audition night there and then

cajoled a couple of dozen of their friends into packing the place. The London Fog didn't find itself with a lively capacity crowd too often and the owner of the club promptly signed the Doors up to be his main attraction six nights a week.

" *I went to the very first London Fog gig. It seemed like there were maybe a dozen people there. I must say, I was taken. Jim didn't have any stage presence and didn't really know what he was doing – but that sound. 'Light My Fire', 'Crystal Ship' – we could hear it was special. At clubs in general the hip people had stopped dancing – there were just the dances for squares that had names like 'the Monkey' or 'the Swim'. But at the Doors shows, we young artists and film students couldn't help but dance to that music. I remember feeling proud of them. There really was some magic in the music."*
Judy Raphael

At first, what little magic the Doors could conjure up within the confines of the London Fog was witnessed exclusively by the friends that they talked into showing up. But soon a buzz began and people who didn't know the Doors were wandering in to check them out.

The band became tighter and more confident in their own material and Morrison began to assert himself on stage. At some shows, he still couldn't face the audience, but when he did he sometimes let himself go crazy, engaging in all manner of antics as he gave himself over to the music.

The Doors still weren't known to many by name, but word of "the weird band with the wild singer" began to spread. Unfortunately, reports weren't always positive. The Doors were already drawing starkly polarized reactions. Still at least nobody seemed to leave the London Fog apathetic about what they'd seen.

Above all, the Doors were hoping that some of the good words would percolate to the Whisky A Go Go, the premier rock-'n'roll club on the Strip.

Early in 1966, the reigning kings of the Whisky were Love, Arthur Lee's extraordinary band. Other high-profile groups on the Strip included the Seeds, the Turtles, the Buffalo Springfield, the Byrds, the Standells, Frank Zappa's Mothers Of Invention and Captain Beefheart's Magic Band. The fact that the Doors were top dog at the London Fog didn't mean anything to the bookers at the Whisky. When Columbia finally made it official that the

Doors no longer had any contract with the label, the band was dispirited.

Things got even worse one spring night when the management at the London Fog decided that the Doors were taking liberties on stage and had had a hand in encouraging too many property-damaging bar room brawls. Band members were told they could finish out the week and then they were fired. The end seemed near – after all, where did a band go once it had been kicked out of the London Fog?

Morrison took care of that. He'd struck up a friendship with Ronnie Haran, who booked the shows at the Whisky. After pleading for months to get her to come see the band, he finally got her to agree to come down the street and see them.

So the group's final night at the London Fog ended up being the Whisky audition that they'd craved for months and they ended their tenure with one of the finest nights of music they'd managed yet. And what Haran saw that night impressed her sufficiently to hire the Doors as the new house band at the Whisky. There, they continued to frighten, delight, shock and outrage whatever audiences happened to come their way.

"*I went to see Them at the Whisky and opening were the Doors. Ray denies it – but I swear they were billed as the Swinging Doors. I thought Ray looked a lot like John Sebastian, and I remember talking to him in the Whisky bathroom. I thought he was a real nice guy, but I hated the band. I really didn't like watching Morrison drape himself over the microphone. I got pissed off and went up to the owner, Elmer Valentine, and said, 'Hey, I've got a band that's better than this – can we get a job here?'*"
Chris Darrow, who played the Sunset Strip as a member of Kaleidoscope

"*I used to show slides at the Whisky on a couple of screens – not so much a light show, just colourful close-ups of everyday objects. I had a picture of a flaming toilet – someone had poured lighter fluid in a motel toilet and I got a great shot of it. It was mixed in with my slides at random, but I remember it came up once right as the Doors started playing 'Light My Fire'. That's the way it seemed back then – things would just fall into place very nicely.*"
Rock'n'roll photographer Henry Diltz, who would later shoot the cover for *Morrison Hotel*

"*A friend and I drove by the Whisky and saw Jim literally sitting in the gutter, all by himself. We were on our way to a party at the home of Eric Burdon of the Animals, so we picked him up and took him to the party. On the way there he was leaning out of the car and I kept trying to pull him back in – he was yelling and I thought he was going to fall out. We got a little concerned about showing up at Burdon's house with Jim acting so crazy, but it turned out to be a pretty wild party and Jim fit right in.*"
Rodney Bingenheimer

It was at the Whisky that the band finally came into its own and "the Doors", a struggling local Los Angeles act, became the Doors – rock'n'roll's smartest, darkest prophets.

At the Whisky, Jim Morrison discovered and perfected his shaman's power to transport an audience and the musical interplay that Ray, Robby and John mastered became the supercharged vehicle for that act of transport. The band's material grew deeper and stronger and a large audience became receptive to the troubling visions offered up in Morrison's lyrics. At the Whisky, the Doors were both loved and hated and the same words of praise and/or scorn that were heaped on them back then are still kicked up every time a Doors record is put on.

Those records were also made possible at the Whisky, when the sharp-eared founder of the Elektra label, Jac Holzman, was convinced by Ronnie Haran to come by and catch a Doors performance. Holzman thought he hated the band, but had to come back the next night to make sure. He ended up seeing them four nights in a row and the depth of the music, along with the wild reactions of the crowd, finally got him to think about signing them.

When Holzman's brilliant staff producer, Paul Rothchild, came to the Whisky and underwent the same conversion, a contract was offered to the Doors. When they accepted, the Doors began in earnest their strange journey into rock'n'roll history.

An organ-based sound, a love of the blues, an explosive lead singer – the Doors had a few things in common with Britain's Animals. And when lead singer Eric Burdon relocated to Los Angeles in the late Sixties, he and Morrison became drinking buddies, with his home often being used as a Morrison crash-pad.

the doors

The Doors' debut album was a beautifully complete, shockingly original, wholly unnerving message of passion, dread and liberation.

Revolutionary hype: Elektra's Jac Holzman was the first to promote a rock band's album on Sunset Boulevard hoardings. Rock'n'roll billboards quickly became conventional on the Strip.

The improvising style of much of the Doors' music came in part from Ray Manzarek's and John Densmore's love of jazz. The bold, soaring explorations of John Coltrane's "free jazz" were a particularly strong source of inspiration for both band members.

The Doors still holds its place in rock'n'roll history as one of the all-time great debuts. After a year of writing, arranging, rehearsing and performing together, the band entered the studio with a fully realized sound that was as potent as it was unique. Before the first tracks for *The Doors* were cut, Jim Morrison, Ray Manzarek, Robby Krieger and John Densmore had already established the kind of musical chemistry that distinguishes all memorable groups – they'd created an inspired sonic whole much greater than the sum of its individual parts.

The Doors' body of work has now become so familiar that it's difficult to imagine just how striking the band were in 1967.

Right away, the absence of a bass player was a startling departure from rock norms. Ray demonstrated a preternatural ability to fill out the bottom end of the sound by playing a Fender piano bass with his left hand, while his right hand seemed to do the work of an entire orchestra on his Vox organ.

Ray was a classically trained player, but he'd developed an enduring love of the charged blues of his Chicago hometown. He'd done time as a GI and been a talented, uncompromising film student at UCLA. He'd seen John Coltrane play at the Manne-Hole in Los Angeles and heard Beat poets like Ferlinghetti and Gary Snyder read their works in Berkeley, California. All that experience seems to be packed into the innovative, angular keyboard parts that are the meat of the Doors' music. Ray was also a basketball fanatic; in his arrangements one can almost hear elaborate passing lanes and pick-and-rolls.

If Manzarek was the band's point guard, Robby Krieger was their stylistic superstar. He was trained in flamenco guitar and, with the Doors adapted that style's finger-picking technique to the electric guitar. While many rock'n'roll guitarists of the time were recycling Chuck Berry riffs, Krieger seemed to invent an entirely new language with his.

At times, he hardly seemed to be playing at all, so ethereal was his presence, but he unerringly added just the right atmospherics to every tune and, when called upon, was capable of stunning displays of power. From the frantic, hard-edged chords of 'Break On Through' to the exquisitely loopy solo of 'Twentieth Century Fox', then on to the haunting ragas of 'The End', the unassuming Krieger coloured the Doors' compositions from an unparalleled musical palette.

If Manzarek and Krieger had rested their estimable skills on just any competent rock drummer's backbeat, the music would not have soared. John Densmore was an avid fan of Art Blakey and Elvin Jones, influences which led him to power the Doors' songs with an astonishing blend of jazzy finesse and garage-band flail. He never just simply held a beat. Instead, he played to create drama – supporting the lyrics, teaming with the keyboard parts, echoing guitar licks. And he did it all with stylish abandon. Densmore didn't just play drums – he performed them.

Manzarek, Krieger and Densmore's talents were given a vibrant, commanding voice in the person of Jim Morrison. With his keen intelligence, absurdist sense of humour, classic beauty, stirring physical presence and a willingness to sacrifice himself completely to the music, how could Jim Morrison have been anything but a sensation – the youngest Rock God, the icon's icon.

However, the truth is that Morrison's sheer charisma didn't constitute the pulsing heart of the Doors – his words did. While living on a Venice, California, rooftop in the summer of 1965, Morrison had meticulously compiled an inspired series of poems and lyrics: he had no idea he'd soon be a member of a band, but he later explained that he could hear a concert in his head and that's what he wrote for. The real concert began when Morrison's notebooks turned into Doors' songs.

Jim's lyrics redefined the thematic boundaries of rock. Previous rock'n'rollers had looked to older blues performers for inspiration, but Jim's work was informed by a literary canon. His song writing was infused with the spirit of Artaud, Nietzsche, Baudelaire, Kafka and Kerouac. Without them, his music could not have existed.

The Beatles had brought wit and intelligence to pop music, and the Rolling Stones demonstrated a brash frankness about life in the modern world, but Morrison and the Doors asked rock'n'roll to do some heavy thinking.

Boy meets girl stuff – even boy spends night with girl stuff – wasn't enough for Jim. He filled the music with ancient legends, treatises on existentialism, psychic unravellings, moments of terror and the deep release of laughter. He spoke of rock performance as shamanistic ritual and, on *The Doors*, the shaman was indeed breaking on through.

In September 1966, the Doors went into Sunset Sound Recording Studios at 6650 Sunset Boulevard with producer Paul Rothchild and engineer Bruce Botnick and began their first sessions.

Rothchild turned out to be a perfect match for the band. His brilliantly transparent approach to production assured that, while he would use all his skills to capture the Doors on tape, in the end a listener would be hearing their music, not studio trickery.

Rothchild and Manzarek quickly agreed that, on tape, keyboard bass did not have the strong punch they were looking for, so ace session bassist Larry Knechtel, from Phil Spector's Wrecking Crew, was brought in on some tracks. The album was recorded in two weeks on a four-track machine and another five weeks were needed to mix the tracks down.

Along with nine original songs, the Doors also recorded two of the cover tunes that had served them well at the London Fog and the Whisky A Go Go – a growling rip at Willie Dixon's 'Back Door Man' and 'Alabama Song' from Kurt Weill and Bertolt Brecht's German opera of the late Twenties, *The Rise And Fall Of The City Of Mahogany* (this had been a favourite of Elektra founder, Jac Holzman, when he saw the band at the Whisky).

"Our first album has a certain unity of mood," Morrison told Jerry Hopkins in a 1969 *Rolling Stone* interview. "It has an intensity about it. It came after a year of almost total performance, every night. We were really fresh and intense and together."

The Doors was recorded, and still plays, like a timeless, perfect-world live album. "We tried to strike a very fine line between being fresh and original and being a documentary – making the album sound like it really happened live," Paul Rothchild recalled in a 1981 interview with Blair Jackson for *BAM* magazine. "We wanted it to sound new. I didn't want it to sound gimmicky by using things that sounded really trendy. For instance, everyone was using wah-wah pedals at the time because Hendrix had just hit and guitar players were blown away by what he did with wah-wah. I prohibited Robby from using wah-wah. When he asked me why I said, 'Because I want people to still be listening to Doors' records in 20 years.'"

The Doors was released in January 1967 and went gold after 'Light My Fire' became a Number 1 hit single in July. The week the album was released by Elektra they took an unprecedented step to promote it; the Doors became the first rock'n'roll band ever to be featured on a Sunset Strip billboard.

Another attention-grabber was the publicity bio that went out with the first record – in it, Ray suggested that the band was a reflection of America at large and Jim was quoted as saying, "I'm interested in anything about revolt, disorder, chaos – especially activity that seems to have no meaning" and "The world we suggest is of a new Wild West. A sensuous evil world."

Billy James, who had opened Elektra's West Coast office, remembers the meeting when those words were spoken. "That was pure Doors. They were just sitting around on the floor of the office at 6725 Sunset with me putting questions to them and transcribing their verbal improvisations. I think it showed that they already had a well-developed sense of their unique aesthetic. It wasn't the sort of stuff you'd expect to hear out of the mouths of rock'n'roll musicians in 1966. For a New York snob like myself to hear that level of self-perception from a bunch of young guys performing in a style I'd considered trivial until a year before was really a great kick."

A triumph of musical chemistry: by the time the Doors began recording their debut album in September 1966, the four members' very different personalities and playing styles had merged to create a unified, distinctive band sound.

break on through

'Break On Through' was released as the Doors' very first single in January 1967 and, as far as introductions go, it was an explosive, white-hot statement of purpose.

With the pop charts topped by the likes of the Monkees' 'I'm A Believer', the New Vaudeville Band's 'Winchester Cathedral' and 'Snoopy And The Red Baron' by the Royal Guardsmen, the revolution-minded 'Break On Through' came as a warning shot across the bow of the pop *Zeitgeist*. As it turned out, not all that many people heard the shot – the single failed to crack the *Billboard* 100. But for a band that had been collecting $10 a night in the dingiest of clubs only a year before, a record deal and a national single felt like the big time.

In essence, Jim Morrison had begun a new life for himself when he broke with his parents' wishes and transferred from Florida State University to the theatre arts department of UCLA in early 1964. At UCLA, he finally found a circle of friends who embraced and invigorated his voracious intellect and his desire for new experiences. (Ray Manzarek, a free-thinking film student, was a member of that circle.) By the time Jim Morrison graduated from UCLA in June 1965, he had transformed himself from a shy, short-haired, baby-faced student into a remarkably handsome, wild-haired adventurer.

With college behind him, Morrison did not slip into casual aimlessness, but continued with fierce dedication his mission of personal exploration. The lyrics to 'Break On Through' came from the notebooks Morrison kept while living in Venice in the summer of 1965. At that time, he was committed to achieving higher, deeper levels of consciousness and awareness. He was partly inspired by Aldous Huxley's book *The Doors Of Perception*, in which the author describes his attempts to achieve a higher consciousness through the use of mescaline. Jim was fascinated by the idea of allowing his mind to break away from the everyday world and into the realm of magic and mysticism.

As a young, inspired writer, Morrison may have been after a grand language of the mind, but some of his finest words were often triggered by small, decidedly earthly experiences. "I wrote 'Break On Through' one morning down in the [Venice] canals," he explained. "I was walking over a bridge. I guess it's about one girl, a girl I knew at the time." The song came together at early Doors rehearsals, with Densmore developing the tune's engaging, bossa nova groove, Manzarek fleshing out the arrangement and Krieger adding a mix of elegant licks and raw guitar power.

"There are things you know about, and things you don't … and in between are the Doors. That's us," Ray explained in 1967. "Hell seems so much more fascinating and bizarre than heaven. You have to 'break on through to the other side' to become the whole being."

Despite the song's urge towards abandon, the lyrics had to be tamed down before the song could be released as a single. Originally Morrison yelled "She gets high" four times in the middle section, but Elektra felt that any perceived drug references in the song would kill its chances of radio play. The section was changed to "She get" four times, followed by a Morrison moan. (In later live performances, the Doors would stick with the edited "She get", although the moan would often become an emphatic "High".)

'Break On Through' didn't bring the Doors overnight national success, but it did cause their stock to skyrocket on the LA scene. Len Fagan is currently the booking manager of the Coconut Teaszer, a popular LA rock club, but, in the spring of 1967, he was in a band called Spontaneous Combustion. That group was supposed to be billed above the Doors for a gig at the Cheetah on the Santa Monica Pier.

"We were booked prior to their getting big," he recalls, "but by the time of the show, 'Break On Through' was getting airplay and they were developing quite a reputation. It came time for what we thought would be the Doors' set and the promoter came up to us and said, 'You guys have to go on – the Doors aren't ready.' We got a little upset so he brought Ray and Robby over. We said 'What's the problem?' and I'll never forget Ray's answer – 'Jim has lost his way.' We still thought it was a ploy, but when we saw Jim, he did look lost and he didn't look ready to perform. We played, and then the Doors went out and put on

British novelist and critic Aldous Huxley, probably best known as the author of the dystopic *Brave New World*. But it was his book *The Doors Of Perception*, in which he describes his attempts to achieve psychic freedom through experiments with mescaline that greatly influenced Jim Morrison's "break on through" approach to music.

a hell of a wild show – I think Jim fell off the stage that night. By that summer, they were huge and we were more than happy to have shared a bill with them."

soul kitchen

Early in the summer of 1965, Jim Morrison did some of his most important writing for the Doors while living on a Venice rooftop and surviving primarily on a diet of acid and poetry.

By the end of that summer, he had moved into a small beach apartment with Ray and Ray's girlfriend, Dorothy Fujikawa, and quickly discovered that he could get cheap, substantial meals at Olivia's, a tiny, somewhat seedy soul food restaurant near the intersection of Main and Ocean Park.

Olivia herself was happy enough to cook for the ragtag bunch that patronized her place, but she was implacably strict about getting her customers out of the door when it was closing time. Morrison may well have been one of those patrons whose dining pleasure was cut short when Olivia was ready to call it quits for the day: if so, then 'Soul Kitchen' was Jim's bluesy rejoinder – a plea to be allowed to stay in the warm, comfortable kitchen all night rather than face the "cars ... stuffed with eyes" and the formidable "neon groves" of night-time Los Angeles.

The song was another remarkable lyrical triumph for Morrison, as he again created mysteriously compelling words to describe a very small, human moment. Especially notable is the refrain "Learn to forget", which could be taken as something of a Morrison motto at the time, given his attempts to distance himself from his family and his past.

Even before the song was recorded, 'Soul Kitchen' had already served an important purpose for the Doors. At a very early rehearsal, when Jim and Ray were still looking for the right drummer, Ray showed a lyric sheet for the song to John Densmore as an example of Jim's work: John was impressed enough to become a band member.

Musically, the song rides out a straightforward blues groove, albeit with a few distinctive Doors flourishes – a quirky, trademark Manzarek keyboard intro and a wonderfully off-kilter Krieger guitar solo. But the song's slippery rhythms and pulsing bassline may have been influenced by a song the band first heard on the jukebox when they began gigging at the London Fog in January 1966. The late author Albert Goldman, while compiling research for a Doors book, discovered that the London Fog jukebox then featured a song by producer/songwriter Kim Fowley called 'The Trip' – a song with a bass-heavy groove that bears a remarkable similarity to 'Soul Kitchen'.

If the groove was in fact "borrowed", Fowley isn't too bothered. "I think we all got riffs from everywhere," he says. "We were all mostly picking up stuff from Chuck Berry and Muddy Waters. Rock'n'roll in Los Angeles at that time still owed a lot to Chicago blues. The great bluesmen are who we truly did our 'borrowing' from."

The cooking at Olivia's may have satisfied the Doors' appetites, but, in a 1978 interview, Manzarek explained that the fiercely energized work on their first album was the result of deeper hungers. "I think that any artist creates from a driving inner need, but there's an outer need that's very important too, and that's acceptance by some people, somewhere, somehow. Someone saying to you, 'I like this work you've created.' That's what being an artist is. So *The Doors* was that incredible, existential first time – 'Here they are, first time out, fresh, brand new, and hungry as hell.'"

'Soul Kitchen' received a punk rock updating when it was covered by the LA band, X, on their Ray Manzarek-produced debut, *Los Angeles*.

Some of the Doors' early creative sessions took place over cheap meals in the diners near Venice Beach. One of the Doors' favourite soul food joints, Olivia's, became renowned when it was celebrated in their song 'Soul Kitchen'. (Left) Kim Fowley's song 'The Trip' may have given the 'Soul Kitchen' groove some of its seductive flavour.

the crystal ship

While many of Jim Morrison's early songs reflected his LSD-fuelled efforts to run through the doors of perception, as well as his headlong attempts to break on through societal constraints, he was also quite capable of creating a gorgeous, delicately poetic piece of work like 'The Crystal Ship'.

The lyrics are at once soothing and ominous, and the gentle, smoky baritone voice Morrison employed to deliver them may have surprised those who were tempted to write him off as a one-dimensional rock'n'roll ranter.

The mysterious, seemingly inscrutable nature of 'The Crystal Ship' also got Doors-listeners used to developing their own interpretations of Morrison's wordplay. "It's about methedrine, isn't it?," asks Kim Fowley, who was duly impressed by the song when he saw his first Doors show at the Los Angeles club Ciro's in April 1967. "Good old-fashioned speed certainly was a drug of choice on the Sunset Strip back then."

In fact, Morrison had composed the song well before the Doors' first gig on the Strip and the lyrics had their genesis in the pairing of both worldly and arcane inspirations – a romantic break-up and Celtic mythology.

Using a disentanglement from one of his many girlfriends at the time as a starting point, Morrison went on to dramatize the song's aching entreaty for "another kiss" with a unifying image borrowed from the legend of the Irish hero Connla. In the ancient *Book Of The Dun Cow*, the hero was wooed by a goddess who whisked him away to "the earthly paradise beyond the sea" in a magical ship that belonged to the sea god Manannan – a ship that was made of crystal, knew its pilot's mind and was capable of flying over sea or land.

A deep understanding of Celtic legend isn't necessary to appreciate 'The Crystal Ship', but its literary origin does demonstrate just how particularly well-read Jim Morrison was. As the Doors' first album took off, Jim was often picked out as a wild-eyed sex symbol or a drugged-out prophet of doom. What was often missed was the fact that Morrison was primarily driven by a scholarly passion for knowledge and a hunger for ancient wisdom and new ideas.

In any case, the song's underlying allusion didn't go completely unnoticed. "I remember discussing literature with Jim," says writer Patricia Kennealy Morrison, who first met the singer at a January 1969 interview and married him by way of a Celtic pagan handfasting ceremony in June 1970. "I quickly realized that he was one of the best-read people I'd ever met. We talked about the Celtic derivation of the Crystal Ship motif, and I was particularly impressed that he knew about all that because it's a fairly obscure legend".

A line in the final verse of the song at one point read "a thousand girls, a thousand pills" but was changed to "a thousand girls, a thousand thrills" before the song was recorded. And, despite the somewhat sombre tone of the song, its concluding phrases – "When we get back, I'll drop a line" – show a flash of the wry Morrison sense of humour that was so often overlooked.

The song was released as the B-side of the 'Light My Fire' single in April 1967 and is still deeply evocative of that time for some of the Doors' Sunset Strip contemporaries. "All I have to do is hear 'Crystal Ship' and I'm immediately transported back to the summer of 1967," says drummer Bruce Gary, who played in a series of Strip bands back then, going on to fame in the late 1970s as a member of The Knack. "It conveys all the memories and smells and tastes of that period for me. It takes me right back to all the mystical feelings that were in the air that year".

twentieth century fox

On its surface, this snappy, perfectly turned out tune is simply a pun on the name of the famous movie studio, but it also serves as a pointedly humorous jab at the twisted values of LA as the pop culture Mecca – a world in a plastic box that prizes youth and sex appeal over all else.

The song was a favourite of Elektra's Jac Holzman and was going to be the follow-up single to 'Break On Through', until the demand for 'Light My Fire' made it the obvious choice for a second single.

Beginning with an oddly graceful Robby Krieger riff that seems to turn the beat on its head 'Twentieth Century Fox' sweeps up listeners in a seductive rush and deposits them right in the middle of the Sunset Strip circa 1967. While most of the songs on the Doors debut album were built of imagery with a timeless, almost universal feel – fire, death, darkness, highways and snakes – 'Twentieth Century Fox' offered up a neon-bathed vision of up-to-the-minute, modern American decadence.

The fearless, tearless, self-conscious mores of 1967's hippest hipsters appear to be fully embodied in the fashionably lean, fashionably late she-fox of the title and, as Morrison asks the listener to watch the way she walks, the music seems perfectly designed for such a creature to strut her stuff.

In fact, the compulsive, pop drive of 'Twentieth Century Fox' is partly the result of one of Paul Rothchild's many clever innovations during the making of *The Doors*. To add power to the song's rhythm track, he recorded band members stomping along with the beat on a wooden platform – this is particularly notice-able during the choruses, the guitar solo and on the two big beats between "She's a … " and "Twentieth century fox".

"It sounds like a small German Army," Rothchild said in a 1981 interview with *BAM*. "I'd just done a flamenco record where I'd used a similar idea. I thought it would be great to put it on a rock'n'roll record."

The tone of 'Twentieth Century Fox' was something of a departure for Morrison, in that, while the sexual imagery in most of his lyrics has a resonant, deeply psychological quality, the sexually-charged lyrics of 'Twentieth Century Fox' are slyly playful. Ultimately, the song was further evidence of Morrison's developing ability to capture the mercurial spirit of his adopted home town of Los Angeles in his songs.

As a man who had described himself in his first Elektra press bio as "primarily, an American, second, a Californian, third, a Los Angeles resident", Morrison had a sharp eye for the foibles and fundamentals of the West Coast and Twentieth Century Foxes were a particularly fanciful part of the landscape.

"'Twentieth Century Fox' is so perfectly regional," says poet Linda Albertano, who met the Doors when they were shopping their demo around and cheered them on at early Gazzari's gigs. (Today Albertano manages the building in Venice where Morrison lived while he was doing his rooftop writing – it's now called The Morrison.)

"Jim had a magnetic, panther-like maleness that was a pleasant jolt to experience, but I think it was his lyrics that people really connected with at the early shows. LA had become a part of his blood and, just like the rest of us, he saw it as a doomed city, but he didn't want to be anywhere else. We knew exactly what he was talking about in 'Twentieth Century Fox' – youth culture and the attraction of LA. It's a process that's still taking place. Young people are drawn to Hollywood, and their excitement at being here in turn excites the people who are ready to consume them. 'Twentieth Century Fox' is about fresh meat, as it were, about to enter the abattoir with a smile."

Poet Linda Albertano first met Jim Morrison when he was beginning to develop a critical eye for Hollywood's "twentieth century foxes". Today she manages the apartment building on whose roof he wrote the material that became the basis of the Doors' first two records.

Images inspired by Southern California often featured in Morrison's lyrics; "Twentieth Century Fox" was a subtle satire on Hollywood's youth culture. In his first publicity release for Elektra the singer declared, "We are from the West. The whole thing is like an invitation to the West."

light my fire

The first and biggest hit song of the Doors' career began as something of a homework assignment.

When Robby Krieger joined the Doors line-up in the fall of 1965, the band quickly fell into a steady rehearsal schedule and both Manzarek and Morrison became increasingly eager for the band to develop more original material. At a rehearsal in December 1965, Ray made it clear that all four Doors should try their hands at song writing for the band, with Jim adding the stipulation that lyrics should somehow relate to the elements – earth, water, air or fire. The idea paid off early in 1966, when Robby Krieger showed up at rehearsal with the first song he'd ever written – 'Light My Fire'.

"I never even thought about writing until one day Ray said, 'Hey you guys, we need some songs! Everybody go home and write some songs,'" Krieger later explained to writers James Riordan and Jerry Prochnicky. "So I went home and wrote 'Light My Fire' and 'Love Me Two Times'. Those are the first two songs I ever wrote. They took about an hour or so".

The basic melody, lyrics and chord progressions all came from Krieger, but the resulting hit is a perfect example of the Doors' group approach to crafting and arranging their material.

As the group first played the song the day Robby brought it in, Ray got the feeling that the verse began too abruptly. He asked Robby, Jim and John to take a break while he tried to work out an introduction. The three headed for a stroll on nearby Venice Beach, but almost instantly Ray's hands found inspiration and he quickly perfected the quasi-classical swirl of chords that would become the Doors musical signature. John Densmore added to the tune further by developing a modified Latin beat for the verses, before breaking into a more straight-ahead rock beat for the choruses and solo sections. He also came up with a distinctively simple bit of drumming genius – the single crack of the snare drum that heralds Manzarek's intro sections.

Robby's lyrics were almost complete when he brought them to the band, but he was short of one rhyme for the second verse. So it was Morrison who added a typical touch of poetic darkness to Krieger's otherwise upbeat love song, matching " ... wallow in the mire" with "funeral pyre". (Producer Paul Rothchild would later tell Morrison that this was the one part of the song he didn't like, unaware that it was the one verse to which Morrison had contributed.)

All of the Doors' unique strengths were strongly evident in 'Light My Fire', though as the album cut ran to seven minutes, it was not considered usable as a single. Instead, Elektra planned to use 'Twentieth Century Fox' as the follow-up single to 'Break On Through', but among the progressive deejays working in the blossoming world of American FM rock stations the long version of 'Light My Fire' was an oft-requested hit, and the requests soon started pouring into AM stations as well.

At first, the Doors resisted cutting the song for AM use, but,

LIFE PRESERVERS

when Rothchild and engineer Bruce Botnick expertly edited the song down to AM length by clipping the middle solo section, the band was satisfied. In April 1967, the song was released as a single and, in the last week of July, it bumped off the Association's 'Windy' to become Number 1 in the American pop charts. The song returned to the charts the following year when it was covered by Jose Feliciano.

'Light My Fire' was also at the heart of a particularly ugly argument within the band. At the conclusion of the Doors' 1968 European tour, Jim and girlfriend Pamela Courson snuck off to London without telling anyone in the band. Krieger, Manzarek and Densmore headed back to Los Angeles, where they received the offer of a sizeable sum of money if 'Light My Fire' could be used in a Buick automobile ad campaign ("Come on Buick, light my fire!").

Morrison couldn't be contacted, but Krieger, with the support of the others, decided to sell the rights to the song, perhaps feeling that it had already become "commercial product" anyway. When Morrison returned a few days later and heard of these plans, he was horrified, and insisted that the deal be undone.

"To us it was a way of coping," remembers former Doors manager Bill Siddons. "Jim's gone, nobody knows where, the offers came in, it was Robby's song, and he didn't have a problem with it. But to Jim it was complete betrayal. That's really when he began to leave the band. Emotionally that's when he no longer trusted them."

'Light My Fire' had quickly become a burden to the Doors. As the group moved ahead musically and, as Jim Morrison forged into deeper and darker lyrical territory, they found it frustrating to be greeted with young fans' screams for 'Light My Fire' wherever they played.

"I think there's a certain moment when you're right in time with your audience and then you both grow out of it and you both have to realize it," Morrison reflected in a 1971 *Rolling Stone* interview with Ben Fong-Torres. "It's not that you've outgrown your audience; it has to go on to something else."

The Doors never abandoned 'Light My Fire', but they responded to its success by continually re-inventing the song in concert, never quite playing it the same way twice and allowing the solo sections to stretch into heady explorations. Morrison even began to temper the tune's pop sentiments by intoning his macabre 'Graveyard Poem' in the middle of it.

On December 12, 1970, to cap off a concert at the Warehouse in New Orleans, 'Light My Fire' became the last song the Doors ever played as a quartet, and the last song Jim Morrison ever sang on-stage.

When 'Light My Fire' became a Number 1 hit single, the Doors were transformed overnight from rock band to pop celebrities. When the group played Steve Paul's club The Scene in New York in June 1967, they were watched by Andy Warhol and a coterie of personalities from his Factory studio.

i looked at you

'I Looked At You' is the slightest offering on the Doors' debut – a simple, musically upbeat love song with a few great pop hooks like John Densmore's Latin-flavoured drum intro, Manzarek's sparkling keyboard solo and the great "trick" double ending.

But even in what at first sounds like a sunny pop tune, Jim Morrison managed to weave some disturbing thoughts. While the song catalogues an exchange of lovers' looks, smiles and words like any other love song might do, the driving messages here are that the lovers can't turn back, and "It's too late". Maybe it's simply too late for the lovers not to be deeply in love, but the edginess and weariness in Morrison's vocals suggest a more sinister subtext. Not exactly 'Happy Together'.

Keyboardist Jimmy Greenspoon was playing constantly on the Sunset Strip in 1966 and 1967 and later achieved fame creating unashamedly old-fashioned love songs with Three Dog Night. He remembers that it was the Doors' ability to add a darker twist to the pop scene that made them stand out.

"At first they were like a best kept secret – they went unnoticed for a while. But there was nothing like them. The music was totally different. We didn't hear what they did as 'pop' or 'psychedelic'; it was just intense and brooding. My bands were playing happy, fluffy pop songs, and the Doors were just heavier than anybody around."

Ray Manzarek elaborated on that point in a 1968 interview. "Our music has to do with operating in the dark areas within yourself. A lot of people are operating on the love trip and that's nice, but there are two sides to this thing. There's a black, evil side as well as a white, love side, and what we're trying to do is to come to grips with that and realize it. 'Sensual' is probably the word that best fits it."

end of the night

Like 'The Crystal Ship', 'End Of The Night' not only showed off Jim Morrison's ability to deliver a moody ballad, it also again demonstrated the depth of his literary frame of reference. The title and general conceit of the song came from a book Jim had read, *Journey To The End Of The Night* by the French author Louis Ferdinand Celine (1894-1961). "College usually doesn't help out rock'n'roll too much," observes Kim Fowley, "but Jim brought a lot of that academia to his music, and used it in a very effective way."

Celine, who was also a doctor, packed his phantasmic novels with all kinds of grotesquerie – frightening giants, murderous dwarves and scenes of bloody physical torture. The characters in Celine's novels are continually overwhelmed by waves of both despair and apathy, and his stories convey a gloomy, exceedingly pessimistic view of the world. That view was reflected in Celine's personal life – the writer was prone to near-psychotic rages and bouts of madness.

In 1944, Celine was accused of collaborating with the Nazis and fled his homeland, first to Germany and then Denmark. He was condemned in absentia to one year in prison by a French court in 1950 and, though he was considered to be a national disgrace, he returned to France when he received a pardon the following year. The pardon didn't change his outlook on the world – his later novels are even more wildly misanthropic than the earlier ones.

Jim Morrison's lyrical vision brought mystery and depth to the Doors material, but it was Ray Manzarek's skill at arrangements that gave the vocalist's ideas appropriately dramatic and sensual musical settings.

Though Celine was clearly an unusual role model, his unique voice, powerful images and unapologetically sour philosophy must have impressed Morrison. At first, Morrison began his song by changing Celine's "journey" to "the trip" as in "take the trip to the end of the night." But by the time the Doors recorded the song, Morrison felt that the word "trip" had already become over-used and somewhat trite, so he turned to one of the many "road" images that he would so often use to great effect and went with "take the highway to the end of the night".

'End Of The Night' features some of the earliest lyrics that Morrison penned in his Venice notebooks and was one of the six songs featured on the Doors demo tape recorded before Robby joined the band.

Actually, it's hard to imagine the song coming fully to life without the ghostly bottleneck guitar parts that Krieger developed for it. Somewhat curiously, this sombre, haunting song was released as the B-side of the frenetic 'Break On Through', perhaps suggesting to listeners that the end of the night is where one might end up after breaking on through.

With the album completed and the first single out in 1967, the Doors began a busier road schedule. In May, when the band booked some weekend gigs in San Francisco, they took on an energetic 18-year-old, Bill Siddons, to help them lug their equipment around.

Within a year, Siddons was to become the band's manager when they asked for his assistance and talked him out of going back to college. Siddons says he was never surprised to hear that there were literary inspirations behind Morrison's powerful words.

"He was the smartest man I've ever known," he explains. "He had the most expansive intelligence of any person I've ever met. There was more than one occasion when I had to make him stop talking because I felt he was making me unstable. I'd start listening to him, and all of a sudden I didn't know where the fuck I was."

Los Angeles is a city dependent on cars and freeways. Jim Morrison often used images of automotive travel in his songs, as is the case in 'End Of The Night'.

A calm moment at Venice Beach, early 1967. Venice was a focal point during the Doors' early days – it was where Jim and Ray decided to get a band together, where first rehearsals took place, and where Jim did his formative writing for the band.

Maharishi Mahesh
Yogi earned himself
a spot in rock'n'roll
history in 1968 when
the Beatles attended
a celebrity studded
retreat at the guru's
Himalayan *ashram*.
But the Maharishi's
ties to the rock world
pre-dated that event.
A few years earlier,
his meditation centre
in Los Angeles had
been visited by some
novice meditators
who were soon to be
famous – members
of the Doors.

take it as it comes

The UCLA film school is where Jim Morrison and Ray Manzarek serendipitously crossed paths, but it was at the Maharishi Mahesh Yogi's Third Street Meditation Center in Los Angeles that the rest of the band came together.

'Take It As It Comes' was written by Jim after he attended a meditation lecture on the advice of John Densmore and Robby Krieger. Meditation didn't have much appeal to Morrison, who

at the time preferred the psychic challenges of hallucinogens and the intellectual comforts of books. But after looking deeply into a meditation instructor's eyes and deciding that the instructor had indeed achieved an enviable sense of contentment, Jim composed the Zen-like verses of 'Take It As It Comes' in tribute.

By 1965, Robby Krieger had begun studying Indian music at Ravi Shankar's Kinnara School and he also became interested in

the eastern practices of yoga and meditation. He was playing in an amateur folk-rock group called the Psychedelic Rangers, whose drummer was an old University High School acquaintance of Krieger's, John Densmore. Krieger convinced Densmore and other band members to accompany him to some preliminary meetings for a meditation course at the Maharishi's newly opened centre. Krieger and Densmore liked what they heard at the first meetings and decided to go through with being initiated into the Maharishi's course of transcendental meditation sessions. At one of those sessions, Densmore was disturbed by another initiate who seemed to be approaching meditation with a very sceptical outlook.

In his book, *Riders On The Storm*, Densmore recalled feeling embarrassed by the actions of this irreverent initiate. While most class members clearly hoped that the journey towards transcendence wouldn't take too long, one guy acted as if the whole concept was a scam. Densmore was further nonplussed when the doubter approached him after the class, said he'd heard John was a drummer, and asked if he wanted to get a band together. Densmore wasn't sure what to make of this guy, but he said "Why not?" The sceptical meditator then explained that it was not yet time for the band to begin, but John would be called when it was. The sceptic was Ray Manzarek.

Densmore eventually got the call from Ray, met Jim and quickly became excited about being a part of the music they were developing. Unlike Ray and Jim, he also became increasingly dedicated to meditation. When Ray's guitarist brother Rick dropped out of the band's first line-up, John suggested Robby, who Ray had also met at meditation. Robby's unique approach to guitar made a big impression at

THE YOGI.

the first rehearsal he came to and the Doors were on their way.

The Maharishi also had bigger days ahead and received a great deal of attention in 1968 when the Beatles took part in a retreat at his Himalayan *ashram*.

the end

While 'Light My Fire' proved that the Doors could make music that had broad appeal, 'The End' proved that the band could also scare the hell out of people.

This phenomenal work of entrancing sound, chilling imagery and Oedipal fury began as something much less formidable – a lover's good-bye sung over some hypnotically pretty chords. But Ray, Robby and John had a knack for free-form improvisation and, on long nights at the Whisky A Go Go in the summer of 1966, 'The End' became one of the songs they would stretch out into all kinds of musical directions.

As the song's musical scope increased, Jim Morrison followed up by incorporating some grander, more enigmatic lyrics from his Venice notebooks into the piece and he began to use the band's shifting, dramatic musical interplay as a backdrop for his own free-form flights of half-sung poetry.

The Sunset Strip began to buzz with talk of the Doors' unfettered, wildly entertaining shows at the Whisky and it was that buzz, along with invitations from Whisky booker Ronnie Haran, that got Elektra's Jac Holzman down to check out the band. He was not immediately impressed.

"I didn't like them at first," he later explained, "But I was drawn back. I went four straight nights, then spoke to them and said I wanted to record them."

Before a deal was finalized, Holzman flew Elektra's senior staff producer, Paul Rothchild, out to see a Whisky show. "I thought, 'These guys suck,'" Rothchild told Blair Jackson in *BAM* magazine. "I caught a horrible show. At the same time they were awful, I could tell they were different from anything I'd heard before. They were totally unique. That's usually a signal

Though Jim Morrison often seemed to be interested in much more wrenching means of breaking on through to a higher consciousness, he conceded that transcendental meditation seemed to work well for some of its practitioners, including his bandmates. 'Take It As It Comes' (p36) was a sly nod to the powers of transcendental meditation.

Robby Krieger was interested in Eastern music and philosophy – he studied sitar and sarod at UCLA and at Ravi Shankar's Kinnara School. This influenced the music he created on songs like 'The End'.

Portrait of an all-American family. Father and mother Morrison couldn't have known that the gleam in little Jim's eyes would one day lead him to produce songs like 'The End'.

that someone is either terrible or on the verge of brilliance. This intrigued me, so I decided to stay for a second set. Well, they were still rough around the edges, but they were brilliant. I heard 'The End', 'Light My Fire', 'Twentieth Century Fox', 'Break On Through' and a few others, and I was convinced."

A contract was soon drawn up. And two nights after the Doors were signed to Elektra, they had another show at the Whisky – their first big gig as a hot new band with a fresh label deal. Morrison didn't show up. Manzarek and Densmore grew panicky and headed over to Morrison's place of residence, the Alta-Cienega Motel, a flophouse on La Cienega Boulevard.

At first, they thought Morrison wasn't in his room, but when they heard some shuffling around, they demanded that he open the door. Allegedly, Jim came to the door and greeted his band-mates with three words – "Ten thousand mikes" – meaning that he had consumed ten thousand micrograms of LSD, roughly 40 times the average dose.

Manzarek and Densmore helped their singer get dressed, which proved not to be such an easy task. He was humming and mumbling and barely able to communicate. Finally, he was trundled into a car and taken over to the Whisky.

Morrison had a rough time getting through most of the Doors' set that night, but when the band launched into 'The End', Morrison suddenly was completely in synch with the music and

began to give one of the most riveting performances of his career.

When he came to the extended middle section, Morrison performed for the first time the spookily concise Oedipal drama that was to become the song's hallmark. The nearly silent Whisky crowd watched intently as Morrison built to his crescendo.

Avid rock fan Paul Body was a recent high school graduate, who had been catching the Doors at the Whisky all summer, and he was there that night. "When Morrison said 'Father? Yes, son. I want to kill you. Mother? I want to … fuck you!!', my buddy and I looked at each other and asked, 'Did he say what we think he said?'" Body remembers that the crowd didn't quite know what to make of the performance. "Quite a few people just couldn't believe he'd really said it, and others just tried to pretend it wasn't a big deal. The teenybopper scene had faded out, Dylan was on the charts, and I guess some people figured the next logical step was 'Mother, I want to fuck you.'"

This kind of logic escaped Whisky owner, Elmer Valentine, who promptly fired the Doors after the show.

While Morrison may have created the Oedipal section of 'The End' on stage that night, there is some evidence that he was already fascinated by the myth of Oedipus (who unknowingly killed his father, married his mother and then ashamedly plucked his own eyes out). In the winter of 1965, Judy Raphael was a UCLA film student and friend of Ray Manzarek. She was trying to get a term paper finished one night when she had a visit from Ray, Jim and their UCLA buddy John Debella.

"They'd all been drinking at the Lucky U and Jim had gotten himself doped up on somebody's asthma medication. My paper was supposed to be about the history of documentary film, and all Jim kept saying was, 'I think it should be about Oedipus – Kill the father. Fuck the mother.' He went off on that until I made them take him away. I never did get the paper done and I had to repeat the course."

After the Whisky show, the Doors continued to play 'The End' with the Oedipal section and, when it was time to record the song for the first album, it hadn't lost any of its power to shock and transport listeners. But Morrison, who came to the first sessions for 'The End' full of a disorienting combination of LSD and alcohol, couldn't focus enough to pull the vocals off.

"We tried and we couldn't get it," Rothchild told *Crawdaddy* in 1967. "Jim couldn't do it. He wanted desperately to do it. His entire being was screaming 'Kill the father, fuck the mother!' He was very emotionally moved."

The next day, however, Morrison was in peak form. "We took almost a whole day to set up the studio," Rothchild told *BAM* in

1981, "Because it was a very complex piece to record. When we finally got the tape rolling, it was the most awe-inspiring thing I'd ever witnessed in a studio. It's still one of the top musical events of my life. We were six minutes into it when I turned to Bruce [Botnick] and said, 'Do you understand what's happening here? This is one of the most important moments in recorded rock'n'roll.' When they were done, I had goose bumps from head to foot. It was magic. I went into the studio and told them that, and then I asked them to do it again, to make sure we got it. They did it again and it was equally brilliant. Afterwards, Ray said, 'I don't think we can do that any better.' I said, 'You don't have to. Between those two takes we have one of the best masters ever cut.' It turns out we used the front half of take one and the back half of take two."

The recording of 'The End' was a triumph, but it also proved to be emotionally taxing for Morrison. After the sessions, for reasons unknown, he snuck back into the Sunset Sound Recording Studios during the night and hosed down the room they'd recorded in with a fire extinguisher.

Billy James was one of the group that discovered the mess the next morning. "That was pretty disconcerting. It was pretty clear what had happened, and it was sad. But it didn't surprise me to see that side of Jim. I never knew exactly what to expect from him, but I was never surprised by extremes."

Many of the phrases and images in 'The End' remain as enigmatic as when Morrison first sang them, but Los Angeles-native, poet, journalist and record producer Harvey Kubernick, can shed light on one piece of the puzzle. A teenage fan at the time *The Doors* was released, Kubernick went on to give college lectures on Jim Morrison's poetry and has collaborated frequently with Ray Manzarek on various record projects over the last 20 years. Kubernick doesn't know where the "ancient lake" is, or what the "seven mile snake" looks like, but he does know about "the blue bus".

"Back then, we all had a sense of regional pride when we heard Jim Morrison say, 'Meet me at the back of the blue bus.' We knew that the blue bus was the bus that went down Pico Boulevard – the bus that took us to the beach for a quarter. I believe it was the Number 7. As young fans of the Doors' music, we didn't talk too much about Freud or Oedipus, but we got very excited every time Jim mentioned that blue bus."

Jim Morrison had been fascinated by the myth of King Oedipus and his disturbed family relationships long before he created the murderous, incestuous scenario that made 'The End' so powerful.

strange days

Ugly faces, lost little girls, drowning lovers and mute nostril agony: *Strange Days* is the music of fantastic nightmares.

With their first album, the Doors had got their rock'n'roll journey off to an undeniably dazzling start. In October 1967, they followed that triumph with a masterpiece – *Strange Days*.

The 10 songs on the Doors' sophomore effort showed them to be at the height of their creative powers. They'd had time to grow into much of the material: 'Moonlight Drive' and 'My Eyes Have Seen You' had first been recorded for the demo tape that the Doors first brought to Billy James at Columbia; 'Love Me Two Times' was one of the earliest songs that Robby Krieger had written for the band; and the extended drama of 'When The Music's Over' had been perfected on the stages of the London Fog and the Whisky A Go Go.

When the songs for *Strange Days* were first developed, Jim was still mining his Venice notebooks for lyrical inspiration and the confidence he'd developed on stage as a performer subsequently helped him to deliver some of the finest vocal work of his career.

On *Strange Days*, all the trademarks of the Doors' sound were again in place. Manzarek's enlightened keyboard parts held the arrangements together, Krieger's graceful guitar work swung from delicate counterpoints to screaming epiphanies and Densmore convincingly furthered his explorations into high-concept drumming.

There were strong stylistic tie-ins with the first album: the same driving, sycopated attack that had kicked 'Light My Fire' to its climax showed up again in 'When The Music's Over' and 'Love Me Two Times'. Meanwhile, 'People Are Strange' sounded like a cabaret companion for 'Alabama Song'.

'When The Music's Over' may have started off like Take Two of 'Soul Kitchen', but it grew into the kind of climactic album-closer that 'The End' had been on the first record.

The band showed astonishing signs of growth on *Strange Days*. If *The Doors* gave listeners a sense of what the band might sound like playing through a flawless set at the Whisky, *Strange Days* offered a startling glimpse into the Doors' eerie cosmos. This was an exhilarating, disconcerting and fearsome place to be, full of ugly faces, tiny monsters, lost little girls and moonlight drives that ended at the bottom of the ocean: all this darkness at a time when the Summer of Love was still a warm memory and the Beatles were insisting 'All You Need Is Love'!

Strange days were arriving for the Doors, and some of the ultimate LA band's strangest and best days of 1967 were spent up in San Francisco. The Doors quickly moved from being at bottom of bills there, to becoming top-drawer head-liners. Their first big gigs after the release of *Strange Days* were at the Fillmore and the Winterland in San Francisco.

Morrison's songs didn't reach out to the listener, nor did they ask to be embraced, yet the music was powerful enough to pull the listener in anyway. The moonlight drive couldn't be refused.

The band returned to Sunset Sound in August 1967 and spent a couple of months assembling the tracks, excitedly seizing upon the opportunities offered by Elektra's newly expanded eight-track recording system. (In those days, this was cutting-edge technology – even *Sgt Pepper* had been recorded on 4-track machines.)

The Doors' innovative use of the recording process, under the guidance of producer Paul Rothchild and engineer Bruce Botnick, was a tremendous factor in the artistic success of *Strange Days*. "That was when we began to experiment with the studio itself, as an instrument to be played," Ray Manzarek said in 1978. "We thought, 'My goodness, how amazing. We can do all kinds of things. We can do overdubs, we can do this, we can do that – now we've got eight tracks to play with.' So, at that point, we began to play – it became five people; keyboards, drums, guitar, singer and studio."

Actually there was a sixth person as well. The band again recruited a bassist to fill out the bottom end of the sound and this time it was a left-handed player named Doug Lubahn, borrowed from one of the Sunset Strip's most psychedelic bands, Clear Light (who took their name from some particularly potent acid).

Paul Rothchild was exceedingly proud of the work he and the band accomplished on *Strange Days*. "There are no weak songs on it," he told *BAM* in 1981. "We had lots of meetings to talk about the concept of the record, how adventurous it would be, things we could improve on from the first record. We knew we wanted to explore additional sounds and rhythms, because we had decided that it would be difficult to sustain a career with a band consisting only of organ, guitar, drums and a singer. So our challenge was to expand the Doors' sound without over-producing it. We had Ray play harpsichord and piano. Robby got new guitar sounds. John played more percussion instruments. Jim was singing with the confidence of a man who had just put out the Doors' first album. We were all at our hottest. We had a ton of ideas and we went to the moon with it all. Even the cover won all sorts of awards."

The cover of *Strange Days* featured a kind of stylized, carnivalesque street scene and the fact that it was not a shot of the band was considered important by them, especially Morrison. During the media blitz that surrounded the first album, Morrison gamely accepted the old saw that sex sells and, to some extent, allowed himself to be focused upon as the group's sex symbol. But he soon realized that the attention paid to his looks and leather pants came at the expense of attention to the music, and the sex symbol role grew wearisome very quickly.

"I hated the cover of our first album," he told John Carpenter of the *Los Angeles Free Press* in 1968. "So for *Strange Days* I said, 'I don't want to be on this cover. Put a chick on it or something. Let's have a dandelion or a design…' and, because of the title, everyone agreed, 'cause that's where we were at, what was happening. It was right. Originally I wanted us in a room surrounded by about 30 dogs, but that was impossible because we couldn't get the dogs, and everyone was saying 'What do you want dogs for?' And I said that it was symbolic that it spelled God backwards. Finally we ended up leaving it to the art director [William S Harvey] and the photographer [Joel Brodsky]. We wanted some real freaks though, and they came out with a typical side-show thing. It looked European. It was better than having our fucking faces on it though."

The Doors' faces were in fact featured on the cover, but only as part of a pair of posters for the first album that were inconspicuously plastered to the buildings framing the photo. Across each of those posters was a bold sticker that announced the second album's title. *Strange Days* had arrived.

By this time, there were two kinds of Doors fans. Those who dug 'The End' and thought of Jim as a mysterious poet, and those who liked 'Light My Fire' and thought of him as a pin-up.

"I ran right out and bought *Strange Days* when it first came out and it blew me away," remembers Doors fan Paul Body. "But I'll never forget the reaction of my friend's little sister when we brought the record over to his house. She got one look at the album sleeve, which had lyrics on one side and a band picture with Jim shirtless on the other side. She ripped the thing right in half, ran away and put the picture up on her wall. I don't know if she even knew who the band was. That's when it dawned on me that there was another appeal to the Doors – that not everybody was going to be buying *Strange Days* just to listen to 'Horse Latitudes'."

The shaman's powers were at their peak on *Strange Days*. Jim Morrison was again pulling fine dark visions from his Venice notebooks to create the lyrical phantasmagoria of the Doors second album, and the band supported him with exceptional musical backdrops.

strange days

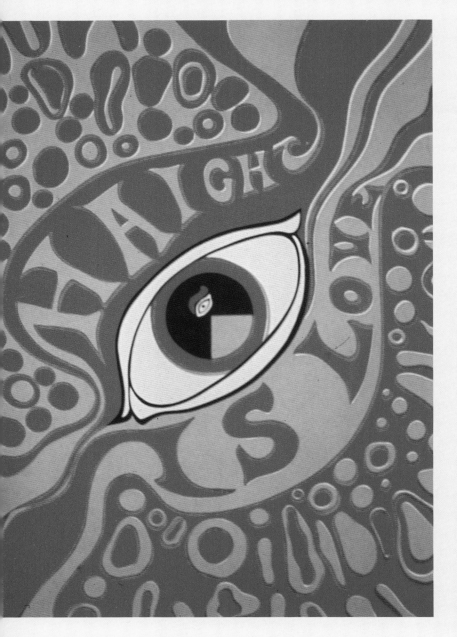

Even within the general excellence of the *Strange Days* album, the song 'Strange Days' stands out as a masterwork.

Morrison may have considered his poems and his lyrics sprang from distinctly separate muses, but in fact, as this song proves, some of his finest poetry was to be found in his lyrics. The strange eyes, sinful guests and confused bodies described here are the creations of a darkly brilliant wordsmith.

Morrison sings the song with coiled power, ready to be unleashed. As he sings, each word spreads and stretches, until it begins to sound like he is chanting some ancient prayer. Morrison is the sage observer of all around him, but he seems to make no judgement about what he sees. He sings of the destruction of casual joys without anger or regret: it is simply a statement of fact.

The world at large and the world within have become, in a word, "strange". But each coolly-delivered Morrison ·verse builds to a moment of abandon. When he hollers, one can almost picture him taking a leap into some yawning abyss and then the band rises to support him with an anthemic instrumental break that is perhaps the most stirringly cathartic piece of music the Doors ever created. As the song comes to its swelling conclusion, Morrison leaves us with one final, frightful image – a "night of stone".

Having made the decision to make full use of their studio, as well as the talents of Paul Rothchild and Bruce Botnick, 'Strange Days' was brought to life with some state-of-the-art techniques. Jim's voice was electronically processed to sound as strange as the days he was singing about and Ray's keyboards were given a ghostly warble.

The group also brought in sound technician Paul Beaver, the West Coast's Moog synthesizer specialist. He helped the band come up with some particularly effective sounds on both 'Strange Days' and 'Horse Latitudes'. This was one of the first uses of the Moog on a rock record.

By 1967, the Summer of Love was in full swing and the prevailing ethos was "the stranger the better". Acid was taken to fuel inner journeys and a premium was placed on personal experimentation. But Jim Morrison knew that voyages of self-discovery weren't always warm and fuzzy – the advent of "strange days" meant that dark and disquieting moments were also at hand.

The Doors had something in common with a fellow Los Angeles band that put out a very different sound – the Monkees. Both bands worked with sound technician Paul Beaver and pioneered the use of the Moog synthesizer as a rock instrument.

(Just exactly who used the Moog first seems to be a toss-up between Ray Manzarek and, somewhat surprisingly, Micky Dolenz of the Monkees, who also enlisted Paul Beaver's equipment for the track 'Daily Nightly' on his group's 1967 album *Pisces, Aquarius, Capricorn & Jones Ltd.*)

Jim Morrison rarely revealed much of himself directly through his songs – he wasn't interested merely in creating dramatic personal confessions, he wanted to produce something more. At the same time, it is hard not to imagine that he was speaking directly from the soul when he penned '*Strange Days*'. After all, in the space of three short years, Jim Morrison had gone from being a bright, troubled "Navy brat" to a wildly liberated, poetry-obsessed film student, who next became a shimmying rock'n'roll frontman with a Jay Sebring haircut, before being transformed in turn into an adulated Rock God with a Number 1 record, a photo-spread in *Vogue* and a spot on *The Ed Sullivan Show*. Strange days indeed.

Musician Chris Darrow describes an encounter with Jim that seems to indicate just how much stranger those days were soon to become. Darrow first saw the Doors at the Whisky, when he was a member of the highly regarded LA band Kaleidoscope. In November 1967, a month after the release of *Strange Days*, he was working as a member of the Nitty Gritty Dirt Band, when they shared a bill with the Doors at Hunter College in New York.

"I was backstage walking around and walked past a little dressing room and Jim was in there by himself. He called out to me by name, and I was a little impressed that he knew who I was. I went in and said hello, and he said 'Man, have you ever tried ether?' I said no, and that was the end of the conversation. I just remember that he had this real Lord Byron aura about him – he was the Romantic who was willing to try anything. I think that attitude worked itself into the music too. There was a folk music undertone to what most of the bands were doing at the time – electric folk – but the Doors had nothing to do with that. They were something else entirely."

Morrison was beginning to grapple with his personal demons, but '*Strange Days*' also showed prescience about the trials and troubles ahead for the world at large.

Riots raged in the ghettos of Newark, Detroit and Cleveland throughout 1967. The month the album came out, 100,000 demonstrators marched on the Pentagon and hippie activist Abbie Hoffman attempted to levitate it. The Vietnam war was clearly only going to get bloodier and shortly, at the 1968 Democratic Convention, there would be furious demonstrations on the streets of Chicago. By the end of 1968, Martin Luther King Jr and Robert F Kennedy had been struck down by assassins' bullets.

Though the Doors had their first great run of success during the so-called "Summer Of Love", Morrison and the band hadn't ever copped to any prevailing vibes of peace and love. The forces of darkness out in the real world could not be kept at bay with love beads. The only hope lay in learning to find one's way through the darkness.

you're lost little girl

While Jim Morrison was locking in his male teen audience with 'People Are Strange' and images of jettisoned horses, young female Doors fans were drawn toward the material which seemed to be aimed directly at them – such as *Strange Days*' second track, 'You're Lost Little Girl'.

Ironically, few suspected that the writer of the song was not the band's alluring lead singer, but low-key guitarist Robby Krieger – a fact obscured by the group's decision to go with a collective "Doors" song writing credit and to evenly distribute song writing royalties.

Fewer still would have believed that, at the time, the band had half-seriously pondered whether no less a crooner than Frank Sinatra might eventually deign to cover the track. The tough-tender melody seemed to make it a perfect song for Ol' Blue Eyes. John Densmore later said that it would have made a great serenade to the waifish Mia Farrow, who was briefly Sinatra's wife. The Doors-Chairman connection wasn't so far-fetched – Jim had listed Sinatra alongside Elvis Presley as his favourite singers on his first press bio.

TV host Ed Sullivan, who had fretted that the word "higher" in 'Light My Fire' would be detrimental to the morals of the nation's youth, would have been further shocked to discover how Jim Morrison achieved the tranquil, dreamy tone of his vocals on 'You're Lost Little Girl'.

Paul Rothchild was concerned that Jim should not push the vocals too hard and felt that, for the track to work, Jim had to sound completely relaxed. Jokingly, he suggested hiring a prostitute to join Jim in the vocal booth and perform oral sex on him while he sang.

Jim's on-again-off-again girlfriend Pamela Courson overheard the suggestion and objected strenuously; such work was her responsibility. She joined Jim in the booth, lights were dimmed and tape began to roll. Jim began to sing, but then stopped. All that could be heard in the control room was some rustling from the booth. The mikes were switched off and the two were left alone for a while.

A later take made it on to the album – apparently without involving any unzipping at all. It had just the right sound – the kind of serene "afterglow" Rothchild had been after in the first place.

In fact, no matter what Jim Morrison did in the studio, and no matter what the Doors did around him, the singer's sex appeal made it through the speakers to those fans who were smitten with him as rock's finest heart-throb. Already he was growing tired of being in that kind of celebrity spotlight, but he couldn't get away from it. Not only did Jim find the adulation distasteful, he also began to sense some disdain among his Sunset Strip contemporaries.

"I've often wondered if Morrison was just too good-looking for his own good," says Chris Darrow. "Nobody else at the time had that kind of sex appeal, and that brought a whole different kind of attention. Look at Buffalo Springfield, the Byrds, Iron Butterfly or the band I was in, Kaleidoscope. We were just regular guys up on stage playing in bands. Nothing special to look at. We knew the Doors were making some interesting music too, but I have to say that there really was some resentment among us musicians over Jim's looks."

The Byrds were the kings of the electric folk-rock sound that many Southern California bands sought to emulate. But, for a while, no band and no frontman could match the fiercely sensual charisma that Jim Morrison brought to the stage.

love me two times

The Doors had had the word "high" taken out of 'Break On Through' and "fuck" taken out of 'The End', but it was Robby Krieger's relatively innocuous 'Love Me Two Times' that became the true measure of the band's notoriety – it was their first "banned" single.

Krieger's career as a songwriter got off to a phenomenal start: 'Light My Fire' was the first song he ever wrote and 'Love Me Two Times' was the second. The idea for 'Love Me Two Times' came to him as he thought about lovers who were separated by forces beyond their control. The thought of soldiers having a night of romance with their lovers before heading off to Vietnam was partly the inspiration. So was the idea of the Doors themselves being out on the road and only having a single night with each of their love interests.

The leering, upbeat tune, which had been a part of the band's sets since the London Fog days, was built around a clever Krieger guitar riff. In the studio, Manzarek and Densmore called upon their feel for jazz to give the track a swinging groove. Morrison wasn't crazy about the lyrics, but he gave them a ripping, testosterone-drenched delivery.

For teenybopper fans, who had fallen in love with 'Light My Fire' and who thought Jim was the cutest thing in leather, 'Love Me Two Times' made ideal listening: the record sold hot and

fast. But at some radio stations, the fact that the "love" in the title could be tallied up made it a little too obvious that this was love of a, well, clinical nature and the record was deemed obscene.

It got a lot harder for the Doors to argue that their love was innocent when, on 9 December 1967 at the New Haven Arena, Jim Morrison became the first rock'n'roller to be arrested on stage during a performance.

In the middle of a short tour to promote *Strange Days*, the band arrived in New Haven having played a less than sizzling show at the Rensselaer Polytechnic Institute in Troy, New York, the night before. Backstage in New Haven, Morrison ran into a young female fan that he took an immediate liking to. Looking for a spot with some privacy, he led her to a dressing room shower stall. They were quickly interrupted by a New Haven policeman, who thought he had discovered some backstage interlopers. The cop attempted to kick Morrison out and Jim put up verbal resistance, so the officer went to his belt and promptly maced the evening's headliner.

Chaos ensued, with Morrison's screams bringing manager Bill Siddons and the Doors' support staff to his aid. Even when Jim was identified to the police, they still wanted to take him into custody. Siddons wisely pointed out that the show was a benefit for a scholarship fund and that it would be dangerous to tell the capacity crowd that they weren't going to see the main attraction. When Jim recovered, the Doors took the stage.

But Morrison couldn't shake off his anger at having been brutalized. He performed a powerful version of 'When The Music's Over', but, when he got in to 'Back Door Man', Morrison started to digress. Instead of belting out Willie Dixon's lyrics, he described what had happened backstage, taking pains to stress his own innocence and painting the cop who sprayed him as a ridiculous "little man in a little blue suit and a little blue cap". He relayed the whole incident to the crowd in a classic Morrison-style rhythmic rant. He ended by saying, "The whole fucking world hates me", and then swung right back into the final verse of the song.

Before the band could finish, the house lights came up. Morrison asked the crowd what was happening and asked them if they wanted to hear more music. They let him know loudly that they did. But the music was over. Lieutenant James P Kelly came out on stage towards Morrison. The singer pointed the microphone at the cop and delivered a memorable line, "Say your thing, man." Kelly had nothing to say, except that the concert was indeed concluded and Morrison was under arrest.

At this point, the crowd truly did turn dangerous, as chairs were hurled and angry fans rushed the stage. While all hell broke loose, Morrison was hauled off to the police station, where he was charged with "breach of the peace, resisting arrest, and indecent or immoral exhibition".

A few weeks after the concert, the resistance and indecency charges were dropped and the breach of the peace was taken care of with the payment of a $25 fine. No big deal. But at many more of the country's fickle, sponsor-fearing radio stations, the charms of Robby's 'Love Me Two Times' didn't stand a chance against the taint of the New Haven bust.

The Doors had been called dark, bleak, sexy and strange before – now they had taken their first real step towards becoming the band that Square America would love to hate. For these upstanding citizens, the "goin' away" part of "Love me two times, I'm goin' away" couldn't come soon enough.

unhappy girl

'Unhappy Girl' was another of the band's older tunes that finally made it to tape for the second record. In the Doors' pre-demo days, before Ray had discovered the wonders of the Fender Rhodes piano bass, 'Unhappy Girl' was one of songs the band had used to audition bass players. The song was usually played as a straightforward, soulful love song.

But when they recorded it for *Strange Days*, it became a triumph of studio atmospherics. Part of that atmosphere came from Robby's doleful bottleneck parts, but a larger part came from Ray's piano part, which he played backwards. "A backwards piano. Boy that was a bitch," he told Pete Fornatale in a 1981 *Musician* interview. "I wrote the whole song out backwards. They played the song, the tape came back to me in the earphones backwards. But the beat was there. I started on the lower right-hand side of the chart rather than the upper left-hand side and read backwards as the song progressed."

Once Ray was done and the master tape was played forward again, the piano alone had an eerie backwards quality, though now the part fitted perfectly into the song.

Producer Paul Rothchild felt such techniques had a chance of putting *Strange Days* right up there next to *Sgt Pepper* as a monumental mix of studio craft and artistic vitality. "We were confident it was going to be bigger than anything the Beatles had done", he told Blair Jackson in *BAM*. "It was filled with ingenuity, creativity, great songs, great playing, fabulous singing. But the record died on us. Oh, it went platinum immediately, but it never really 'conquered' like it should have. It never conquered like the first one did or the next one would."

The Doors never developed any kind of a flashy stage show, but on a good night all they needed were the players' instrumental prowess and Jim Morrison's estimable talents to produce a performance that mesmerised their audience.

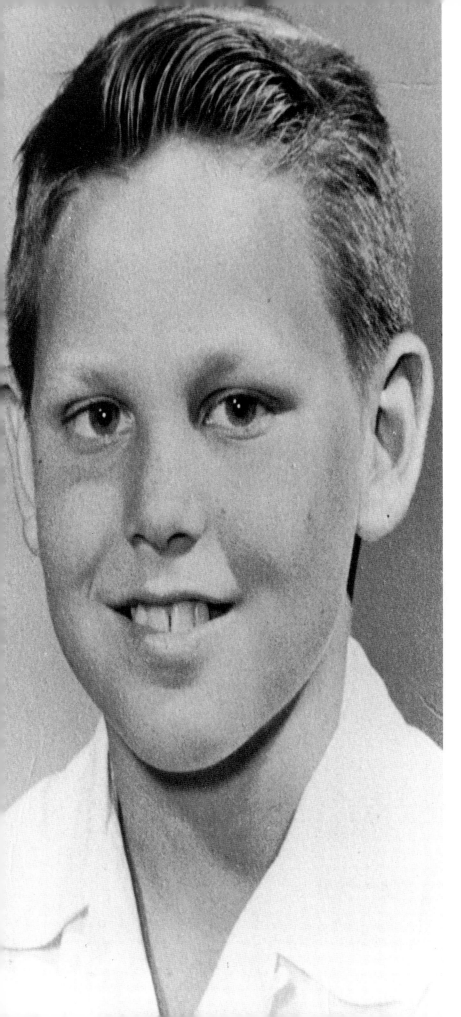

'Unhappy Girl' was the flipside of the 'People Are Strange' single and, despite the ingenuity that went into it and some fabulous singing from Jim, it became something of a throwaway song — basically, it took the message of 'Break On Through' and softened it into a gentle lover's encouragements.

Listening to the song today, Bill Siddons says that he can't help but think the lyrics reflect on the situation Morrison found himself in back in 1967. "He eventually abandoned music because he became a victim of what he created. Suddenly he didn't have the freedom that he went into music to find. Like the person he describes in 'Unhappy Girl', he became a prisoner of his own devise. He devised a prison by being so outrageous that everybody said 'Man, he's great.' He knew he couldn't top himself, and he didn't have any desire too. But others' expectations became a prison."

The product of some of Jim Morrison's earliest poetry efforts,

horse latitudes

'Horse Latitudes' has the longest history of any Doors song.

Throughout elementary school, junior high and high school, Jim was a voracious reader who was intrigued by innovative use of language. He loved the anarchic satire of *Mad* magazine, but he was also powerfully attracted to the Übermensch philosophies of the German Friedrich Nietzsche. He was particularly taken with a Nietzsche work called *The Birth Of Tragedy (Out Of The Spirit Of Music)*. Here, the philosopher analyzed two contrasting approaches to life: the Apollonian, which represented an aesthetic of harmony and order, and the Dionysian, which was given to chaos, impulse and carnality. By the time *Strange Days* was out, Jim was regularly quoting Nietzsche in interviews and discussing the Apollonian-Dionysian split in the Doors' music.

Morrison was deeply influenced by other writers and artists: Balzac, Molière, Cocteau, French existentialists and

Beat poets such as Lawrence Ferlinghetti, Allen Ginsberg, Michael McClure and Gregory Corso. James Joyce's *Ulysses* showed him how powerful language could become when it was used unconventionally and Jack Kerouac's *On The Road* may have eventually given him the strength to break away from his family and travel across the country from Florida to Los Angeles.

The existentialist writing of Franz Kafka also had a profound effect on Jim. He was fascinated by Kafka's famous short story *The Metamorphosis*, but he was even more affected by the journals and diaries that Kafka had kept. In high school, he began to keep a journal himself and that is where 'Horse Latitudes' first appeared. The poem was inspired by the illustration on a paperback book that showed horses being thrown from a Spanish galleon.

"It's called 'Horse Latitudes' because it's about the Doldrums," Morrison explained in 1967, "where sailing ships from Spain would get stuck. In order to lighten the vessel, they had to throw things overboard. Their major cargo was working horses for the New World. And this song is about the moment when the horse is in the air. I imagine it must have been hard to get them over the side. When they got to the edge, they probably started chucking and kicking. And it must have been hell for the men to watch, too. Because horses can swim for a little while, but then they lose their strength and just go down … slowly sink away."

It wasn't the first time Morrison had used horse imagery in a poem. "Around the fifth or sixth grade I wrote a poem called 'The Pony Express'," he told Jerry Hopkins of *Rolling Stone* in 1969. "That was the first one I can remember. It was one of those ballad-type poems. I never could get it together, though. I always wanted to write, but I figured it'd be no good unless somehow the hand just took the pen and started moving without me having anything to do with it. But it just never happened."

The Doors decided to give 'Horse Latitudes' special treatment when they recorded it for *Strange Days*. The sonic foundation for the song – a terrible howling wind – was created in the studio control booth by manually spinning a tape of white noise at varying speeds. To create the appropriate accompanying frenzy, various odd percussion effects were recorded, including bottles being flung into a trash can. Some dissonant counterpoint to Jim's frightening intonation was added by opening a piano and playing its strings from the inside.

"We were scraping on them, plucking them, hitting them with drumsticks, and putting a delay on it," Ray explained to Paul Laurence in a 1983 *Audio* interview. "If you hit it once, the delay sound keeps happening so it sounds like a lot of people doing it. I imagine everyone got their fingers in for a couple of picks. It was too much fun." For additional sound effects, the band brought in Moog expert Paul Beaver.

As important as the studio effects were in providing essential depth to the short piece, the song was still effective in live shows and it became one of the most chilling moments in their sets. "I heard 'Horse Latitudes' at one of their early gigs at the Hullabaloo," remembers songwriter/producer Kim Fowley, "and I decided right then that Jim Morrison was the greatest white frontman in rock'n'roll."

It was also a performance of 'Horse Latitudes' at one of their early San Francisco gigs that cemented the band's relationship with future manager Bill Siddons. "It wasn't their music that grabbed me – it was Jim's words. I had come from LA with them to help to carry their amps that night, not because I was a fan, but because I just wanted to get away for the weekend. But then I heard Morrison do 'Horse Latitudes'. That was the moment. I went, 'Oh my God'. It had nothing to do with any music I'd ever imagined. I was awed. And the reason that song can still give you chills all these years later is that Jim believed every word he was saying."

One striking phrase from the piece, "mute nostril agony", was John Densmore's favoured choice for the title of a documentary film detailing the Doors' travels throughout 1968. The band eventually went with one of Ray's suggestions, a phrase taken from 'When The Music's Over' – *Feast Of Friends*.

Ray Manzarek has said that if Jim Morrison had never read novelist Jack Kerouac's (above) Beat manifesto, *On The Road,* the Doors might never have happened.

Even as a young child, Jim Morrison (p.50) was a voracious reader and an ambitious writer. His fascination with equine imagery first turned up in an elementary school poem entitled 'The Pony Express'.

As a teenager, Jim was greatly intrigued by *Beyond Good And Evil,* German philosopher Friedrich Nietzsche's (left) treatise on how an exceptional human could rise above societal norms.

moonlight drive

Though it didn't show up until the second album, 'Moonlight Drive' actually marks the beginning of the Doors' history as a band.

In July 1965, Ray Manzarek was enjoying a sunny day out lazing around Venice beach when he spotted a friendly acquaintance from UCLA that he hadn't seen for some time – Jim Morrison. The two exchanged greetings and, when Ray asked Jim what he had been up to lately, he was surprised to hear that Jim had been writing songs.

"I said, 'Well, far out'," Ray remembered in a 1981 interview. "'Why not sing one for me?' So what he did was sing 'Moonlight Drive' and when I heard those first four lines, I said, 'Wow, those are the greatest lyrics I've ever heard for a rock'n'roll song.' As he was singing, I could hear the chord changes and the beat – my fingers immediately started moving. I asked him if he had anymore, and he replied, 'Yeah, I've got a lot of them,' and he went through a few more. I said, 'Listen, those are the best rock'n'roll songs I've ever heard, and I've been into music since I was seven years old. Why don't we do something about this?' Jim said, 'That's what I had in mind. Let's start a band together.' I said, 'Let's do that, and make a million dollars.' And that's how the Doors got started."

There were some who thought those million dollars would be a long time coming. Judy Raphael, a UCLA classmate, remembers the day Ray excitedly approached her with the news of his new endeavour. "He said he was going to form a rock band, and I was a little floored, I guess I was a little jealous – I wanted to be in the band. I asked if I could sing with him, and he said 'Oh I don't think so. We've got Jim Morrison.' Morrison? That was a shock. Then he showed me 'Moonlight Drive', written out on a piece of lined paper and he read it to me. I thought it was dreadful," she laughs. "It didn't sound like the lyrics to any of the folk or rock music I was listening to at the time. But I still wanted to be a part of it somehow, so I suggested a name – I can't remember what. Ray said, 'I think we're going to go with 'the Doors' and I remember saying to him, 'The Doors? That's stupid – that'll never work.'"

The song had come to Jim as he filled his notebooks with poetry early in the summer of 1965. Morrison only had a few piano lessons worth of musical training, but occasionally the words that came to him came clearly in the form of songs rather than poetry. If he concentrated hard enough, he could hear the whole musical arrangement – a concert in his head. "To me a song comes with the music, a sound or rhythm first; then I make up words as fast as I can, just to hold on to the feel, until the music and lyric come almost simultaneously," he said in 1969.

The first song to arrive that way was 'Moonlight Drive'. Writing one night on his Venice rooftop, with a clear view of the beach, the surf and the moon before him, and the busy streets below him, Morrison created a wonderfully evocative invitation to a night-time swim – a swim to the moon – that ended rather mysteriously in either watery romance or a suicide pact.

The song also played an important role in bringing Densmore and Krieger into the Doors. The lyrics to 'Moonlight Drive', along with those of 'Soul Kitchen', were what convinced Densmore at an early rehearsal to throw in with Ray and Jim. And at Robby's first rehearsal with the group, it was during a run-through of 'Moonlight Drive' that the band members realized that they were playing with a remarkable chemistry, that they had just created an entirely unique sound.

"Robby came down with his guitar and bottleneck," Ray recalled in 1972. "The first song we played as a group was 'Moonlight Drive', because it didn't have too many difficult chord changes and, after playing that, I said, 'This is it. This is the best musical experience I've ever had.'"

A version of 'Moonlight Drive' had been recorded for the group's very first demo tape and it was a staple of their live sets. It was going to appear on the first album, and it was the first track the Doors worked on at those sessions. But, perhaps because they were uncomfortable or nervous that first day in the studio, they ended up with a take of the song that they weren't happy with.

They shelved the song and recut it during the *Strange Days* sessions. The song had a basic blues structure, but the group's knack for unorthodox arrangement turned it into something much more compelling. It begins with Ray's sprightly piano riffs, a martial drum beat from Densmore that tapped his experience in the Uni High marching band and some almost cartoonish floating bottleneck figures from Robby.

Morrison sang clearly and calmly, with just a touch of grit evident in his powerful baritone pipes. But as the song modulates up into the second verse, things start to get a little crazy and more active – it becomes a wilder drive. By the final verse, the band is white hot and Morrison is screaming his invitation

Judy Raphael was a friend of Ray Manzarek's at UCLA. She was initially sceptical about songs like 'Moonlight Drive' or a band called "the Doors" ever amounting to much. A couple of years later, she was working as an exotic dancer in San Francisco. Her speciality number was a hit single called 'Light My Fire' by none other than her friend Ray's band – the Doors.

to climb to the moon and sink in the ocean. In live versions, Ray and Jim would often engage in some bluesy vocal interplay, and the final "down, down, down" section would turn into an extended vamp. In a performance included on the 1983 release *Alive She Cried*, Morrison wove 'Horse Latitudes' into this section.

Throughout their career, the band continued to have fun with 'Moonlight Drive'. Bill Siddons remembers it being played on a special occasion at the Doors Workshop during the rehearsals for *LA Woman*. "It was my wife's birthday. She loved 'Moonlight Drive' — it was always her favourite. When she came by the office Jim said, 'Hey Cheri, come on in — we've got something for you.' She walked in, Jim walked up to the mike, and they played 'Moonlight Drive' just for her."

people are strange

'People Are Strange' served as a harbinger of *Strange Days*. Backed with 'Unhappy Girl', it was released in September 1967, while the Doors were still in the process of completing their second album.

This catchy tune was a misleadingly jaunty profession of alienation and it worked so well precisely because of the odd blend of bleak Morrison imagery — ugly faces, uneven streets, wicked women — and rollicking music, especially Ray Manzarek's barrelhouse piano parts. The song's lyrics may have struck some listeners as having sprung from a well of deep depression, but while Morrison's angst was honest, this song was actually more the result of Jim using his wily, self-depre-cating sense of humour to fight off depression.

When the band began recording again at Sunset Sound, Morrison may have been under some pressure as a songwriter. His greatest songs so far had come from the Venice notebooks he'd been keeping two years before and, as the band became more and more successful, he realized that he was going to

have to continue coming up with the goods. If he had any fears about running out of ideas, they were allayed when 'People Are Strange' came to him in a flash on one of the band's days off in August.

Robby Krieger was surprised when Morrison turned up at the rented house Krieger and John Densmore shared on Lookout Mountain Drive in Laurel Canyon. The band members spent so much time together for their music by this point, they did not often see each other on a strictly social basis. Krieger was further surprised that Morrison, who was in an agitated, depressed state, talked openly about his conflicted feelings concerning the band's success. "He just didn't think it was all worth it anymore and life was horrible," recalled Krieger. "So we spent all night talking him out of killing himself, like we did many times, and finally in the morning he said, 'Well, I'm going to take a walk up to the top of the hill.'"

The tight, wildly twisting streets through this area of the Hollywood Hills were not designed to welcome pedestrians — there are no sidewalks. But Jim hiked up the hill from Robby's house to a street called Appian Way, where various vista points offer, on a clear day, magnificent panoramic views over Los Angeles.

Just off Appian Way, Morrison found a comfortable spot to perch and take in the view. The sprawling landscape before him cleared his head and brought a sense of calm — and then, inspiration. A while later Morrison showed up again at the house and this time he was wildly happy. "He was in the best mood I'd ever seen him in," said Krieger. "He said, 'Man, I've just seen the light, man, it was so beautiful up there and I just wrote a song on the way back down the hill.'"

Morrison proceeded to sing Krieger his spanking fresh song about how strange the world is when one is a stranger to begin with. It sounded like a winner to Krieger and the band worked it into shape over the first couple of weeks of the *Strange Days* sessions. The single failed to tear up the charts the way 'Light My Fire' had done, but it did reach Number 12 on the *Billboard* charts and helped *Strange Days* become a Top 10 album.

But, in typical Morrison fashion, the song develops a more sinister edge – it's not just the confessions of a lusty Peeping Tom. In the third verse, the "eyes" observe someone "gazing on a city under television skies". Is the watcher now being watched? And in the final verse, the "eyes" become a camera that can photograph a soul on an endless roll of film. So who's doing the watching? Jim? An omnipotent being? A little of both? The nightly news? The CIA?

Some of Jim Morrison's finest writing was produced in a heated, acid-driven rush during the summer of 1965 on this Venice rooftop. Looking out to sea, he saw the water he wanted to sink into on his 'Moonlight Drive'. Facing inland, he was "gazing at a city under television skies".

my eyes have seen you

'My Eyes Have Seen You' was first developed by the band in the garage at Ray's parents home in Manhattan Beach before Robby joined them. It was another of the six tracks that were recorded for the first pre-Robby Doors demo at World Pacific Sound, and it was one of the songs that came to Morrison in his first inspired rush of song writing on the Venice rooftop in the summer of 1965.

Knowing that it was written on a rooftop makes sense as one listens to Morrison snarl out the title phrase over and over – this is one of rock'n'roll's greatest tributes to voyeurism. From his perch three stories above the street, Morrison takes in every move that the objects of his infatuation make: they stand in a doorway, turn and stare, fix their hair.

As is usually the case with Jim's strongest work, a literal understanding isn't really necessary because the words, backed by the Doors' driving accompaniment, aren't telling a story but creating a mood. 'My Eyes Have Seen You' is, in some ways, one of the Doors' simpler rockers, but it also calls up questions of power and privacy, obliquely sends up the hunger for "pictures" in the age of modern media and tosses in a hint of dread for good measure.

Jim had come up with a basic melody for the song and the band invented one of their usual, ingenious arrangements to put it across. Instead of giving the song a steady rock'n'roll feel, Ray conceived of it as "a rock'n'roll tango" and created the catchy stop and go rhythms of the verses. Robby ratcheted up the excitement with some great distorted guitar lines and a brief but explosive solo.

The expression "television skies" is a particularly good example of Morrison's ability to find strong simple words to build a uniquely creative image. From his rooftop, he was looking down at blocks of bungalows and small walk-up apartment buildings, each of which was crowned with any number of television antennae. He must have thought of all those television sets pulling signals through their roofs, all those signals bouncing about in the atmosphere above the city, and he came up with a powerfully concise description: "television skies".

i can't see your face

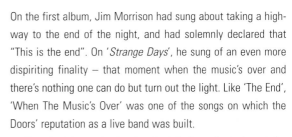

At the Doors early shows on Sunset Strip, Linda Albertano realized that the power Jim Morrison exerted over the club crowds wasn't just down to his beautiful face. The face didn't hurt, but it was Jim's words, like his poetic riffs during 'When The Music's Over', that really held his audience spellbound.

'I Can't See Your Face' isn't generally seen as a tremendously important Doors track, but in some ways it is thoroughly representative of their work. It has a conventionally beautiful melody and a pop theme – a romantic break-up (Morrison gives the break-up a dark edge – he's searching for the right lie that will free him). But Jim's sad voice and otherworldly images blend with the group's hauntingly delicate arrangement to create a very affecting piece of music.

In feel and content 'I Can't See Your Face' is perhaps opposite to '*Strange Days*' but it's still odd – and a perfectly realised Doors track. Robby again used subtle bottleneck lines to set a mood and Ray combined his organ parts with some mallet work on marimba to add new range to the group's sound. Most interesting of all, John Densmore's cymbal track was recorded backwards, to get the soft, rhythmic whoosh that underlies the track.

When the *Strange Days* sessions were concluded, Jim Morrison felt that all the studio experimentation had paid off handsomely and that the Doors had created an album that lived up to every bit of their potential. "He always thought it was their best album," says Patricia Kennealy Morrison. "It was his favourite of all of them. He thought that *Strange Days* was the one that would stand out when the Doors were history."

when the music's over

On the first album, Jim Morrison had sung about taking a highway to the end of the night, and had solemnly declared that "This is the end". On '*Strange Days*', he sung of an even more dispiriting finality – that moment when the music's over and there's nothing one can do but turn out the light. Like 'The End', 'When The Music's Over' was one of the songs on which the Doors' reputation as a live band was built.

They had begun to develop it at their earliest gigs at the London Fog. Bookended by verses in which Jim gently sang the title phrase and then heatedly insisted that "Music is your special friend ... ", the band used the piece as a springboard for their long, shape-shifting improvisations.

Over these passages, Morrison would add his polished poetry and some random, improvised thoughts and phrases. He learned to let the music his bandmates were making guide him towards lyrical inspiration – and Ray, Robby and John learned in turn to follow Jim's lead and answer his words with the appropriate musical expressions. With the band working as a single-minded entity, 'When The Music's Over' became a thrilling, 10-minute excursion into that frightening place where the light has been turned out.

Shortly after the Doors had been fired from the Whisky A Go Go because of Jim's Oedipal excesses, the band played a gig at Gazzari's in which 'When The Music's Over' was used as a climactic part of the set. Morrison went wild during the perfor-

mance, hurling himself about the stage recklessly and smashing his microphone into the floor. He later explained his behaviour this way: "You never know when you're giving your last performance."

Lyrical themes of personal mortality and the despoiling of the planet became more pronounced as the piece developed further. And the more the Doors played the tune, the more it began to develop a form, until finally the band knew quite well what to expect from Jim's words in the middle section. A final important piece of lyric came to him during one of the band's trips to New York. Driving through Times Square, Jim noticed a marquee for an adult theatre advertising their latest feature – *The Scream Of The Butterfly*. If Jim could borrow from Celtic legend, Greek mythology and French existentialism, why not from some Times Square pornography as well?

The piece evolved into a poetic *tour de force* for Jim. His words alternately soothed and seethed, seeming at one and the same time a mournful warning, a bitter indictment and a vibrant celebration. Poet Linda Albertano heard the piece performed at Gazzari's and was moved by the power of Jim's lyrics. "Now spoken word performances are consigned to coffee-houses, but Jim was actually creating the people's poetry back then, in his actual poetry – but even more so in his lyrics. Jim wasn't 'dabbling' in poetry, he was the real thing. What always came through was the immediacy of the message and a love of the language."

The band planned on 'When The Music's Over' being the musical cornerstone of *Strange Days* and hoped to capture it on tape as effectively as they had 'The End'. But the night it was to be recorded at Sunset Sound, Jim didn't show up. For most songs, it would have been no big deal to lay down background tracks and then add the vocal later – but for a piece as depen-

dent on vocals and "interactive" as this one, it was going to be difficult. Ray, Robby and John went ahead and laid down their parts, pacing it just the way they had for so many live performances. The next day, Jim did show up and put the vocal track down.

Somehow, through the tape machine, the live chemistry of the band was recreated. Densmore's guesses at where to add percussive accents were almost perfectly in synch with Morrison's performance and Robby's "butterfly scream" was right on the money. The song's greatest moment came at the end of the middle section, when Jim said that he and his like-minded listeners wanted the world and wanted it now." "Now" was first whispered, and then, brilliantly, asked – "Now?" There was an anxious pause – just long enough to contemplate the terrible possibility of actually getting what you ask for – and then the screaming affirmation, the apotheosis – "Now!" The Doors had another head-expanding epic locked in for posterity.

The song was taken by some to be Morrison's first overtly political anthem, but Jim continued to be more concerned with the world of the mind and spirit than he was with current events. "Back then you knew a Doors song right from the first three notes," says Patricia Kennealy Morrison. "Nobody sounded like them and nobody ever has, which is why their stuff holds up. They weren't just ahead of their time, they were outside their time. Jim wasn't as political as some of the other songwriters of the day who were singing explicitly about revolution. I think the Doors were after bigger game, a more complex revolution. They really did believe that rock could be a shamanistic ritual – that they could explore that relationship between people and power. Some people thought it was hokum, and still do. But they believed it."

Robbie Krieger wasn't the only guitarist making butterfly screams – 1967 was the year Jimi Hendrix released his debut album, *Are You Experienced?* The Doors were in the middle of a three week run at The Scene in New York when Hendrix made a splash at the Monterey Pop Festival. The following year, when Hendrix was jamming at The Scene, Morrison introduced himself by crawling up on stage and grabbing Jimi around the legs while he was playing.

waiting for the sun

waiting for the sun

Jim Morrison wanted the Doors' third album to be their crowning achievement – a bravura mix of drama and music, taking its title from the poem that would be its signature composition, 'The Celebration Of The Lizard'. But Jim was distracted by personal demons, the band grew weary and the celebration did not take place.

The Doors clinched their position as commercial heavy-weights with their third album, *Waiting For The Sun*. The record's irresistible second single, 'Hello, I Love You', was as big a smash as 'Light My Fire' and, consequently, the album was hugely successful. But success came at a price.

The band began the record wanting to equal or surpass the artistic achievement of *Strange Days* – and their ambitious plans included using Jim Morrison's epic poem 'The Celebration Of The Lizard' as the heart, soul and entire second side of the album. That was also the working title of the record, which Morrison wanted to release with a faux snakeskin cover. But in the final analysis, in the eyes of their most serious fans and by their own admission, the band stumbled with *Waiting For The Sun*.

'Hello, I Love You' was as sweet, odd and heady as a spiked sugar cube, but it played like pure pop, rather than the kind of vision from the end of the night that had made the band so formidable on their first two efforts. And the more they'd wrestled with it, the more 'Celebration Of The Lizard' had refused to take shape – only a small portion ever made it out of the studio (though the original poem was written out in full inside the album's fold-out cover). The rest of the album included several swooning love songs ('Love Street', 'Wintertime Love') that, at least on the surface, seemed to be entirely out of character for the Doors.

Part of the problem was simply a lack of time. *Waiting For The Sun* was assembled only 18 months after the band's debut and barely half a year after *Strange Days*. While the first two albums had centred on songs that the band had developed in live settings and had carefully crafted before bringing to the studio, now, for the first time, they were pressed to come up with material.

"That natural, spontaneous, generative process wasn't given a chance to happen, as it had in the beginning," Morrison told Jerry Hopkins in *Rolling Stone*. "We actually had to create songs in the studio. Robby and I would just come in with a song and the arrangement already completed in our minds instead of working it out slowly."

On *Waiting For The Sun*, Krieger took a further step forward as a songwriter, penning three of the 11 tracks but he wasn't completely happy with the results. "Third album syndrome," Robby called it. "Usually a group will have enough songs to record one, maybe two albums, then they'll go off on tour and not have time to write any more material. So by the third album, you find yourself trying to write stuff in the studio ... and it shows, usually."

True, it often did show on *Waiting For The Sun*, but there were still flashes of brilliance as well. The rallying cry that Morrison had issued with 'When The Music's Over' was re-voiced a bit more explicitly with the powerful 'The Unknown Soldier'. 'Five To One' was an even more powerful exhortation, although the ratio in the title never did get properly explained. And the stark 'My Wild Love' sounded like a spectral lament from a chain-gang in Hell.

Even working on the stronger material, the *Waiting For The Sun* sessions were never easy. Morrison no longer relied on LSD to help fuel his imagination, but his growing disenchantment with the omnivorous demands of rock stardom led him to seek refuge in alcohol and he became an increasingly undependable performer in the studio.

"We got into heavy vocal compositing because Jim would come in too drunk to sing decently," Paul Rothchild told *BAM*. "Sometimes we'd put together eight different takes of a song to make one good one. Every single song from the third album was done that way. I don't mean a verse at a time, either. Sometimes it was a phrase at a time, from one breath to the next."

Rothchild also found he had to push harder to get usable tracks from the rest of the band. It often took dozens of takes to get even the simplest music recorded.

Dallas Taylor got a taste of rock stardom as a member of Crosby, Stills, Nash & Young in the late Sixties and early Seventies. But in 1968 he was still the drummer for Clear Light, the popular Sunset Strip band that loaned bass player Doug Lubahn to the Doors for many of their sessions, including *Waiting For The Sun*.

"Clear Light was one of Paul Rothchild's projects too," says Taylor. "So I'd hang out at Doors sessions and Morrison would hang out at our sessions. When he drank, he had that Jekyll and Hyde personality. He was mostly a lovely man, very sweet and very articulate. Then he'd get drunk and go wild. But we were all sort of expected to be as outrageous as possible. I remember Paul Rothchild suggesting we all read Marat/Sade for inspiration."

It became increasingly difficult for the Doors to pull their material together. A song Jim brought in called 'Orange County Suite' failed to impress his bandmates and was scrapped after a few run-throughs. Not even the song that gave the album its title could be recorded satisfactorily — it didn't show up on vinyl until *Morrison Hotel.*

Writer Joan Didion sat in on one of the dispiriting *Sun* sessions and incisively captured its entropic feel in a piece for the *Saturday Evening Post.* She described the Doors hanging about listlessly, with not much to do but hope that Jim would show up. The piece was called "Waiting For Morrison".

At the sessions Jim did attend, he often brought along outsiders — hangers-on, groupies, drinking companions — and their presence further soured the mood in the studio. At one point, the atmosphere of unproductive decadence sickened John Densmore so much that he quit the band for a day. By the time the album was finished, Morrison too was talking about quitting.

With the release of *Waiting For The Sun* in July 1968, the

Doors found themselves with a new musical/popularity status completely reversed from the one they had imagined for themselves.

Once they had been a subversive, resolutely intellectual underground band who had lurched into the pop charts despite themselves. Now they were a commercial cash cow and many arbiters of hip were deeming the Doors decidedly uncool. On the Sunset Strip, they were talked of as an act that used to have "it", before they had sold out to the teenyboppers. *Waiting For The Sun*'s bubble gum pink back cover didn't help allay this impression.

"It was pretty clear that they were a better band than most of what the rest of us were in," says Dallas Taylor. "They were just a more talented band. But as their records took off and they left us in the dust, that's when you started hearing some jealous comments about how they'd gone commercial. Among us musicians, they weren't so dark and cool anymore. They became laughable. But I think we made fun of them mostly because we were jealous. And to his credit, when Jim realized that success actually destroyed the music's mystique, he wanted to get away from it."

In some ways, *Waiting For The Sun* is the hardest Doors album to listen to, simply because it calls to mind the album that it is not: *Celebration Of The Lizard.*

With less pressure for a hit single, with more time, with Jim working hard in the studio rather than drinking hard at Barney's Beanery (a favoured watering hole), the Doors' third album might have been another masterpiece.

Author Lew Shiner, in his wistful, affecting novel, *Glimpses,* sends a character back in time to witness the successful completion of rock'n'roll's great "lost" albums and *Celebration Of The Lizard* is one of them. "I grew up a huge Doors fan," says Shiner, "and I can remember the growing anticipation for the third album. We couldn't wait to get our hands on it. But it was a disappointment. There was no 'The End' or 'When The Music's Over'. Instead we got 'Hello, I Love You' and 'Love Street.' Something seemed lost. My feeling for *Celebration Of The Lizard* as a great lost rock album began the day *Waiting For The Sun* came out. I felt like there was always a Lizard-shaped hole in my life, and it was the first record that came to mind when *Glimpses* started to take shape."

hello,
i love you

"When it became clear that 'Celebration Of The Lizard' was not going to come to fruition on the Doors' third album, the group found themselves in a very tight bind. The song that was supposed to have been one full 24-minute side of their record was suddenly gone and they needed to come up with something to replace it fairly quickly.

Flicking through some of Jim Morrison's old Venice notebooks at the studio, Jac Holzman's son Adam came across the

Ray Davies generously dismissed criticism that 'Hello, I Love You' and his 'All Day And All Of The Night' were similar.

The 'Love Street' Jim sang about was a real place – Laurel Canyon Boulevard. When Jim was sharing an apartment with Pam Courson just off the boulevard on Rothdell Trail, Laurel Canyon was home to a multitude of musicians, including chief Mother Of Invention Frank Zappa.

lyrics to 'Hello, I Love You' and suggested the band work that into shape. It wasn't too hard – the song had been one of the six the Doors recorded for the early demo tape that had eventually found its way on to Billy James' desk.

The band pumped up the song with a new arrangement that included some elegantly freaky Manzarek keyboards, a full-bore pummelling of the drums from Densmore and some ear-grabbing fuzz tone guitar licks from Krieger. Jim double-tracked his somewhat lecherous vocals over the highly danceable track and the Doors had the second and final Number 1 single of their career.

The song was one of Morrison's earliest – one of the five or six he had written before his fateful meeting with Ray on Venice Beach. It was the product of another day on the same stretch of beach, when Morrison had seen a tall, thin, very attractive black woman walking along towards him.

"Actually, I think the music came to my mind first and then I made up the words to hang on to the melody, some kind of sound," he said later. "I could hear it and, since I had no way of writing it down musically, the only way I could remember it was to try and get words to put to it."

So inspired was Morrison that he found himself calling out the title phrase to the woman. Whether or not he got a phone number out of the encounter, he did get a chart-topping song.

For young Los Angeles fans still listening to Doors songs for local colour – 'Hello' offered an interesting turn of phrase. "As kids in LA, and as Doors fans, we felt the band had a real presence around town," remembers Harvey Kubernick. "You'd go into Norm's restaurant on La Cienega Boulevard and hear that the Doors had just been in – Elektra was just up the street. I was thrilled just to think I might have the same waitress Manzarek had. And in 'Hello, I Love You', Jim talked about making the queen of the angels sigh. I thought that was a great line, because I was born at Queen of the Angels hospital on Sunset and Alvarado – about as LA as you could get. As a Jewish kid who happened to be born in a Catholic hospital, I loved that line."

The first few lines of the song's verse had an unfortunate musical resemblance to the Kinks' 'All Day And All Of The Night', a similarity that occurred to Ray Manzarek back when the song was first cut for the demo. But it was really just that one opening vocal phrase that matched the Kinks' tune – lyrically, rhythmically and tonally the rest of the song was original Doors work.

Ray Davies of the Kinks thought so too and said he wasn't bothered by the song at all. But critics across the country smirked that not only had the Doors gone bubble gum, they'd stolen a song to do it.

In Los Angeles, the Doors still had their core of local defenders. "I think we understood that the Doors were up against the pressures of radio," says Kim Fowley. "That's what the record company wanted from them. I think we heard 'Hello, I Love You' as a stupid song, but it was a great stupid song. Some of the finest records in pop history happen to be great, stupid songs, and this is one of them. The Doors were smart, but they were also good with lowest common denominator stuff."

Questions of bubble gum and sell-out didn't much matter to most of the record-buying public, who rushed out to buy the single when it was released in June. The same radio stations that had refused to play the band's last two singles – 'Love Me Two Times' and 'The Unknown Soldier' – were quickly flooded with requests for 'Hello, I Love You' and they duly obliged their listeners.

love
street

This song, the B-side of 'Hello, I Love You', was often pointed to as evidence that Jim Morrison no longer had the edge that had once made him so interesting – this stroll down 'Love Street' clearly showed that the man who had brought Oedipus and Artaud to the rock stage had gone soft.

Musically, this was too harsh a judgement. The song was not a dark epic or a fiery mind-blower, but it was within previously staked out Doors territory – somewhere between the cool melodicism of 'Crystal Ship' and the cabaret lilt of 'People Are Strange'.

The thing that was also missed by some critics was the streak of somewhat bitter humour that turned up towards the end of the tune and turned its dreamy enchantment on its head. A love song sung by a lover who says he's fairly happy "so far" isn't exactly a doe-eyed paean to romantic commitment. That hint of doubt on 'Love Street' suggested a more jaundiced view of things than the song's tunefulness implied: Morrison still had the edge, but he had become a subtler writer. The rock'n'roll shaman had not by any means given in to colourful visions of hippie-dippy contentment.

In fact, Love Street was a real street – Laurel Canyon Boulevard, running from the Sunset Strip through the Hollywood Hills, across Mulholland Drive and out into the San Fernando Valley. Though Jim still spent a fair amount of time crashing at the Alta-Cienega Motel while *Waiting For The Sun* was being recorded, he was also sharing an apartment with girlfriend Pam Courson. Their place was a small house at 1812 Rothdell Trail, a little street off Laurel Canyon just a few blocks from the Strip. Their house was up behind the boulevard's general store and, from a balcony, Jim could watch the comings and goings of much of the neighbourhood, which happened to include the pads of a couple of popular drug dealers.

While the song was considered slight, the fact that it was based on a real place delighted local fans. "When you heard 'Moonlight Drive' it was nice to know that it was written in Venice," says Harvey Kubernick. "Or that the Soul Kitchen was in Venice. You found out that the Doors were singing about the neighbourhood. They didn't use street names or addresses, but they'd give you regional information. Finding out that 'Love Street' possessed a direct correlation to Laurel Canyon was a real kick."

Jimmy Greenspoon of Three Dog Night happened to be a resident of 'Love Street', when the song first came out. "Danny

Hutton and I lived in Laurel Canyon, two doors down from Jim. Gene Clark of the Byrds was around the corner and Roger McGuinn, David Crosby and Chris Hillman were across the street. John and Michelle Phillips were right there, and Cass Elliot was a little further up the street. So was Frank Zappa and his family. Everybody would be running back and forth to each other's houses exchanging brownies and drugs. On the weekend, everybody would leave their doors open and you'd hear this amazing amount of music just flooding through the air."

One of Jim Morrison's greatest interests was the study of the mystic rituals and religious practices of early civilizations. He grew to believe that the rock concert was just an update of the ritualistic celebrations that were a part of most primitive cultures.

not to touch
the earth

'Not To Touch The Earth' was supposed to be the pivotal central section of 'Celebration Of The Lizard' (and was later to appear as such on *Absolutely Live*), but, when the *Waiting For The Sun* sessions stalled and dragged, it became the only section of the epic poem to make it on to the record.

The poem's as a whole described a kind of mass exodus from modern civilization and a return to a more tribal manner of existence. The roving travellers of 'Celebration' are stopping during their journey to recount their adventures and restate their purpose, and that's what creates the poems phantasmagoric stream of images. The non-linear tale was to come to a frenzied climax with 'Not To Touch The Earth'.

The origin of the 'Not To Touch The Earth' section again points to the depth of literary knowledge that Jim Morrison had accumulated. The first two phrases of the song, "Not to touch the earth, not to see the sun," are taken from *The Golden Bough*, a study of magic and religion in primitive cultures written by Scottish anthropologist J G Frazer, first published in 1890. The book had become an important resource for Morrison when he developed interests in demonology and shamanism, and Frazer's theories on primitive ritual dance as the origin of all drama actually influenced the way Jim presented himself on stage. (Jim's trademark "circle dance" is one example of this.)

Using 'Not To Touch The Earth' as a title was Jim's subtle way of paying tribute to someone whose research and writing he respected, although the song doesn't really have any other tie to Frazer's ideas. In fact, Jim was simply using Frazer's words as a starting point. They also became the title of a short documentary on the band put together by Bobby Neuwirth. He had been hired by the Doors during the *Sun* sessions supposedly to shoot a film, but that was a cover for Neuwirth's real job, which was to serve as guardian angel for Jim. He was to keep an eye on Morrison, follow him when he went out drinking and make sure he didn't get into too much trouble. But Morrison was more aware of what was going on than his bandmates thought. He quickly realised that Neuwirth had been hired as a babysitter, and resolutely refused the service. However, Neuwirth stayed with the Doors, even making a film eventually.

'Not To Touch The Earth' was actually taken from the table of contents of *The Golden Bough*, explains Patricia Kennealy Morrison. "There are chapters right after each other called 'Not To Touch The Earth' and 'Not To See The Sun'. They're mainly concerned with menstruation taboos, because in some primitive cultures menstruating women were sent outside the village and put up in huts that were built up off the ground on poles – they did not touch the earth. They were also often built without windows, so that's where not seeing the sun comes from. Those themes aren't really reflected at all in Jim's poem, but he'd read the book and he liked the way the titles sounded as lyrics."

On an album, which some people found too loaded with soft, soothing moments, 'Not To Touch The Earth' proved the Doors could still give a listener bad dreams. The repetitive riff the song is built on seems to come at once from a gloomy past and a creepy future and Densmore's bashing beat is relentless.

Morrison's ragged description of dead presidents, cars that run on glue and tar and a minister's daughter in love with a snake had the old shaman's touch to them – Jim could still lead us into the darker realms. And the message that came through

strongest – Run with me.

As the piece came to a frenzied apocalypse of sound, Morrison delivered the lines that may have been quite apt for a man of his mysterious talents – lines that may have been completely tongue-in-cheek, but he would have a hell of a time living up to: "I am the Lizard King. I can do anything."

summer's almost gone

Ray's stately, layered keyboards and Robby's bottleneck give 'Summer's Almost Gone' the sound and feel of a Doors' song, but at face value the lyrics seem to have been nicked from the band that provided the sunny antithesis to the Doors' vision of California – the Beach Boys.

This probably wouldn't have bothered Jim Morrison, who, on his first Elektra press bio, listed the Wilson brothers' band along with the Kinks and Love as his favourite singing groups. "Jim thought Brian Wilson was a genius," says Patricia Kennealy Morrison. "We had huge fights over that. I said, 'C'mon, he writes about convertibles and surfing!' Jim said, 'No, no – *Pet Sounds, Smile* – the man is brilliant.' I don't think it was something he used as an influence very often in his own music, but it was something he loved to listen to."

Built around a delicate, mournful blues progression, 'Summer's Almost Gone' seems to find Jim Morrison taking on a rather standard pop theme – the inexorable passing of a warm, fun summer into a cold, cruel, unpredictable winter.

The song was actually written during what was turning out to be a rather depressing winter for the Doors, what with the memory of the New Haven bust lingering and the *Waiting For The Sun* sessions off to a dismal start. 'Summer's Almost Gone' is guileless, but it picked up a little depth simply through Morrison's voice, which was beginning to show some signs of wear and tear. When Jim sings of winter's approach and summer's imminent demise he sounds so sad that one can

Part of what made *Waiting for the Sun* a No.1 album was undoubtedly the beckoning sex appeal of Jim Morrison. Gloria Stavers the New York-based editor of 16 magazine was one of the pivotal image-makers who helped define the Doors' lead singer as a sex symbol extraodinaire.

assume he's thinking about more than seasons. In the world at large, "summer" was over and a winter of war, unrest and assassination was on the way.

For the Doors, too, the days were getting colder. Making music was not as much fun or as easy as it had been back at the London Fog and Jim Morrison was getting awfully tired of being the sexy, crazy "Jim Morrison" that people paid money to see. It was a more troublesome question than some might have suspected: when summer really was gone, where would he be?

wintertime love

On *Waiting For The Sun* , 'Wintertime Love' stands out as a curiosity. Despite some interesting chord progressions and a sort of fetching drowsiness in Morrison's vocals, this Robby Krieger composition doesn't really seem to have the heart of a Doors tune. A sprightly, Renaissance Faire waltz with a jazzy breakdown in the middle, 'Wintertime Love' finds Ray mixing harpsichord parts with what sounds like a skating rink organ, while Robby's guitar part is barely noticeable. Robby's lyrics are an unabashedly romantic expression of the best way to keep warm during a blue and freezing winter – stay very close to a cherished lover.

While Robby's songs are full of nicely turned phrases, his words are easily distinguished from Morrison's by their directness and innocence – there's none of Jim's penchant for dark visions, wry humour or sly irony in 'Wintertime Love'. The fine, winding melody of the song is also a trademark of Krieger work. "As a guitar player, Robby's more complex," Jim explained, "and my thing is more in a blues vein, long rambling, basic and primitive. It's just that the difference between any two poets is very great."

Krieger had proved he was capable of strong song writing with 'Light My Fire' and 'Love Me Two Times' and, as Jim Morrison's creative drive began to flag, Robby would step in and begin to develop more of his material for the band. But the circumstances around *Waiting For The Sun*, particularly the time crunch, wouldn't allow Krieger to craft his material as fully as he would have liked. Ironically, the pressures pinching Robby's song writing during this time were largely the result of the success his first composition, 'Light My Fire', had engendered for the band.

"I think a lot of success can endanger your artistic side," he later explained. "Once you get big like that, you have to be touring all the time, and all the pressures make it hard to create. But as long as you're capable of creating stuff that will bring joy or happiness to people, then you're obligated to do it."

the unknown soldier

The Vietnam War provided a bloody backdrop to the career of the Doors and, for many young men during the mid-to-late 1960s, the possibility of being selected by the local draft board to become part of a questionable undertaking in Southeast Asia

created a constant, underlying fear.

By the time the Doors got together, Ray Manzarek had already served in the Army, interrupting his studies at UCLA to spend two years working as a piano player in a military' dance band. John Densmore avoided service with a bit of misinformation – he checked the box indicating "homosexual tendencies" on his draft registration papers. Billy James wrote a letter to the draft board on behalf of Robby Krieger that helped get the guitarist declared unfit for duty.

In the summer of 1965, Jim Morrison had received a 1-A classification for the draft, but apparently he avoided serving by consuming such an enormous quantity of drugs before a military physical that he failed with flying colours. Widespread anti-war demonstration had not yet begun, but Jim knew that he wanted nothing to do with containing Communism in Indochina. He also felt he'd already had plenty of experience with military life, most of it unhappy, having grown up in the home headed by Captain – later Admiral – George S Morrison. (Jim's middle name, Douglas, was in tribute to General Douglas MacArthur.)

On *Waiting For The Sun*, Jim finally voiced his feelings about the war in 'The Unknown Soldier' – a song received as the Doors' first political protest anthem. The song actually preceded the album and was released as a single in March 1968, backed by the strikingly non-political 'We Could Be So Good Together'.

'The Unknown Soldier' had been developed on the road by the band and, in it, Morrison expressed distaste not only for war in general, but also for the callous way in which death and destruction were now turning up on the nation's television screens. The Tomb of the Unknown Soldier was one of America's most sombre and hallowed monuments, but Morrison suggested that the real "unknown soldiers" were the ones whose corpses flickered across the evening newscasts.

The song's bold proclamation that "War is over" was something of a cruel irony – Morrison's point was that war is over for a soldier when he is killed. But for young Americans looking for some way to get their country out of what they saw as a spiralling tragedy, it felt good to take matters into their own hands for a moment and simply declare the war over along with Jim.

Resentment of his military father may have had a great deal to do with the anti-authoritarian streak in Jim's personality. But when Morrison finally wrote an anti-military, anti-war song, it was not an angry indictment of those who fought, but an affecting tribute to 'The Unknown Soldier'.

The "hipper and cooler" competition between Los Angeles and San Francisco was given its rock-'n'roll embodiment by the Doors and Jefferson Airplane respectively. The two "rivals" toured Europe together in 1968.

The sentiments of the song were powerful and much of the music was forceful and straightforward. But some theatrical flourishes – ringing bells, cheering crowds, an execution drama where the instrumental break might have been – and the fact that it had to be recorded in two main sections meant it was an extremely difficult track to capture in the studio to everyone's satisfaction, especially producer Paul Rothchild's. Reportedly, it took over 100 takes to get the song right. For the execution, the band marched loudly around the studio and then shot off a real rifle loaded with blanks. (Even the weaponry proved difficult – it took hours to get a properly dramatic gunshot recorded.)

As a single, the song wasn't very successful – its political nature simply made it too controversial for radio stations to touch – but the song did become important for the Doors in other ways. First, Manzarek and Morrison took the opportunity to dip back into their film school training and assembled the band's first conceptual film to accompany a song. (They'd previously done a simple, somewhat stylized performance film for 'Break On Through' and had lip-synched their way through a number of "concept" TV clips.)

The film was not tremendously ambitious, but it did have some punch. The Doors (and a dog) are seen walking on a beach – Jim with a bouquet of flowers and Ray, Robby and John lugging Indian instruments. Jim is tied to a piling on the beach –

appearing very Christ-like – while the other three sit on the sand and play their instruments. At the moment of execution on the soundtrack, Morrison is shot – his body twitches violently, his head rolls forward and he spits up some thick red blood on his flowers. Then comes a three-part montage of war images – first, scenes of explosion and destruction, then scenes of prisoners of war and dying soldiers, followed by scenes of the wild celebrations on VJ Day. Finally, the surviving Doors (and the dog) head back down the beach. The film was cutting-edge for its time and, for those paying attention, indicated that, despite the words of certain critics, the Doors were clearly not in a "bubble gum" state of mind throughout *Waiting For The Sun*.

'The Unknown Soldier' also became an increasingly important part of the band's live show. Robby would ease the song in with some tremeloed chords and the band would quickly work their way through the first verse and chorus to the firing squad section. Jim would call out the commands, Ray would rise and hold his arm up in a stiff salute and John would pump out a frantic buzz roll. When Jim was "shot", he'd crumple to the stage and there would sometimes be a very long, dramatic pause before he showed signs of life again, then brought the tune to its exultant conclusion.

The Doors received some negative reviews for their show at the Hollywood Bowl on 5 July 1968, a show that some had hoped would seal the band's reputation as LA's consummate rock outfit. Morrison wasn't that exciting, critics complained – he didn't do anything shocking, he actually seemed light-hearted during 'The End'. But photographer Henry Diltz, who would

later shoot the band's cover photo for *Morrison Hotel*, was at the Bowl that night taking pictures of the band. "I was right there up front, and the whole show seemed pretty exciting to me. When they did 'Unknown Soldier', it really was a mind-blowing experience. You actually felt you were watching Jim get shot. He fell in a heap on the stage and it all just felt so real. Then at the end of the song you could sense this wave of emotion, relief and happiness, like Jim really had ended the war."

In early September, the Doors left for a tour of Europe with the Jefferson Airplane. (One night in Amsterdam, Jim Morrison was to dance himself into a state of collapse on stage during the Airplane's set, thus occasioning the Doors' first performance as a trio, with Ray handling vocals.) European crowds were very taken with Jim's idea of the Doors as "erotic politicians": 'The Unknown Soldier' often earned the band thunderous ovations.

"In Europe, the kids were much more politically-oriented," Robby Krieger explained to journalist Richard Goldstein during a 1969 public television appearance. "If we said anything politically, they'd go into a furore. I mean they loved it, especially anything against America. If we just played they dug that too, but they really dug the political side of it, but in America it's just the opposite really. A lot of people at our concerts don't really come to hear us speak politics. I think they come more for the religious experience."

With the Doors, Robby Krieger quickly developed into one of rock's most original and idiosyncratic talents on electric guitar. He worked flamenco and Indian styles into his sound, but his earliest inspirations as a guitarist came from the founding father of basic rock'n'roll guitar – Chuck Berry – an equally original and idiosyncratic talent.

spanish caravan

Robby Krieger had modified and developed his classical guitar technique into a unique and extremely effective electric guitar style with the Doors. However, on *Waiting For The Sun* Krieger created 'Spanish Caravan' to put some of his un-modified flamenco abilities to use.

As he explained in his original Elektra press biography, "The first music that I heard that I liked was *Peter And The Wolf*. I accidentally sat down and broke the record (I was about seven). There was lots of classical music in my house.

When I was 17, I started playing guitar. It was a Mexican flamenco guitar. I took flamenco lessons for a few months. I switched around from folk to flamenco to blues to rock'n'roll."

Krieger's conversion to rock'n'roll came after he saw a Chuck Berry concert at the Santa Monica Civic Auditorium. He was so impressed with Berry's mix of raw energy and winning technique that he stopped thinking about becoming a jazz or classical player: he decided he was going to have to be in a rock'n'roll band.

The day after the Berry concert, Krieger traded in his classical guitar for a Gibson SG. But he didn't dismiss everything he'd learned previously; he began to play his electric guitar in the flamenco style. This meant he played with the thumb of his left hand under the neck of the guitar, while plucking the strings with the fingers of his right hand (he often kept his right-hand fingernails long to help in the picking and plucking).

'Spanish Caravan' begins with some stunning flamenco work on a nylon-stringed classical guitar and, after the first verse and chorus, it heads into some wilder sounds with

Krieger switching to electric guitar and Manzarek coming up with some very spooky organ parts and sound effects. While the lyrics describe a sort of moody travelogue, the real strength and dynamic quality of the song lies in the sense of arrangement and composition that is packed into barely three minutes of music.

With 'Spanish Caravan', Krieger may also have planted a song writing seed for the countless progressive and heavy metal bands that would begin to mix neo-classical composition with rock'n'roll bombast throughout the Seventies and Eighties.

Interestingly enough, 'Spanish Caravan' was the second Doors song to utilize the idea of Spanish galleons in distress. Jim Morrison had imagined such a ship grounded off the coast of the New World and jettisoning its cargo in 'Horse Latitudes' and Krieger describes "galleons lost in the sea" while he hunts for gold and silver up in the mountains of Spain. Doors fans were used to hearing the band stretch its music in challenging, new directions: it was one of the things which made Doors' music instantly recognizable.

my wild love

'My Wild Love' was the first song on which the band departed completely from "the Doors' sound". No keyboards, no guitar, bottleneck or otherwise, no Densmore rhythms. Jim Morrison's voice was the only element that let a listener know that this was indeed a track from the band that had produced 'Light My Fire'.

At this point, the Doors were becoming frustrated with the amount of studio time they were eating up getting their writing and arranging completed for their *Waiting For The Sun* material. In response, they designed this simple lament composed of chants, stomps, claps, sparse percussion and Jim's ghostly, somewhat ambiguous tale of a lover on horseback who encounters the devil. The song has the feel of an early plantation spiritual, or the kind of working song that prisoners doing hard labour might come up with to help pass the time.

Waiting For The Sun sessions were not often graced with the kind of supportive camaraderie that had held the band together in the past, but when 'My Wild Love' was recorded, everybody present pitched in and had some fun.

Billy James, the man who'd first heard something special in the Doors music back when he'd listened to their first demo, was by now working for Elektra and happened to drop by the studio with his young son, just as the Doors were working out 'My Wild Love'. He helped work out the clapping part for the song and, when it was recorded, little Mark James was stomping and clapping along with the band his father had "discovered".

we could be so good together

The squeeze for the band to come up with material on the spot in the studio is probably best evidenced by 'We Could Be So Good Together', the B-side to 'The Unknown Soldier' and perhaps the weakest song on *Waiting For The Sun*.

Built around a unison organ/fuzz guitar riff, the song comes across as Doors-by-numbers. A punchy rhythmic figure from 'Break On Through' shows up when Morrison gets to the end of a verse but this time around the effect is more music hall kitsch than liberating epiphany. It does have one fresh and interesting instrumental moment – a brief, screaming double-tracked guitar break from Robby.

But even when Jim was cobbling together lyrics out of the remaining golden nuggets from his Venice notebooks, he could still come up with mysterious, evocative material. 'We Could Be So Good Together', in title and tone, sounds like some simple boy-to-girl romantic assurance – perhaps a lyrical kiss in Pam Courson's direction. But whereas in 'I Can't See Your Face In My Mind', Morrison had shrugged that he couldn't find "the right lie", here he promises to tell plenty of "wicked lies" – brazen dissembling seems to be the secret of being so good together.

It's also easy to imagine that Jim might have been singing the song partly to his bandmates, or even the counterculture-at-large. Perhaps the days of heady idealism and "breaking on through" were coming to a close and the time for more pragmatic "enterprise, expedition, invitation and invention" was at hand, but, wicked lies notwithstanding, a good time could still be had together.

The grand sweep of the Doors' music was often matched by equally imposing lyrical conceits. Robby Krieger paired deft flamenco guitar work with images of trade winds blowing galleons off course and a hunt for gold in the mountains in 'Spanish Caravan'.

yes, the river knows

At the Doors early rehearsals, when Ray and Jim first encouraged the band to develop original material and Jim suggested basing lyrics on the elements, Robby responded with 'Light My Fire'. *On Waiting For The Sun*, he got around to writing his water tune – the elegiac 'Yes, The River Knows'.

Water imagery was often used to great effect in Doors songs ('Crystal Ship', 'Moonlight Drive', 'Horse Latitudes') and Robby comes up with some beautiful lyrics here. The sorrowful – possibly suicidal – feelings of the song are backed with Manzarek's cascading piano parts and Densmore's subtle brushwork on drums. Robby also adds his usual gorgeously restrained guitar to the mix.

This song, more than other Krieger works, seems to be written specifically for Jim - particularly the line about drowning in "mystic heated wine". Here was a line that not only showed the influence that Morrison's use of language had on Krieger, but was also a message from the guitarist to a singer and writer who was beginning to compromise some of his gifts as he drowned his troubles in alcohol.

"I've never seen anybody else from our generation who could put words together like Jim could," Krieger told Robert Matheu of *Creem* in a 1981 interview. "If he'd been more disciplined, he could have done greater things…but there was nothing you could do about it. People would tell Jim to drink less, and he would just take them out and get them drunk."

five to one

While most songs of protest lose their potency when they go out of date, the rage packed into 'Five To One' can still make a listener's skin crawl. Of course, what exactly Jim Morrison was protesting against when he belted this one out was never made clear. He refused to tell the other Doors or anyone else what the ratio in the title represented and various conjectures were ventured around the studio: the proportion of whites to blacks, dope-smokers to straights, or under-25ers to over-25ers in the population.

Some of the rage Morrison brought to the vocals had nothing to do with the lyrics – the song was recorded within a day or two of the group making the decision not to pursue

'Celebration Of The Lizard' any further.

In his book *Riders On The Storm*, John Densmore explains how 'Five To One' was hammered into shape in the studio. He and Robby had just finished a 15-minute meditation break, when Jim demanded that John get back to the drums and play a loud, basic, primal beat. Densmore wasn't particularly happy with the suggestion, since he was hoping to start working some more of his jazz training into the *Waiting For The Sun* material and wasn't too excited at the prospect of a tune built on a pounding 4/4 beat.

Densmore finally obliged Morrison and the singer began screaming out the opening line of the song. Robby began working his way from a delicate riff to a screaming solo and Manzarek quickly found some simple, powerful keyboard parts. The song was supported from below by a monstrously fat bassline – a part somewhat reminiscent of Ray's piano bass figure from the "butterfly scream" section of 'When The Music's Over'. Suddenly, the Doors had created their most blistering anthem to date, for an album that would feature some of their gentlest songs.

But was the song a call to arms against the establishment, or a mockery of the failures of the counterculture? Morrison's boast

The Doors' sound, and the spirit in which it was created, constituted something of a rock'n'roll revolution. The closing track on *Waiting For The Sun* was an impassioned call-to-arms, but against who and what? Jim Morrison never told anybody to what the ratio 'Five To One' referred.

that a vast number of people were ready to go up against the authorities' guns seemed calculated to put a shiver up the spine of Lt Kelly back in New Haven, but, when Morrison sang of ballroom days being over and trading in hours for handfuls of dimes, he seemed to be interested in a revolution but at the same time disgusted by the revolutionaries.

Sadly, one of the reasons that 'Five To One' has such a harrowing edge to it is that, when Morrison recorded his vocals, he was decidedly drunk. His voice cracks and gives out, he seems to hiccup in the middle of one line and conspicuously falls out of time with the band. One can even hear what sounds like an instruction from the control booth for Jim to wait "One more" measure before coming in at the beginning. He breaks into a lunatic laugh at the end. His improvisations aren't clever – just sheer raging howls. He says "Love my girl" at the beginning and end of the track, which may have been meant for the song but may also have been Jim talking to Pam Courson somewhere in the studio.

Even for long-time Doors fans, the fury of the track was frightening. "I remember the first time I heard 'Five To One' right after it came out," says Paul Body. "I happened to put the record on at 3 am one morning, and that song scared the shit out of me. This was supposed to be the Doors' teenybopper album, but that didn't sound like bubble gum to me."

Morrison's drinking was used to good effect on 'Five To One', but otherwise it was beginning to take its toll on him. Rather than being celebrated on the Sunset Strip as an all-conquering rock'n'roll hero, more often Morrison was being tossed out of the clubs where he had once headlined.

Musician Jimmy Greenspoon remembers engaging Morrison in a drinking contest at the Whisky A Go Go around the time of the *Waiting For The Sun* sessions. "We went to see a group there, and I matched him drink for drink. I got quiet, but he was screaming his head off. Mario the manager came over and told him, 'I don't care who you are – open your mouth one more time and you're out of here.' Of course Jim orders a couple more rounds for us and is right back up on the table screaming again. Mario comes over and – boom – Morrison's thrown out. I'm rolling on the floor laughing, and Mario says, 'You too, Greenspoon,' and boom, I'm out on the curb sitting next to Morrison. I said, 'Now what?' And Jim said – very calmly – 'Well, now let's go to the Galaxy.'"

the soft parade

At once misguided and brilliant, *The Soft Parade* unfolds as the grand oddity of the Doors' career.

Cracks in the glass became apparent during the recording of *The Soft Parade*. Members' diverging ideas about what musical direction the band should take took a toll on the sublime chemistry the four Doors had previously shared.

By the spring of 1969, the Doors had become many different bands: the value and importance of their music changed according to who was listening to them.

There were still die-hards standing by for more of the dark Doors missals such as 'The End' and 'Strange Days' and to those fans, after *Waiting For The Sun*, the Doors were fallen heroes of the underground.

There were, however, newer, fresh-faced fans, who had fallen in love with 'Hello, I Love You' and who'd made *Waiting For The Sun* the band's first Number 1 album. To them, Jim and the band were still exciting pop idols.

For the band itself, the benefits of having a Number 1 album were offset by the controversy surrounding their March appearance at the Dinner Key auditorium in Miami. Spurred on by the performances of Julian Beck's activist, expressionistic Living Theatre, and loosened by alcohol, Jim had taken to the stage in Miami and, depending on which witness you listened to, either did or didn't publicly celebrate his lizard. Anyway, he ended up being charged with lewd and lascivious behaviour, indecent exposure, public profanity and public drunkenness.

For the self-appointed judges of the rock press, the Miami debacle was taken as further reason to declare Jim Morrison a tiresome buffoon: according to them, the Doors' story was over. And newspaper accounts of the shocking Miami show and its ugly aftermath led concerned parents around the country to believe that Jim Morrison was a scary cross of the Pied Piper and the Devil himself

Obviously, the Doors couldn't keep everybody happy, but, with the release of *The Soft Parade* in July, they demonstrated that they could at least keep everybody confused. Friends and foes alike just weren't sure what to make of this record.

In the first place, though it was released a full year after the previous album, *The Soft Parade* offered an alarming amount of material already familiar via previous single releases, including 'Touch Me', 'Wild Child', 'Wishful Sinful', 'Tell All The People' and 'Easy Ride'. Secondly, the group's haunting bare-boned musical style seemed to be "evolving" for better or worse into occasionally over-produced slickness – *The Soft Parade* saw the group teaming up with orchestral strings and horns. There was even country fiddle on one tune. And when the band wasn't making such unseemly artistic leaps, it seemed to be treading water as a turbo-charged whiteboy blues band.

"It kind of got out of control and took too long in the making," said Morrison. "It spread over nine months. An album should be like a book of stories strung together, some kind of unified feeling and style about it, and that's what *The Soft Parade* lacks."

"We liked it, but no one else seemed to," shrugged Robby Krieger.

Putting *The Soft Parade* together wasn't much fun for anybody. The band began recording in November 1968 and didn't finish until July 1969. *Waiting For The Sun* had taken six months, but that spell of studio work had at least been interspersed with many gigs.

After the debacle at Miami, the Doors essentially became a studio group and, for the increasingly disaffected Morrison, the studio was no longer a happy place to be.

"Jim was really not interested after about the third album," Paul Rothchild told *BAM* in 1981. "He wanted to do other things. He wanted to write. He wanted to be an actor. Being lead singer of the Doors was really not his idea of a good time. It became very difficult to get him involved with the records. When we made *The Soft Parade*, it was like pulling teeth to get Jim into it."

"They were all kind of lost at that point," says Bill Siddons. "They'd lost focus as a band. Jim was out crashing cars and getting arrested and behaving erratically and nobody could trust the friendships that the band had been built on. As manager, I never knew what phone call I'd get or what I'd do about it when it came."

While songs like 'Touch Me' introduced a new level of polish to the Doors' music, Morrison himself began to develop a much rougher physical appearance. He allowed his sturdy frame – nearly emaciated in the band's early days – to fill out to a comfortable plumpness (and was consequently scoffed at for being grossly overweight). The mane of hair that stylist-to-the-stars Jay Sebring had once coiffured was now a wild tangle and by May 1969, when the group appeared on a public television special for an in-depth interview and to debut some *Soft Parade* material, Morrison was sporting a thick, sizeable beard. (Patricia Kennealy Morrison, writing in *Jazz & Pop* magazine at the time, referred to Morrison's appearance as "Che Guevara drag".)

Jim was tired of being a rock star and the band was tired of worrying about Jim but occasionally the deep chemistry of spirit that had first brought them together still showed. And occasionally, Jim, Ray, Robby and John could still have a good

time jamming the way they used to at the London Fog.

Towards the end of *The Soft Parade* sessions, when the band's spirits had finally been lifted by the work they were accomplishing, they attempted to fill out the remaining space on the album with an improvisational jam. "We needed another song for this album. We were racking our brains," Morrison told *Rolling Stone* in 1969. "Finally we just started playing and we played about an hour, and we went through the whole history of rock music – starting with blues, going through rock'n'roll, surf music, Latin, the whole thing. I call it 'Rock Is Dead'."

The session was fun, but the musical magic wasn't quite there. The song was later scrapped, to become available only on bootlegs. "When we recorded it, it was just a bunch of drunks fooling around and jamming in the studio," Manzarek explained in a 1983 *Audio* interview. "Then we started to get into something. Unfortunately, the tape ran out halfway through and by the time they got it back on, five minutes had elapsed and we were right in the middle of doing surf music. We went into the control room and said, 'Gee that was really great, hope you guys got it down on tape.' And they said, 'Well, we got it all down, except we missed some of the last 'Rock Is Dead'.' And I said, 'That was the only thing that was any good.'"

The Doors had hoped that *The Soft Parade* would bring back some fun and fire to their music-making – Ray and John were particularly excited about working more jazz elements into the songs. But the album's sessions were frustrating and, when it was finally released, sales were a disappointment too.

Waiting For The Sun had topped the American charts for four weeks, but *The Soft Parade* failed to enter the *Billboard* Top 5 and dropped out of the charts after only 28 weeks. It was the group's worst showing to date. And in the wake of Miami, wary American concert promoters began cancelling scheduled tour dates, fearful of Morrison perhaps providing an "encore" performance for which they would be legally liable. (Jim's joking about such an encore during a Pittsburgh show later became a part of *Absolutely Live*.)

About this time, the band was becoming the ideal sacrificial goat for the residual fury which conservative Americans felt towards all things countercultural. Jim's songs were "pro-drug", "anti-family", "anti-war" and now he was wagging his great snake about in public! The fact that the group's most popular single at the moment was called 'Touch Me' did not escape the decent folks' attention. "Things didn't go so well after Miami," remembers Bill Siddons. "But still, they were able to work. Basically we had to cancel a 10-day tour. We kept booking a weekend here and there, and tried to cope with the world around us coming at us."

On March 23, three weeks after the Doors' scandalous show, over 30,000 clean-minded citizens gathered at the Orange Bowl to witness a high-spirited Rally for Decency. Entertainment was provided by Anita Bryant, the Lettermen, Kate Smith, the Miami Drum and Bugle Corps and Jackie Gleason, (whose own boozy, high-rolling private life was hardly the model of suburban decency that was ostensibly being promoted that day).

Nowadays, *The Soft Parade* can be heard as an album that is both flawed and fascinating – a compelling curiosity among the Doors' body of work. With the heavy expectations the band faced at the time gone, what has lasted on the record are some powerful, appealing songs, some great playing, some fine production and some classic Jim.

After *The Soft Parade*, the band was dismissed to an extent – they could no longer hold their own as either Rock Gods or Rock Demons. That is perhaps the greatest charm of *The Soft Parade*. Though flawed, it is the first Doors album on which the music is greater than the *mythos*. Ultimately musicians and not self-conscious myth-makers, the Doors would do quite well without the burden of such *mythos* on their backs. On *The Soft Parade* and all the albums to follow, the Doors existed simply as a uniquely talented, often inspired, all-too human rock'n'roll band.

tell all the people

The last thing Jim Morrison wanted to be telling the world in May of 1969 was "follow me," especially to a backing of celestial trumpets. He was finishing off his first film, *HWY*, which he starred in, wrote, directed and produced himself. In April, two self-published collections of his poetry, *The Lords: Notes On Vision* and *The New Creatures*, were combined and published officially in a hard cover edition by Simon & Schuster.

The Lizard King could do anything, it seemed, but what he wanted to do most of all was stop being the Lizard King. The idea of continuing to play the role of rock star demagogue was repulsive to him. Nonetheless, he was still lead singer of the Doors and the band needed to keep making music. Morrison's Venice notebooks were close to exhaustion and his poetry and film projects were taking up most of his creative energies.

So it was Robby Krieger who stepped up his song output on *The Soft Parade* to keep the band well-stocked with original tunes, and 'Tell All The People' was his. He thought it was an excellent vehicle for Jim and was very excited about showing it to the band at the beginning of rehearsals for *Soft Parade* material. Morrison hated the song and almost refused to sing it, but finally consented – with the understanding that the number would be credited to Krieger, and not "the Doors". The song was released as the third single prior to the release of the album, and it was the third song to feature the string and horn arrangements of orchestrator Paul Harris.

"*Soft Parade* was a moment of adventure for them," remembers Bill Siddons. "Paul Rothchild proposed strings and they said, 'You're crazy – we're a rock band.' But he was bright and persuasive and they were looking for some way to make the music more interesting. Paul got them to like the idea, and then to fully embrace the idea of a "Doors orchestra". They even did some dates with the full orchestra on stage with them."

Later on their own, when they taped a public television special in New York in May, the group gave the song a convincing bare-bones performance.

Though 'Tell All The People' has a stirring, triumphant lilt to it, its subtext is less pleasant. As difficult as it was for Morrison to be viewed as a rock'n'roll icon, the spotlight which fell on Morrison was equally bothersome to Manzarek, Krieger and Densmore.

They had begun the band with an all-for-one camaraderie – that was the reason songs prior to *The Soft Parade* had simply been credited to "the Doors". But by now, the group was publicly perceived as having two identities – first of all came Morrison and then there were the other guys. Ray was making an effort to stay friendly with Jim and to provide guidance, but, in general, relations within the band had become strained. (There may be more than a hint of irony in Krieger's writing the lyric "follow me down" for Jim to sing.)

But the fact is that, by virtue of his natural magnetism and the power of his presence, Morrison was a born leader. Henry Diltz, a member of the Modern Folk Quartet who was developing a reputation as one of the finest rock'n'roll photographers, remembers the band dynamics during a publicity shoot around the time *Soft Parade* was being recorded.

"We spent a few hours walking around Venice Beach with a bottle of wine. A nice little adventure. Jim was very quiet. He was definitely the observer-poet. Very introspective and almost shy. He just liked to watch people, and he always had a smile on his face. He was a good listener. But he was obviously the leader of the group. He was quiet, but he was the one the others rallied around. He'd walk off in one direction and everybody would just naturally kind of follow him."

touch me

With his wicked sense of humour and fine-honed sense of irony, Jim Morrison may well have enjoyed the fact that he had a song called 'Touch Me' in the national charts at the same time he was fighting indecent exposure charges in Miami's courts. But that enjoyment would have been at least partly tempered by the knowledge that the song – the first single prior to *The Soft Parade's* release – was not his: it was Robby Krieger's.

Morrison wasn't crazy about the song, but he felt its title was at least better than the one Krieger had originally given it, 'Hit Me'. "That was the title," Krieger said later, "but Jim said, 'No way am I going to sing those lyrics.' So we changed it."

The song had been written by Robby as a kind of loving taunt after a spat with his wife, Lynn Krieger. Everyone who bought the single knew that this was Robby's tune – the most revealing of all the additional changes on the songs that made up *The Soft Parade* was the introduction of individual song credits. Though original material on the band's three previous albums had been uniformly credited to "the Doors", this time all song writing attributions were specific.

It was an eye-opener for fans - Jim Morrison, who had generally been considered the group's fount of inspiration, in fact, had only written half of *The Soft Parade's* material. Quiet, humble guitarist Robby Krieger had written the remainder. (Immediately following *The Soft Parade*, he was listed as "Robbie" rather than "Robby". He'd go back to "Robby" after *LA Woman*.) Krieger and Morrison also shared one song writing credit on

The Soft Parade, which, curiously, was for 'Do It', the song that seemed to involve the least writing skills of any on the album.

On previous work, Krieger's graceful melodies and open-hearted lyrics made his contributions quite distinct from Jim Morrison's music. These distinctions became even clearer on *The Soft Parade*. Firstly, it was Krieger's tunes that carried the extra string and horn accompaniments. And secondly, Morrison now seemed very uncomfortable singing Robby's words. He'd made 'Light My Fire' partly his own through his fierce delivery and he'd been game even for 'Wintertime Love'.

But the sentiments of 'Touch Me' just didn't sound like they had any connection with what was going on in Morrison's turbulent soul. Some fans gave Morrison the benefit of the doubt and considered his performance to be the archest of parodies. (This interpretation may have been strengthened by the fact that, over the song's final dramatic notes, you could hear a *basso profundo* voice sing "Stronger than dirt", poking fun at a then-current commercial for Ajax cleaner.) Irony of ironies: the song became the third-biggest hit single in the Doors' career.

Finally, there was no denying that Elektra Records – who perceived the Doors, their biggest act, as the very lifeblood of the label – had entirely cast their lot in with Krieger's songs, not Morrison's, as the biggest potential hits.

Between December 1968 and August 1969, the label released exactly four Doors' singles: 'Touch Me', 'Wishful Sinful', 'Tell All The People' and 'Runnin' Blue'. Effectively, this meant that Jim Morrison was now writing B-sides for Robby Krieger records.

"Jim had a strong sense of trust that Ray would find the right arrangement for his stuff," says Patricia Kennealy Morrison. "But Jim didn't trust the band as much with Robby's songs. He often really disliked Robby's songs,

Tommy and Dick Smothers hosted what was considered to be the hippest and most "political" of network variety shows. In December 1968, the Doors gave their fans a sense of what was forthcoming on *The Soft Parade* when they performed 'Wild Child' and 'Touch Me' on *The Smothers Brothers' Comedy Hour*.

Jim Morrison sincerely believed that the liberating power he wielded during Doors' performances was akin to the magic of a shaman. As he explained to Lizze James in a 1969 *Creem* interview, "I see the role of the artist as shaman and scape-goat. People project their fantasies on to him and their fantasies come alive. People can destroy their fantasies by destroying him."

I think partly because they weren't his. There was definitely some artistic vanity there."

For Doors fans, the strangest of strange days came in December 1968, when the Doors appeared on CBS Television's extremely popular *The Smothers Brothers Comedy Hour*. In that pre-MTV era, an American network television performance by a highly regarded rock'n'roll group was an event, and millions sat in their living rooms awaiting a glimpse of Morrison & Company.

The first sight they got was reassuring – the group gave a solidly bluesy performance of 'Wild Child'. Fans surely were not expecting what they saw next though, yet here it was: immeasurably hip underground sensations the Doors had gone "orchestral" and 'Touch Me' was the rather odd-sounding result. The band's butterfly screams were now being made by an unwieldy aggregation – Manzarek, Krieger and Densmore were augmented on-stage by the tuxedoed, union-wage string and horn players of the Smothers Brothers studio orchestra.

And up on a riser at the back, looking even more out of place than Morrison, was saxophonist Curtis Amy in yellow flares, yellow shades and a suede top, blaring away at his extended solo. The new line-up didn't find Morrison in very good form – he blew a "C'mon, c'mon, c'mon, c'mon now … " that left a gaping hole in the second verse.

Composer Krieger didn't look particularly happy either. He was on national TV performing his successful new song – once called 'Hit Me' – with a large, conspicuous, painful-looking black eye.

shaman's blues

What kind of blues could possibly be more appropriate for Jim Morrison in the summer of 1969 than a 'Shaman's Blues'?

After all the hours of magic he had produced, Jim Morrison was now bone tired of being the Lizard King. He had wanted the world, and wanted it now, and, for better or worse, he had got

it. Unfortunately, now the world wasn't sure whether it wanted him in return…and those who did still want him seemed to want a Jim Morrison that didn't exist anymore.

Those who slagged off *The Soft Parade* may not have listened closely to work like 'Shaman's Blues'. Musically, the song showed the Doors in top form, especially Robby, as they swung through a flowing, "down-with-the-ship" jazz-blues waltz. And, at the end of the track, there was an exhilarating Doors moment – a barrage of Morrison phrases ("optical promise…Isn't it amazing") created as Jim's ad libs on various vocal tracks were punched in and out. (Multiple Jims becoming one Jim – an act of shamanism right there on the studio tape.)

Jim's lyrics throughout the song were not only personal and haunting, but they were also remarkably reflexive. The song functions in two directions – either as a lament from the shaman to the village which has stopped believing in him, or as a plea from the village that is sadly hoping to see magic again from its cherished madman.

"I don't think the shaman, from what I've read, is really too interested in defining his role in society," Morrison told journalist Richard Goldstein during the interview on the WNET television special. "He's just more interested in pursuing his own fantasies. If he became too self-conscious of a function, you know, I think it might tend to ruin his own inner trip."

And indeed, the trip was becoming bumpy. Jim felt that the connection between performer and audience was a spiritual one, and that the performance could be a sacred ritual, but increasingly – looking back at Miami, or the sloppy, riotous shows at the Singer Bowl in New York, the Public Hall in Cleveland and the Phoenix Coliseum – the sacred had degenerated into the profane. Battling his own formidable personal demons, Jim could not possibly tap the shaman's magic night after night for endless "feasts of friends".

"In my whole career with them, they were never overworked, overbooked, and chasing the American dream," says Bill Siddons, "Because Jim was just not stable enough to work on a heavy touring basis. If he worked a weekend, by the third day it was always a question of whether he'd pull it off or not. He wasn't a normal person in that sense. He wasn't completely nuts, but he was someone who really didn't deal with the pressure of being a hard-working rock star because he really wasn't interested in that. He became a rock

star almost as a challenge – as a game at first. When he accomplished that, he said, 'OK, I'm done.' And the audience said, 'We're not.'"

One of the ways a shaman achieved his state of higher consciousness was through ritual dance. When he was particularly moved during a Doors set, Jim Morrison often broke into a "circle dance" based on those performed during American Indian ceremonies.

The Doors realised that they had stumbled with *Waiting for the Sun*, and wanted to recapture their group spirit and challenge themselves musically on *The Soft Parade*. It wasn't a complete success. Songwriting credits on tracks like 'Do It' indicated collaborative efforts, but it would take a while longer to fully rebuild the band's chemistry.

do it

A successful Doors song usually depended on four elements falling into place – Jim's lyrics, Robby's sense of melody and composition, Ray's knack for arrangement and John's sense of rhythmic drama. All four players were integral to the final Doors' sound, but it was Jim and Robby who functioned as the band's songwriters, bringing in the initial song ideas for the band to work out.

The distinction between writing a song and creating a performance could be a fine one in Doors' music, but the writing and the playing were still two distinct parts of the creative process. 'Soul Kitchen' or 'Love Me Two Times' couldn't have come to life the way they did in the hands of anybody but the Doors, but of course they did exist before the Doors got their hands on them as Morrison and Krieger's respective creations.

'Do It' was not the first song that Jim and Robby had shared on a creative give-and-take basis, but it was the first one to bear a "Morrison-Krieger" song writing credit, in keeping with the new individualized credits first seen on *The Soft Parade*.

While 'Do It' isn't of much thematic substance, musically it is one of the band's stronger in-studio compositions. Centred on a

driving guitar riff, the song features some warmly supportive organ work from Ray and a great loose'n'floppy groove from John. There's a catchy scratch-rhythm hook after the verses, a neo-gospel bridge and even a semi-jazz coda. The song also demonstrates that the sometime gruelling *Soft Parade* sessions weren't without their light-hearted moments – you can hear some stereophonic nonsense vocals before the track kicks in with a maniacal Morrison laugh.

Curiously, while Jim Morrison was quite hesitant about asking his fans to "follow me down" by way of Robby Krieger's 'Tell All the People', in 'Do It' he didn't seem to flinch at addressing his listeners as children and urging them to pay attention to him. In fact, that one sentiment made up the main lyrical body of the song. But there were a few Morrison twists – the rock Messiah may be addressing his "children", but the message is not that they should follow him but that they are the ones who will rule the world.

The listeners are the ones with the power to change the world – they shouldn't be just followers. Morrison often seemed concerned with breaking down the distance between performer and audience and wanted to undo the icon-adulator relationship.

"My audiences, they usually get pretty turned on," he told John Carpenter of the *Los Angeles Free Press* in 1968. "It's like

saying at first you're the audience and we're up here, you're down there. Then all of a sudden there you are and you're right there just like us – it's out of sight. When they know 'You're just like us', it breaks down all the barriers and I like that a lot."

But the song isn't just an encouragement for the followers to lead the leaders – the "please listen to me" is also shortened to "please me", and it's clear that this "pleasing" may take all night long. Morrison had voiced his thoughts more eloquently in the past, and would again, but 'Do It's' mix of lust and liberation was unmistakably Jim.

easy ride

Jim Morrison hoped that 'Easy Ride' would be released as a single, perhaps as a smiling response to the doomsayers that said the Miami show marked the end of the Doors' artistic validity and commercial viability. In the song, Morrison announced with blithe certainty that ahead of him he saw not dark clouds, but an "easy ride".

The song did come out before the album, but as the B-side to Robby's 'Tell All The People'. The strings and horns added to the Doors' sound were getting all the attention, but what people overlooked was the fact that Jim was still capable of pushing the band in new musical directions - 'Easy Ride' two-stepped along like an up tempo gospel roof-raiser.

Lyrically, the song was like a high-spirited, anger-free continuation of 'Break On Through', wherein Jim proclaims to the song's subject that it will be all right once they get beyond socially sanctioned poses and pretences. Real happiness and

excitement – an easier ride – are at hand once the restrictive masks and costumes that society demands are finally stripped away. Of course, this was Jim singing and 'Easy Ride' couldn't help but have a more sexual connotation as well, especially when he howls for a bride towards the end of the song.

The song stood out on the album, and continues to stand out, mainly because it's one of the few tracks that sounds like Jim and the band are just having a plain old hoot. The lyrics aren't fluff – "Rage in darkness by my side" isn't exactly a happy-go-lucky suggestion – but the mood of the music and the vocals evoke the kind of excited celebration the band must have felt, when it revved its way through blues covers back in the earliest Venice days. Jim's sense of humour has often shown up in his music in sly and subtle ways, but 'Easy Ride' seems to let the listener in on the laugh.

"Jim was exceptionally funny," says Bill Siddons. "It was a wicked sense of humour at times, and he could be an asshole sometimes ,

In 'Easy Ride', Jim Morrison seemed to yearn for less complicated, more carefree days, like the one captured below in a 1967 Bobby Klein photo, when the band had time to meander around the Branson Caves.

but nonetheless he was cogent, bright, educated, warm and generous and funny as hell. He was playful and frisky – he was all kinds of guys. In fact I can remember the day, after a particularly strong drink, he'd come into the studio and said, in the most cheerful voice, 'I'm feeling a little schizophrenic today.'"

wild
child

Those listeners who heard 'Tell All The People' and 'Touch Me', then promptly wrote off *The Soft Parade* without flipping the record over and playing the second side were missing out on some prime, robust Doors' work.

Jim Morrison saw striking parallels between his childhood experiences and those of French poet Arthur Rimbaud – he was inspired throughout his life by Rimbaud's artful use of language and his musings on the role of the artist.

'Wild Child' kicked off the second side with some ferocious Doors-style blues and some fiery Jim Morrison vocals. This song, originally released as the 'Touch Me' B-side in December 1968, had all the familiar Doors ingredients – a sizzling Krieger guitar lick, a pumped-up organ part from Ray, a loose-limbed beat smacked out by John, plus some dark, mysterious, fully engaging lyrics belted out by Jim. In fact, it was one of the few songs on *The Soft Parade* that was road-tested – it had been on the set-list at the Doors' frenzied, violence-marred show at New York's Singer Bowl in August 1968.

By the time Jim Morrison wrote 'Wild Child', he had read extensively about primitive cultures and the song is something of a tribute to a creature untouched by the constraints of civilization. The climax of the song, and one of the most arresting moments of the album, comes right at the end, when Morrison asks, "You remember when we were in Africa?" At first, it sounds like a bizarre throw-away line, more of Jim's lyrical Dadaism. But in fact, it was a veiled reference to one of Morrison's deepest influences, Arthur Rimbaud.

Rimbaud was a French poet who lived from 1854 to 1891. His father was a military man who turned his back on the family when Rimbaud was seven. When he was 16, Rimbaud began to write and his work embraced themes of exploration and discovery, both of the world at large and the soul within. Some of his works were retellings or updates of classic myths, and others were examinations of life's smallest moments – such as the beauty of a full beer mug at a comfortable inn.

When Rimbaud wrote about himself, it was often highly self-deprecating and ironic. Amazingly, he created the complete body of his literary work between the ages of 16 and 20. From then on, he lived out the kind of exploration he had written about. At a time when global travel was difficult and dangerous, Rimbaud journeyed extensively throughout Europe, Asia and Africa, working as a trader and gun-runner. Eventually, he returned to France for treatment of a tumour on his leg and died in a Marseilles hospital at the age of 37.

The poetry Rimbaud produced and the life he led fascinated Jim and he was particularly inspired by one of the writer's lines, "The poet makes himself into a visionary by a long derangement of all the senses." He often quoted from Rimbaud's most substantial and autobiographical work, *A Season In Hell*. And he was particularly interested in the fact that Rimbaud had created poetry of depth and wit, beauty and terror, and then completely turned his back on the life of an artist and ran off to lose himself in exotic locales and earthy, dirty work. Jim would joke with the band that some day he might also run off to Africa and disappear.

In 1968, Jim sent a note to one of the world's foremost scholars on Rimbaud's work, Professor Wallace Fowlie of Duke University, who had published a book of Rimbaud translations in 1966 that featured a Picasso pencil sketch of the poet on its cover. The note read: "Dear Wallace Fowlie, Just wanted to say thanks for doing the Rimbaud translation. I needed it because I don't read French that easily ... I am a rock singer and your book travels around with me. Jim Morrison. PS That Picasso drawing of Rimbaud on the cover is great." (Fowlie has since explored the connection between Rimbaud's work and Morrison's and, in 1994, authored the insightful *Rimbaud And Morrison: The Rebel As Poet*.)

When they recorded 'Wild Child', the Doors were in the process of assembling a documentary on the band called *Feast Of Friends*, filmed by old UCLA buddy Paul Ferrara with sound handled by Babe Hill, who soon became one of Morrison's closest friends and ablest drinking buddies.

The birth of the song at Sunset Sound was thus captured in footage shot for that project. "Let's do it," Jim says before a take. "But before I begin I must say that the collective archetype is getting me down. You know what I mean? So if there are any desert islands available, please turn me on to them."

As the track is worked on, John is concerned that the band is playing too loud, while Robby is concerned with finding just the right guitar wail. Ray performs his usual role as coach and facilitator – when Jim wants to know how his own song starts, Ray explains, "Robby does two, John does one, Doug [Lubahn] does one, I do two and then you come in," and that's what's on the record.

At the other end of the song, there's some disagreement. John thinks ending on the Africa phrase is "the stupidest ending I've ever heard of". But in a practice run Jim screams it out the way he wants it. "Don't overblow, Jim. You've got a long way to go," Paul Rothchild cautions from the booth.

"Don't overblow" strikes Morrison as very funny. He smiles and asks, "Why not?"

runnin' blue

If it weren't odd enough for Doors fans to get used to hearing their favourite rock'n'roll band backed with regal trumpets and sweeping violins, here was an even odder twist – a bluegrass-flavoured tribute to soul singer Otis Redding.

Mixing the wild abandon of Little Richard and the smooth, warm vocals of Sam Cooke, Otis Redding had become the most vibrant embodiment of the Memphis sound. In the early Sixties, working out of the Stax studio with Booker T and the MG's as a backing band, Redding created such soulful masterpieces as 'Mr Pitiful', 'Pain In My Heart' and 'That's How Strong My Love Is'.

In 1965, 'Respect' showed that Redding had clearly come into his own as an artist and also scored him some unprecedented commercial success. The song would become a further smash when Aretha Franklin did a gender-flipped version of the Redding composition. Redding was a star in the black soul

'Runnin' Blue' was a musical tip of the hat from Robby Krieger to deceased soul giant Otis Redding.

charts and slowly he began to earn respect from a white audience as well. The Rolling Stones had covered him on their records and he returned the compliment with a sizzling cover of 'Satisfaction'. At the Monterey Pop Festival in June 1967, Jimi Hendrix made his American debut and created an excited buzz by setting his guitar on fire, but it was Redding's galvanizing set that was the musical highlight of the three-day festival.

Towards the end of that year, Redding's song writing had started to become introspective. He'd mastered the grooves of soul and R&B and was looking to push his music in a new direction. On 7 December 1967, he went into the Stax/Volt studios and recorded the kind of song he was after — 'Sitting On The Dock Of The Bay'. Unfortunately, three days later, on his way to a show, his private plane crashed and Otis was killed. In March 1968, 'Sitting On The Dock Of The Bay' was the Number 1 record in the American pop charts.

The Doors had wanted to be a part of the Monterey Pop Festival, but at the time the festival was put together 'Light My Fire' had not yet become a big hit and, on the national scene, the Doors were just another band from LA. (Morrison suspected the Doors had been passed over by Festival bookers due to a simmering rivalry between the LA and San Francisco music scenes.) When Otis Redding won over a crowd of 50,000 white hippies at Monterey, the Doors were in the middle of their third trip to New York, packing the largest crowds ever into Steve Paul's club, The Scene, as well as mingling with Andy Warhol and the hipsters from his Factory.

By the time *The Soft Parade* was being assembled, Robby felt that Otis deserved a lyrical homage, and gave it to him with 'Runnin' Blue'. The song begins with Jim's unaccompanied singing of "Poor Otis dead and gone" in a kind of military marching cadence, then the song proper kicks in, with horns amply evident. Robby expands on the kind of search for solace and rest that Redding described in 'Dock Of The Bay" and the "dock" now becomes any place where one can find peace of mind,

it may even be found in Los Angeles. The song may have suffered from a bit too much ambition — instead of being a straightforward soul tribute, (which is probably what was intended) the song is an awkward pastiche of a number of rock and soul sections, combined with a jazz-type bridge and country-bluegrass choruses (sung by Krieger himself in a twangy, semi-Bob Dylan style).

"We were making our *Sgt Pepper*," said John Densmore in a 1972 interview. "Just to show how ridiculous things got, we imported Jesse McReynolds and Jimmy Buchanan, a mandolin player and a fiddler, from North Carolina, to play one solo on one song."

wishful sinful

With the release of *The Soft Parade*, it became clear which Door was writing which song and consequently Robby Krieger's material often suffered cruel comparison with Jim Morrison's.

Generally, Krieger's music was softer and more commercially-oriented than Jim's, but, as 'Wishful Sinful' proved, Krieger was also capable of brilliance. This gorgeous song — almost a companion in feel to 'Crystal Ship' — was an unabashedly romantic love song, but it was also spiked with some Morrisonian darkness. It was also the one song on *The Soft Parade* on which the orchestral backings seemed entirely appropriate.

For younger fans, the affecting compositions that Robby brought to the band were often a large part of the Doors appeal. One such avid Doors fan was bassist/keyboardist Arthur Barrow, probably best known for his work with Frank Zappa's bands.

When *The Soft Parade* was released, Barrow was a teenager living in Texas who was learning to play his instruments, and who often tried to get his garagebands to play convincing covers of Doors tunes. "I remember trying to do 'When The Music's Over' at a GI dance in San Antonio, and just getting a lot of blank stares in return," he laughs. Barrow would later get to work with the Doors themselves when he moved to LA and found that his first big job as a professional studio player would be as a synthesist for the *American Prayer* sessions. Barrow says that back in the Texas days 'Wishful Sinful' was a very instructive song for a young musician.

"I've heard people say 'The music was all Jim

Jim Morrison was widely regarded as the Doors' creative centre, but the band's decision to individualize song writing credits on *The Soft Parade* revealed Robby Krieger to be an equally vital song writing force within the group – he wrote half the material on the album.

The Soft Parade had its moments of Morrison magic but increasingly the singer's energies were sapped by alcohol, lack of artistic focus and an ugly handful of legal troubles.

Producer Rothchild's (p89) encouragements helped send the band off in new directions to create some powerfully memorable music.

– the Doors weren't anything.' I totally disagree with that.

The unit as a whole was essential. On *Soft Parade*, something like 'Shaman's Blues' was OK, but musically it was bluesy and simple.

I was drawn to the more musically interesting songs like 'Wishful Sinful' – a beautiful song with beautiful chord changes. I loved Jim's voice and vibe, but as a young kid learning to play guitar, I was floored by things like 'Wishful Sinful' that were just packed with innovative chord changes that my teenage mind hadn't even dreamed of. I was really into them musically, so Robby's compositions were at least as important to me as Jim Morrison's aura."

'Wishful Sinful' was released in February 1969, the second single to appear before *The Soft Parade*'s release in July. Its B-side was a horn-powered Morrison track, 'Who Scared You', which would not appear on *The Soft Parade* but did show up on the 1972 compilation *Weird Scenes Inside The Goldmine*.

the soft parade

"We don't find our long numbers, they just come out," Ray Manzarek told an interviewer in 1969. "If a song needs six, eight, ten minutes, it gets it."

It took all of eight minutes and 40 seconds to pull off the title track of the band's fourth album, but this was a completely different "long-player" to previous epics such as 'The End' or 'When The Music's Over'. The extended song-poem, 'The Soft Parade', was named after Jim's phrase for the varied, and often very odd, stream of humanity that flowed day and night along

Sunset Boulevard. Instead of growing from a long, improvisational jam as the others had, the piece was very much a collection of separate parts and sections.

"It wasn't designed as one song," Paul Rothchild later explained. "Whenever we got stuck in the studio with a bridge section, I'd ask Jim to get out his notebooks of poetry and we'd go through them and find a piece that fitted rhythmically and conceptually. A lot of the fragments there were just bits of poetry we put together. The song came out kind of interesting I thought."

It began with Jim, in the guise of a most fiery fire and brimstone preacher, speaking of his days back in seminary school, where he learned the lesson that "You cannot petition the lord with prayer". Some very delicate music creeps in and Jim begins asking for sanctuary and soft asylum. This is followed by an insistent dance beat section over which there are some goofy images ("peppermint miniskirts") and a jazzy section with a kind of nursery-rhyme lilt (including the image of women "carrying babies to the river," presumably for a bath but perhaps for something more sinister). Then, the monk buys lunch and, as Morrison puts it, "the best part of the trip" begins.

The final section of 'The Soft Parade' is one of the headiest, most exciting pieces of music the Doors ever created. Paul Rothchild had innovatively begun experimenting with double-tracking Jim Morrison's voice back on the first album, now he went further with multiple Morrisons firing off in all directions. Singing of the soft parade en masse, bubbling up to a climactic boil during the "Tropic corridor" sections and then imploding into white-hot frenzy while "Calling on the dogs", the voices of Morrison are astounding.

Throughout the song the band stayed right with him. "Jim has so much energy it is as if he can't do it all alone," Robby Krieger explained at an interview during the sessions. "We use our musical structure to support Jim's lyrics. There are some people who go out on the edge – and Jim goes out into unknown territory. We keep his exploration of the chaos intact, by keeping his words to the chords and the rhythms."

'The Soft Parade' is another Doors song in which horses are a central feature – and again they fare less than well – the piece ends with Jim offering the ominous advice that, if all else fails, the horses' eyes can be whipped.

morrison hotel

By 1970, many people considered the Doors to be just like the habitués of LA's seedy Morrison Hotel – down and out. But the band rallied on their fifth album and surprised even themselves with some of their tightest, finest work.

The Doors stepped out of the shadows and took to the highway. *Morrison Hotel* describes that journey: it is a rock'n'roll survey of the American landscape.

By the end of the summer of 1969, men had walked on the moon and Aquarian vibes had blossomed at Woodstock. For a brief, shining moment, a brighter future seemed to be, if not at hand, at least possible.

But hope was soon overshadowed by darker moments: some of the high-tech know-how that landed the lunar module was also being put to horrendous use in Vietnam, and the love-in at Woodstock was quickly followed by violence at Altamont. Headlines screamed out news of the My Lai Massacre and the Manson murders.

The music wasn't over, but the tune had become decidedly sombre.

On a personal level, the Seventies didn't seem to be beginning all that well for Jim Morrison, either. He started 1970 with a pair of trial dates: one in Miami on charges stemming from the Dinner Key show, and one in Phoenix on federal felony charges of interfering with the flight of an aircraft. (Morrison and buddy Tom Baker had engaged in some drunken horseplay en route to Phoenix for a Rolling Stones show in November 1969. Morrison was found guilty, then later acquitted when a stewardess on the flight realised that she had confused him with the more troublesome Baker.)

At this point, Morrison was drinking heavily – alcohol must have seemed like an effective antidote to the toils and troubles of rock'n'roll life. But while the drink may have sapped some physical strength (at times he appeared rather haggard and bloated), it couldn't dampen his powerful intellect or ever-mischievous creative spirit and he was still as active an artist as he had ever been.

Morrison was a familiar face in the audience at many of LA's underground theatre productions and he was in the preliminary stages of several film projects. He was working on screenplays with poet Michael McClure. He was continuing to write poetry and, in May 1969, gave his first public readings at the Cinematheque Theater in Los Angeles at a benefit for author Norman Mailer, who was campaigning to become mayor of New York City. (Mailer hoped to have New York City secede from the US.)

with *Waiting For The Sun*.

The Doors simply wanted to keep the sound focused and straightforward this time – they were going to forget about the kind of musical experimentation that had been the hallmark of *The Soft Parade*. By the time the sessions for the new record were over, however, band members had surprised themselves. The result of their work, *Morrison Hotel*, was one of the strongest, sharpest albums they'd ever made.

"We listened to *The Soft Parade* a couple of times, and decided it would probably sound just as good without the brass," Krieger drolly remarked in 1972.

Unheralded by any singles, *Morrison Hotel* was released in February 1970. Musically, the album was as much of a leap forward as *Strange Days* or *The Soft Parade* had been. But what the band had opted for this time was a tighter, harder sound. The music was stripped bare. Gone were the elaborately extended riffs and psycho-histrionics. Gone were the images of seven-mile snakes from ancient lakes. What the music revealed now was an entirely new creature – a sleek, splendid American monster – more a blues phoenix rising from the ashes than a rock'n'roll demon hulking in the shadows.

Morrison was back on form as a songwriter with a writing or co-writing credit on every track – and the album sounded like a combination of reflective Morrison journal entries ('Indian Summer') and a Doors-style travelogue of America's hubs and highways, from the country's roadhouses to its bloody urban streets, all the way to "Tangie Town".

The group that had been nurtured in the smoky clubs of the Sunset Strip now seemed to embody the dusty truths and fragile hopes of the American spirit at large. Somehow, the Doors had become the quintessential American band.

Morrison Hotel purred, leered, laughed and roared ("Do it, Robby, do it") and, in so doing, set forth the proposition that, while the Doors might not change the world, they could still deeply affect the listener and make great music. (The band recorded one song at the *Morrison Hotel* sessions that did not make it on to the album – 'Whiskey, Mystics and Men'.)

Morrison realised that, for some listeners, great music from the Doors simply wasn't enough. "Basically the music has

Norman Mailer's tongue-in-cheek campaign to be Mayor of New York City delighted Jim Morrison and inspired him to read his poetry in public for the first time at a campaign fund-raiser.

These days, the Morrison Hotel in downtown LA is defunct, but the Venice apartment building where Jim did his rooftop writing is now called 'The Morrison'. A plaque on the front door reads: "WC Fields, Jim Morrison & many other artists have passed through these halls since the 1920's."

"Morrison thought that Mailer's campaign was beautifully loony," says poet Michael C Ford, a friend from UCLA days who was instrumental in getting Jim's poetry first published in the *Mt Alverno Review*. "He loved the idea, and wanted to be a part of it. He called me up and said, 'Have you ever read your poems in front of an audience?' I told him I hadn't. He asked, 'Do you want to take that bath?' and we did." (Morrison and Ford did not read completely without support – Robby Krieger backed their poetry with some gentle guitar noodlings.)

In fact, Morrison was more excited about getting attention as a poet than he'd ever been about becoming an anointed rock star. Patricia Kennealy Morrison remarks that Jim's reaction to her lukewarm assessment of *The Lords And The New Creatures* in *Jazz & Pop* may be, "the only time in literary history that a slap-on-the-wrist review occasioned a marriage proposal from the subject to the reviewer."

With so many outside projects vying for Jim Morrison's attention, the future of the Doors was uncertain. But the group was still under contract to make records for Elektra, and so they returned to Sunset Sound in November 1969 to begin work on new material.

The Soft Parade had been time-consuming and expensive, and hadn't sold as well as Elektra would have liked (though it did mark four gold records in a row for the Doors). The record company hoped the band could again top the charts, as they had

gotten progressively better, tighter, and more professional… more interesting," Morrison told Salli Stevenson in a 1970 *Circus* interview. "But three years ago, there was a great renaissance of spirit and emotion tied up with revolutionary sentiment. When things didn't change overnight, I think people resented the fact that we were just still around doing good music."

The public appreciated the music enough, however, to make *Morrison Hotel* the band's fifth consecutive gold record.

The first indication of the unpolished sounds within *Morrison Hotel* was to be found on the album's cover. Far from the kind of "arty" shots the band had chosen on past albums, *Morrison Hotel* featured a raw, unposed photograph of the group inside the establishment that leant the album its title, located at 1246 South Hope Street in downtown Los Angeles.

The shot was taken by photographer Henry Diltz. "The band asked my partner and I to do a cover, even though they didn't know what they were going to call the album. We had a meeting and Ray mentioned that he'd seen this great place called the Morrison Hotel. It was in a seedy area, an old man's hotel – rooms $2.50 and up. We scouted it out with Ray and Jim and then went back a few days later with the other guys.

"We went into the lobby and the guy at the desk said that we couldn't take a picture without an OK from the owner, who wasn't available. We went back outside and said 'Now what?' We were talking about shooting them in front of the hotel, and then I noticed that the guy at the desk was leaving his post and getting into the tiny elevator. I said 'Quick, run in!' They did and just kind of naturally fell into place behind the window. I shot a roll as fast as I could and we got the cover. When we were done, Jim said, 'Let's get a drink somewhere interesting'. We were driving together and spotted the Hard Rock Cafe, and I thought it looked great. The band went in and sat at the bar and ordered beers and I stood just outside the door and shot them from a few feet away. That was the inside cover photo. The old guys in the bar started to notice us and started telling us stories. Ray had a real long talk with one guy, and I could tell Jim really liked listening to all these great tales of the old days. He was very quiet, and very polite to these guys – he just listened with a smile. Eventually the band went home, but Jim and I went to some more bars – he wanted to buy drinks for more old guys so he could hear some more great stories."

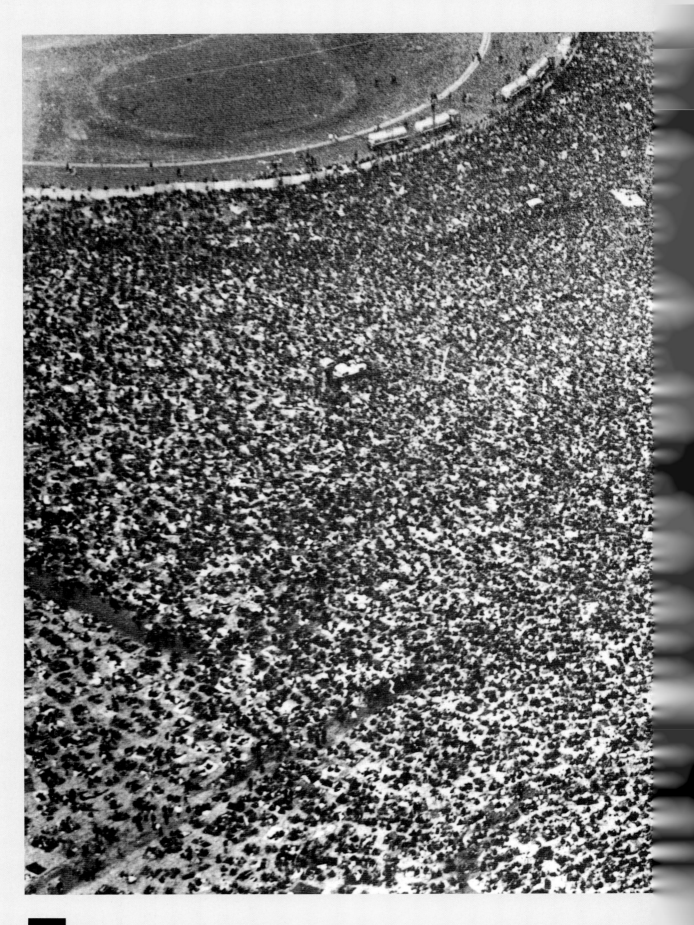

For a major figure in rock'n'roll, Jim Morrison had curious and unfortunate experiences with some of the late Sixties' major rock events. He and the Doors weren't asked to Monterey Pop and refused to be part of Woodstock. When Jim decided to take in the 1969 Rolling Stones tour at Phoenix, he didn't make it to that gig either – he and buddy Tom Baker engaged in drunken shenanigans on the flight from LA and were arrested before they got off the plane.

roadhouse blues

The lyrics of 'Roadhouse Blues' grew out of instructions to Pam Courson on how to handle Topanga Canyon Boulevard's treacherous curves. The song debuted on stage at the Toronto festival (p97).

The Doors decided not to take part in the Woodstock Festival in August of 1969, since Jim and the band were no longer interested in playing large, outdoor venues.

"I really liked it more when we were on the way up, at clubs like the Whisky, and Ondine's and The Scene in New York," said Robby Krieger in 1970. "Once we started the big concerts, it was more showtime, and I didn't like that as much."

After the Festival, Morrison worried that Woodstock had been a safe packaging of a once vibrant revolutionary spirit rather than the flowering of youthful ideals. "Woodstock seemed to me to be just a bunch of young parasites being spoon-fed for three or four days", he told John Toller of *Zig Zag* in 1970. "They looked like the victims and dupes of a culture more than anything else. Of course that may be sour grapes because I wasn't there, not even as a spectator. But some free celebration of a young culture, it's still better than nothing, and I'm sure that some of the people take away a kind of myth back to the city with them."

While the Doors weren't part of the youth celebration at Yasgur's farm, they did play as part of a sizeable tribute to rock'n'roll elders at the Toronto Rock'n'Roll Revival show in September 1969 at the city's Varsity Stadium. The Doors joined a bill that included Chuck Berry, Little Richard, Jerry Lee Lewis, Gene Vincent and Fats Domino. Also on the bill was a young outrageous band fronted by Morrison's drinking pal Vincent Furnier – a group called Alice Cooper.

The show was MC'd by song writer/producer Kim Fowley, although when ticket sales lagged Fowley and the promoters contacted John Lennon to see if he'd be interested in hosting the event. Instead, Lennon offered to get a band together and it was at Toronto that he gave his first post-Beatles performance, debuting the Plastic Ono Band, which included John, Yoko, Eric Clapton, Klaus Voorman and Alan White. As word of Lennon's participation spread, the 22,000 seat stadium rapidly sold out.

The Doors gave a strong performance as the concert's closing act. Jim made a point of telling the crowd how meaningful it was for him to be playing on a stage shared with so many rock'n'roll legends. In the end, though, the sharing of the stage became a bone of contention. "Chuck Berry wanted to come out and jam with the Doors," remembers Fowley. "But Jim laughed and said no, because Chuck hadn't let any of the younger guys come out and jam with him."

When the Doors played 'Back Door Man' towards the end of their set, Morrison had the band work the blues groove hard and slow, and he added some new lyrics that advised an unnamed driver to keep his eyes on the road and his hands on the wheel. The audience may have thought they were hearing some ad lib Morrison riffs, but he was actually testing out his freshest material. The Toronto crowd was the first to hear the first sample of what would shortly become one of the Doors' hardiest signature tunes.

Jim Morrison never bought a house for himself, but he did buy a small bungalow for girlfriend Pam Courson up in LA's Topanga Canyon, when Pam wanted a quieter spot away from

Let it roll – on *Morrison Hotel*, the regrouped and re-energized Doors proved that they could still create some remarkable sounds. On 'Roadhouse Blues', Morrison's dark, subtly-rendered fatalism was powered by some fine, fearsome riffs – the result was the Doors' hardiest, heaviest rock anthem.

perfectly against the vocals, so Morrison went ahead and laid some honking harp on a separate track.

The band wasn't entirely happy with Morrison's playing though and Robby, a more accomplished harp player, was all set to take a crack at it. But Rothchild suggested that John Sebastian, formerly of the Lovin' Spoonful, be brought in to add the harmonica licks. Sebastian came in later that night and aced the part, but felt that, in terms of image, he and the Doors were an uneasy mix. When *Morrison Hotel* was released, the Sebastian harp part was credited to the fictional "G Puglese". The song soon became a favourite opener at Doors shows.

'Roadhouse Blues' has continued to roll along all these years later as a classic party-rock anthem. But those listeners who key on the "beer-for-breakfast" credo promoted by Jim are missing some of the writer's depth.

It's true Jim was a drinker and found in alcohol some respite from being the Lizard King – often it meant he could play the Loud Clown instead. But the image of Jim as a booze-fuelled party monster, incapable of anything more than a catchy toast, is wide of the mark. Even as a man going down to the roadhouse to have a real good time, Morrison offers a substantial bit of dark wisdom in his lyrics, reminding us that the future can't be predicted and that the end is always a little closer than we like to think. (All this is not to say Morrison never had beer for breakfast. In her book, *Strange Days*, Patricia Kennealy Morrison recounts watching Jim down a cold one immediately upon rising from bed. She muses, "And here I thought that was just a song. Silly me.")

Still, Kennealy believes that the focus on Jim's drinking and sex life has made it too easy to write off his talents. "Some people might prefer to think of Jim as a wild drunk and a complete idiot. But listen to his music. How could he not have been a smart man? Where would the songs have come from? It's an insult to the work to think of Jim as just some guy running around screwing everything that moves and getting drunk all the time. Listen to the music."

Singing it like it was – Jim Morrison didn't often reveal too many details of his personal life directly in his songwriting, but he was in fact the owner of a Topanga Canyon bungalow perched behind a roadhouse where locals hung out and had a real good time.

the hustling pace of Hollywood. Laurel Canyon, where Jim and Pam had shared a place and which Jim had described in 'Love Street', was plugged into Hollywood and the Sunset Strip, while the more secluded Topanga Canyon and its winding Boulevard connected with the Malibu Beach area of Pacific Coast Highway.

As Topanga Canyon wound its way into the Santa Monica Mountains, the Boulevard and its curlicue offshoots led to secluded cabins and hillside homes. The lifestyle of area residents was decidedly earthy and laid-back, a relaxed mix of hippies, hermits and some of LA County's bona fide cowpokes.

Pam's place was up a hill behind a small roadhouse, a local, country-flavoured bar that offered little more than cold beer and a jukebox. Jim was inspired enough by this joint to honour it with a tune – 'Roadhouse Blues' – and the words of the first verse were the instructions he often uttered to Pam as she took the sometimes precarious drive along Topanga Canyon Boulevard to her bungalow.

The band as a whole worked the high-energy tune into shape during rehearsals (it ended up with a "Morrison/Doors" song writing credit). When the track was cut at Sunset Sound, the roadhouse rocker received some unexpected and invaluable assistance in the studio.

Bassist Ray Neapolitan, who had been playing at most of the *Morrison Hotel* sessions, was going to be late to the studio the day 'Roadhouse Blues' was ready to be recorded. But legendary blues guitarist, Lonnie Mack, happened to be there at the studio, finishing off a track of his own, and, when Doors manager Bill Siddons asked him to take a shot at laying down a bassline for the Doors, Mack said he would.

Mack and John Densmore worked together to create the extra-fat blues-rock shuffle that powered the song along, and 'Roadhouse Blues' was quickly cut to everyone's satisfaction. Paul Rothchild suggested that some blues harmonica would fit

waiting for the sun

Almost two years after the album of the same name, the Doors were still 'Waiting For The Sun', but now finally the song had found a home.

One measure of just how chaotic the *Waiting For The Sun* album sessions had been is that not even the title track could be properly executed and recorded in time, so that the song, a strong one, had to be held over until the band was looking for material for *Morrison Hotel*. (It had somehow seemed too soon after the *Waiting* album to use the song on *The Soft Parade*, even though there had been a scramble for material during those sessions too.)

When the rehearsals for *Morrison Hotel* began, all of the band members welcomed the new, rawer approach to developing the material and band camaraderie was high.

Often, the Doors began rehearsals playing through some of their favourite old rockers, such as 'Gloria' or 'Money' just to get the juices flowing before moving on to newer tunes. The hard rock feel of the band's club standards helped pull the players together and maintain a high level of energy. That energy was then focused on the new songs, which would be ripped through as if they too were from an old club set list.

'Waiting For The Sun' was a little out of character at these sessions – it sounded more like "old-Doors" and didn't have the same kind of blues-rock heart as the stuff Jim and Robby were coming up with in rehearsal. But it was too good a song to throw away and its mix of graceful melody and raw power made it fun to play.

The number had already undergone some changes – Morrison had originally written the words to fit a melody supplied by UCLA film buddy and *Feast Of Friends* cameraman Paul Ferrara. Robby Krieger had reworked the song into something more fitting for the group – a point he made clear when Morrison suggested sharing his song writing credit with Ferrara.

(Morrison ended up with sole credit.) The song was reworked a bit more for *Morrison Hotel*, which became the only album to feature some exotic instrumentation – a touch of Moog synthesizer to beef up the emphatically heavy riff used as musical punctuation throughout the tune.

Jim's song is an odd meditation on a sun that never seems to arrive. It's Jim's only song about inaction – all that happens is the waiting. Spring has come; it should be the time to live beneath sunny skies and still nothing but waiting. A brighter future is ahead if one just patiently waits and contents oneself with a glimpse of paradise rather than seeking out the whole Garden of Eden.

There's a strange calm in Morrison's voice – but does it signal resignation to the wait or complete confidence in the arrival? How long the wait and how bright the sun is left unclear, but Jim Morrison does deliver one of his most memorable admissions; he says that he is now living "the strangest life" he's ever known.

Jim Morrison was in need of a little sunshine in his life by the time 'Waiting For The Sun' finally arrived on *Morrison Hotel* in February 1970. He was due to stand trial in Phoenix at the beginning of March and in Miami in August.

you make me real

'You Make Me Real' was the A-side of the one and only single from *Morrison Hotel*, released after the album in March 1970.

Backed by 'Roadhouse Blues', the two songs make perfect companion pieces. Lyrically, 'You Make Me Real''s admonition to "Roll now, baby, roll" is fairly close to the advice in 'Roadhouse Blues' to "Let it roll" – and, in spirit, both tunes capture the Doors at their up-tempo, bluesy best.

'You Make Me Real' also allows Ray Manzarek to slip back into his old Screaming Ray Daniels guise for a track: as on 'Roadhouse', he gets away from the organ and creates a great rock'n'roll vibe by pouncing furiously on a piano. The track is also notable for showcasing some of John Densmore's most awesomely frantic drum work. And Robby Krieger further refines his art – the twangy, distorted guitar lines of 'You Make Me Real' are both wildly askew and elegantly precise at the same time.

Though lyrically he was now expressing much more carnal concerns, Jim Morrison was still singing about "breaking on through", as it were, telling a lover that she allows him to forget about his perils and problems until, finally, she makes him free and real.

It's not hard to figure out what this freedom and reality entail – the words "let me slide in your tender sunken sea" are hard to misinterpret.

While Jim clearly worked his unsteady relationship with Pam Courson into much of the material on *Morrison Hotel*, 'You Make Me Real' may have been aimed in Patricia Kennealy's direction.

The two had met in New York at the beginning of 1969, when she interviewed him for *Jazz & Pop* magazine. Kennealy was shocked to discover that the "Pig Man of LA" was in fact a courtly, intelligent, shockingly polite gentleman with a good-natured sense of humour about himself.

For his part, Jim had found someone willing to take him seriously as a writer, artist and human being. They hit it off immediately and were soon lovers bound up in a relationship that was as much a meeting of minds as it was a romance.

The couple got together as much as their schedules allowed, and were married in a Celtic handfasting ceremony in June 1970. The number of people with whom Jim could be "real" was dwindling fast – but when he was with Kennealy he could be free for a while.

'Peace Frog' was another stirring, though oblique, political cry from the Doors, but the line "blood in the streets in the town of Chicago" made it clear that Jim Morrison had not missed the horror of Chicago police brutalizing demonstrators outside the 1968 Democratic Convention.

peace frog

'Peace Frog' is memorable among Doors' songs as the one with the most ridiculous – some might charitably say "cutest" – title.

Morrison often admitted as much himself when the song was performed in concert – "Funny name for a song, huh?" he would remark to the crowd.

But the song itself is far from goofy. It's one of Morrison's more political pieces of work and presents a commentary on America's civil unrest throughout the late Sixties – the epochal moment of "blood in the streets" being a reference perhaps to the 1968 Democratic Convention in Chicago, when Mayor Daley's army of baton-wielding cops pummelled demonstrators for daring to make their voices heard.

The song was one of five on *Morrison Hotel* to be credited as a Morrison/Krieger composition. Actually, 'Peace Frog' is a good example of how Jim's words and Robby's music could be developed independently and then be brought together to create a song bigger than either of them had imagined.

Krieger may have figured that since the Doors were having fun and producing powerful music reworking the blues, they might get lucky with a stab at some white funk. It was he who came up with the distinctive soul-funk guitar scratch that powers the song along. The rhythm of that part kicked up some inspiration for John, who developed a kind of pre-disco funk dance beat for the tune, and for Ray, who came up with some typically ingenious organ lines.

Together, the three refined the main section of the song, and even developed a dramatic turnaround where the rhythm pulled back and the music just swelled. There was room for a wild Robby solo as well as a deceptively quiet section just before the final burst of energy at the song's end. The song was almost all there, but Jim drew a blank: the music was strong, only he wasn't sure where to take it lyrically.

Ray, Robby and John were too excited about the track to let it sit around while Jim tried to work out the right words, so, with bassist Ray Neapolitan, they went ahead and recorded the track one day when Jim was out with his buddy, Babe Hill.

The next time Jim was in the studio, Ray took a look at his notebooks and was immediately grabbed by one of Jim's epic poems in progress, titled 'Abortion Stories'. The poem described a country awash in rivers of blood – blood that represented both large-scale political upheaval and the deepest of personal pains. Ray discovered that the words and rhythms of the poem fitted the new track remarkably well and suggested Jim go with 'Abortion Stories' for the vocals.

Before Jim recorded his part though, producer Paul Rothchild suggested that the poem be interwoven with other lyrics: he and Jim worked out a way for the song to be,

in essence, two sets of lyrics in one. The words from the poem worked against some new words that were chanted in counterpoint. ("She came...") Together, the lyrics created a picture of a world of chaos and carnage, screaming ahead into the future as individuals do the best they can to get along.

The song was not explicitly for or against anything, but it was a shocking series of snapshots of a nation in emotional and physical agony – an idea made even more shocking by the incongruously upbeat feel of the music. (It's perhaps worth noting that although Morrison put blood in the streets of New Haven and Chicago, the West-loving singer hung a bloody red sun over "phantastic LA")

In a few lines towards the end of the song, Morrison quietly and concisely describes an image of "Indians scattered on dawn's highway bleeding". This was a reference to an incident he considered pivotal in his childhood.

When Jim was four, on a family car trip between Albuquerque and Santa Fe, New Mexico, his family had come across a horrible accident – a truck driven by some Pueblo Indians had overturned on the road and most of its many passengers were thrown about the scene, injured, bleeding and dying. This first awesome glimpse of death and tragedy terrified young Jim and deeply affected him for the rest of his life.

In his poems 'Dawn's Highway' and 'Ghost Song', Jim combined some of the same "blood in the streets" imagery of 'Peace Frog' with a further examination of his response to the highway accident.

'Dawn's Highway' and 'Ghost Song' were two of many poems Jim recorded by himself in December 1970. That recorded work would be used by the Doors to create the 1978 album *An American Prayer*.)

After the violently quelled demonstrations in Chicago, America had to admit that it was at war with its own youth. The dark themes of the Doors music didn't seem so fanciful anymore – reality had caught up with Jim Morrison's imagination.

Jim was greatly intrigued by the lore and customs of American Indians. A gruesome encounter with some New Mexican Pueblo Indians, when Jim was just a small boy, proved to be one of the pivotal events of his life and was described in several of his songs and poems.

blue Sunday

Jim Morrison was a being of rampant masculine energies, but when he read the works of Anais Nin (p.105), he discovered a woman whose lusts and passions, both sensual and intellectual, matched and even exceeded his own. Nin wrote her best-remembered works while living in Paris, but, like Morrison, she eventually decided that "the West is the best" and moved to Los Angeles.

Hard on the heels of 'Peace Frog' – the sharpest, most vivid track on *Morrison Hotel* – comes the slightest piece of music on the album. 'Blue Sunday' is nothing more than a romantic's profession of sweet-nothings, complete with Jim crooning "la la la's".

Sequenced almost as a coda to 'Peace Frog', the song picks up strength from the jarring juxtaposition, but is basically little more than lovers' mood music. Luckily, the Doors were able to pull off some rather stunning mood music and, between John Densmore's expert brush work on the drums, Robby Krieger's lazy swirls of guitar notes, Ray's delecately supportive keys and Jim's Sinatra phrasings, 'Blue Sunday' works as an evocative few moments of gliding transport in an album full of wilder rides.

Again, even in the minimal lyrics to this song, Morrison creates mystery. Does a "blue Sunday" refer to a Sunday of perfect, clear skies, or a Sunday of sadness? The minor chords and dolorous melody suggest the latter, but Jim's claim that his girl is the world to him would suggest warmer sentiments.

Jim may have intended the song both ways: his tumultuous relationship with Pam Courson demonstrated equal measures of hurtfulness and tenderness, disinterest and devotion.

ship of fools

Jim Morrison was never far from water, physically and creatively: the Doors take a stroll around Venice, pausing for a sultry shot on a canal bridge.

When Jim and Robby teamed up on a song, the jagged contrast between lyrical content and musical feel often added an odd and intriguing depth to their work.

On 'Peace Frog', they ended up with images of flowing rivers of blood sung to an irresistible dance beat and, in 'Ship Of Fools', the death of humanity is described by way of a tune that's remarkably happy and full of bounce.

In short, the 'Ship Of Fools' is Planet Earth, with we humans the fools. Our curious self-destruction is made clear in the very first verse, wherein Jim bemoans the fact that, though the world has advanced enough to have people walking on the moon, humanity has also managed to create unbreathable air for itself. This echoed some of the ecological concerns he'd first voiced in 'When The Music's Over'. 'Ship Of Fools' wasn't an especially substantial Doors' song but its green sentiments were timely. *Morrison Hotel* was in record store racks when the first earth day was held, April 22 1970.

land ho!

The sea was important for Jim Morrison and frequently recurs across his creative output. He was the son of an admiral and a songwriter whose first flashes of inspiration had come to him while on an apartment block rooftop with a view of the surf.

Oceans and water imagery turn up again and again in his work ('Crystal Ship', 'Moonlight Drive', 'Horse Latitudes'). While assembling the songs for the album *Morrison Hotel*, Jim and Robby came up with a bona fide, traditional-sounding, anchor-hoisting sailor's song – 'Land Ho!'

One of the songs that gives the album its essentially "American" flavour, 'Land Ho!' rolls along with the kind of folksy storytelling gusto one might hear in a rollicking port town tavern. The song is also a satisfactory counterpoint to the angst of 'Waiting For The Sun'. By the end of that song, Jim is still in suspense and some turmoil, but for his crew of sea dogs at the finale of 'Land Ho!', the waiting is over. A welcoming shore holds out the promise of drinks at the bar and love for sale.

the
spy

Even when Jim Morrison seemed to be growling out some simple, hot-blooded blues, there was often surprising literary depth to his words. 'The Spy' and its main line of lyric, "I'm a spy in the house of love", are borrowed from a 1954 novel, *Spy In The House Of Love* by author/diarist Anais Nin.

The daughter of a Spanish pianist and a Danish singer, Nin was born outside Paris in 1903. During her teenage years, she lived in the United States and it was there, during trips to the New York Public Library, that she developed her lifelong passion for language. Still a young woman, Nin moved back to France. Her intellectual curiosity was matched by a desire to fully explore her sexuality and, though she had married young, she became involved in several serious affairs.

In 1931, she met American writer Henry Miller and his wife June when they came to live in Paris. Nin fell in love with June Miller and the two had an affair that ended unhappily. But it was with Henry Miller that Nin established perhaps her most significant relationship. The two became not only lovers but supporters of each other's art. Because of her dedication to freedom of expression in life and in art, Nin underwrote the publication of Miller's wild first novel *Tropic Of Cancer* and he in turn encouraged her to write.

When *Tropic Of Cancer* was finally published in the US in the early Sixties, Nin wrote an insightful preface that might have also stood as a prophecy of the work to come from Jim and the Doors.

"Here is a book which, if such a thing were possible, might restore our appetite for fundamental realities. The predominant note will seem one of bitterness, and bitterness there is, to the full. But there is also a wild extravagance, a mad gaiety, a verve, a gusto, at times almost a delirium. A continual oscillation between extremes, with bare stretches that taste like brass and leave the full flavour of emptiness. It is beyond optimism or pessimism. The author has given us the last frisson. Pain has no more secret recesses."

Anais Nin's letters, diaries, essays and novels are marked by sensitive prose and a gentle, playful surrealism. The collected works provide a look deep into the soul of an artist struggling towards fulfilment and it is easy to imagine Morrison being quite taken with her writing. (In fact, when the Doors were first coming together, Nin was already a fixture on the Los Angeles literary scene, having established a home there in the early

queen of the highway

Another Morrison/Krieger song, 'Queen Of The Highway' is Jim's romanticized look at his involvement with Pamela Courson, backed with Robby's flowing chord progressions and rhythmic riffs.

The opening punches to the tune seem to borrow a bit from Larry Williams' 'Bad Boy' and there's also a kind of high-kicking saloon-rock break in the middle of the song that lets the band have a blast for a few bars. In his book, *Riders On The Storm*, John Densmore explains that he was not happy with the music the band put together for this song: "It had some nice autobiographical lyrics from Jim, but the track never settled into a good groove. It was the first time I ever felt we let Jim down in supporting his words."

Jim had been involved with Pam Courson since they'd met at one of the band's early London Fog gigs. She was born in Weed, California, and grew up south of Los Angeles in the conservative climes of Orange County. (Jim eventually wrote a song called 'Orange County Suite' for her, but it went unrecorded.)

When Pam first met Jim she was a 19-year-old art student at Los Angeles City College, very interested in exploring the big city, particularly the Sunset Strip scene. Pam was a delicate beauty who appeared to be the quintessential "little girl lost", but she could tap a steely will when necessary. She was immediately attracted to the captivating singer she saw working himself into a frenzy on the London Fog's tiny stage and Jim was soon taken with this fine-featured waif with the warmest of smiles.

The two quickly became lovers and began a relationship that, though tortured at times, was hallmarked by a deep, unshakable loyalty. When Jim left for Paris after the *LA Woman* sessions, it was to be with Pam. The dynamic between the two is laid out for all to see in 'Queen Of The Highway', admittedly in a somewhat tongue-in-cheek manner. Pam is a "princess" and Jim is a "monster, black dressed in leather".

But above all, this leathered monster and his Orange County princess are simply an American boy and girl, who Jim claims are the world's most beautiful people. The struggles of the relationship, and Jim's general uncertainty about what the future would bring, are made clear in the song's final line, where Jim simply hopes that things can continue a little while longer.

Though there is a line in the middle verse describing the two as wedded, Jim and Pam were never officially married – in papers filed immediately after Jim's death, Pamela was listed as

Forties. She died in LA in 1977.)

The Doors were so pleased with the way 'The Spy' turned out that it became a crucial part of their live set: a special piano would be wheeled out on stage so that Ray could duplicate his tumbling blues work on the ivories.

Built on a simple but crafty blues progression, the song has Jim taking the role of master-voyeur (a la 'My Eyes Have Seen You'). It also has a touch of the stealth-lover bravado that Jim brought to Willie Dixon's 'Back Door Man'. But, while that song was delivered as a triumphant howl of pure lust, Jim's become a cagier lover in 'The Spy'. He's in the house of love, and he knows the words the object of his attention longs to hear, but most importantly – is it a threat or simply an acknowledgement? – he knows his potential lover's "deepest secret fear".

"People are afraid of themselves," Jim told Lizze James in a 1969 interview. "Of their own reality – their feelings, most of all. People talk about how great love is, but that's bullshit. Love hurts. Feelings are disturbing. People are taught that pain is evil and dangerous. How can they deal with love if they're afraid to feel?"

"I'm an old blues man," Morrison growled convincingly in 'Maggie M'Gill." he learned some of his blues-craft by listening to and borrowing from the best – like Chicago blues legend Willie Dixon. Dixon's 'Back Door Man' and 'Little Red Rooster' were highlights of Doors' performances throughout their career.

"friend". Jim also sings that the couple are "soon to have offspring," but, in fact, Jim and Pam remained childless. However, she was named as the beneficiary of a will he made out in February 1969.

indian summer

Like 'Blue Sunday', 'Indian Summer' is a slight piece of work that nonetheless shows the Doors to be capable of making some beautifully airy music.

Jim is saying, ostensibly to Pam Courson, what every lover longs to hear – "I love you the best." That sweet thought is somewhat tempered by the fact that it is a comparative – "better than all the rest". The lover being sung to may be loved best, but is not the only one loved. The title phrase adds a melancholy atmosphere to the tune. The image of an "Indian summer", a time when summer heat has unexpectedly continued into the autumn, is an intriguing one in the love song context. The title also becomes something of a pun, in that the band backs Jim with gently repetitive sounds that approximate an Indian raga, as John Densmore gets a tabla sound out of his tom-toms and Robby plucks his guitar to get it to sound like a sitar.

It is interesting to note that 'Indian Summer' is one of the first songs the band worked on in their earliest rehearsals and was considered for inclusion on the first album. When deadlines for *Morrison Hotel*'s completion loomed and the band was still a little short of material, 'Indian Summer' was resurrected.

A remarkable couple: Jim Morrison and Pamela Courson – the Lizard King and the Queen of the Highway. Their tortured, tempestuous love affair spanned almost all of Jim's career with the Doors. They could be cruel to each other and both took other lovers, but they were bonded by a strange, loving devotion. Jim's vocals on 'Indian Summer' are proof of just how sweet the couple's sweetest moments could be.

maggie m'gill

Like 'Roadhouse Blues', 'Maggie M'gill' is a Morrison/Doors composition with Jim's oracular blues lyrics backed up by the band cooking away on some of their gutsiest riffs. The song ended up being a showcase tune on *Morrison Hotel*, but its beginnings were far from promising.

In concert, on nights when Jim Morrison was riding the snake – when he was dancing on fire – the band would lift the music to his level. That was when Doors shows became a phenomenal melding of psychic transport and physical release.

But Jim, the rock'n'roll shaman, was never quite able to conjure up his magic on a nightly basis – and there were quite a few shows which were not only devoid of magic but which actually proved embarrassing for Ray, Robby and John.

One of the worst "off nights" came during a short tour of the American mid-West in February 1969. The band was keeping up a hectic schedule, recording *The Soft Parade* in LA during the week and then flying off to gigs at the weekend. At a University of Michigan show in Ann Arbor, Jim ran out of magic.

Given the intensity of his concentration and his commitment to the music, Morrison did not have to be drunk or stoned to soar on stage. But in Ann Arbor, he was in fact drunk – and rather than kicking him into a great performance, the alcohol weighed him down. He missed musical cues, forgot sections of lyrics and slurred through those he could remember. Sensing that he was in front of a crowd that did not connect with him – a crowd of beer-hoisting frat boys and disinterested sorority sisters – Jim took to cussing out the audience.

Towards the end of the set, as another tune fell into a shambles, John Densmore made the bold decision to lay his sticks down and leave the stage mid-song. (In *Riders On The Storm*, Densmore says that the stress and pressure of backing Morrison by this point had caused a severe rash to break out all over his body.) Robby Krieger quickly decided that he'd had enough of a sinking ship as well and he left the stage after one more song.

Only three and a half years before, Ray and Jim had sat next to each other on Venice Beach and had decided to get a rock'n'roll band together "to make a million dollars". Now the two of them were next to each other on a stage, rock stars before a large paying crowd – but their rock'n'roll dream was proving to have rather an ugly edge to it. Ray tried to do what he could to salvage the show, so he moved from behind the keys over to Robby's guitar and began to play a simple blues lick for

Jim to riff to. Jim jumped in with "Miss Maggie M'Gill, She lives on a hill…" and carried on for a while. Ray and Jim played for five minutes or so, but the jam never really clicked. As they left the stage, the room filled with boos.

John Densmore was at the peak of frustration that night and in no mood to encourage Ray and Jim to develop their two-man blues tune. But, later, as the *Morrison Hotel* sessions rolled along, Ray's lick and Jim's opening line stuck with him. He encouraged Ray to try playing the same kind of blues guitar in the studio, over which Robby could cut loose with some bottleneck work. Lonnie Mack had been sitting in on bass for 'Roadhouse Blues' and the Doors asked him to lay down the bottom for one more track. Jim took the opportunity to elaborate further on the tale of Miss M'Gill from the hill who went down to Tangie Town where people "really like to get it on".

Naturally, Jim didn't stick with a straight narrative. After a surprise stop in the music, there's a wobbly blast of guitar noise, Ray's lick picks up again, Densmore kicks back in with his tribal 4/4 and, in the middle verses, Jim sings about "the illegitimate son of a rock'n'roll star". (This turned out to be sadly and somewhat chillingly ironic – by the end of the year, Patricia Kennealy Morrison would abort Jim's child when Jim insisted that he wasn't ready for fatherhood.)

Then Jim makes the rather remarkable statement "I'm an old blues man…I've been singing the blues ever since the world began." Perhaps no other white rock'n'roller could pull off such a line. But not only does it make sense coming from Jim – it's a minor revelation.

Of course that's who he is: unlike most white performers, Morrison was never attempting to either duplicate or erase the "blackness" of the blues. Instead he went to the soul-source of the music – the well of pain, lust and hellfire that gave the blues its spirit, which is what he connected with. (No mean feat for a Navy brat child of the suburbs.)

There was nothing precious or studied in Jim's blues. He was, by some measure of spirit, an "old blues man" and he sang his blues music with the voice of an enduring ancient.

In February 1970, a year after 'Maggie M'gill' had been dismissed with boos at its disastrous debut, the song had people dancing in the aisles at the Allen Theatre in Cleveland, Ohio. An extended version of 'Maggie' was now a highlight of every Doors' concert.

He was the monster dressed in black leather. Jim Morrison was not able to keep up with, or live up to, the image of sleek danger and exquisite beauty that he had radiated in the Doors' early days. But the brightest moments of *Morrison Hotel* demonstrated that, beyond "the face" and the leather, his talents were still burning brightly.

absolutely live

The perfect party album: *Absolutely Live* couldn't deliver all the awesome transport of a prime Doors' show, but it was heavy, high powered fun.

After the Miami incident, the Doors started to attract a crowd that was paying to either witness further obscenity or another riot. But the band was still capable of pulling together and delivering powerful moments of musical transport, and a good deal of those moments were captured in the 1969-1970 concerts that made up *Absolutely Live*.

"I think it's a fairly true document of what the band sounds like on a fairly good night," Jim Morrison said of *Absolutely Live* shortly after its release in July 1970. "It's not the best we can do, and it's certainly not the worst. It's a true document of an above-average evening."

Talk of a Doors live album initially began for economic rather than artistic reasons. As *The Soft Parade*'s budget began to swell, Elektra started pushing for a live recording that would help the company make some money back. The recording was originally scheduled for a pair of Whisky a Go Go shows in May 1969 and the album was intended to document the Doors' return to the humble hometown stage where they'd first made a name for themselves.

Possibly because the post-Miami buzz was still fairly ugly, these shows never happened. But by the end of July, *The Soft Parade* was finally out, the Doors had played some great shows on the road and the band, their LA fans and their record company were ready for a high-profile recording of the homecoming.

At this time, Elektra used the Aquarius Theater in LA to showcase its acts on Monday nights – it was the one night of the week when LA's production of the musical *Hair* left the theatre dark. On Monday 21 July, the Doors did two shows at the Aquarius – a pair of 90-minute sets to sell-out crowds.

Those expecting to witness the antics of a trouser-dropping lunatic were in for a disappointment – for most of the performances, Jim Morrison simply sat on a stool centre-stage, calmly puffed on a cigar and sang with more sensuality, intensity and forcefulness than anyone expected. Of course, there were a few crazed moments – Morrison scaled the scaffolding of the *Hair* set to deliver 'The Celebration Of The Lizard' from on high and finished by grabbing a rope and swinging out over the audience like a rock'n'roll Tarzan.

The Doors' love of blues and classic rock'n'roll came through strongly on *Absolutely Live*. The two-record set opened with a wild, extended jam on Bo Diddley's 'Who Do You Love'.

Mostly what the crowd saw was not a shaman at work, but a music-minded craftsman of impressive abilities.

The shows were recorded in their entirety, including the sound check, but, when Jim and the band listened back to their performance, they didn't feel it was representative of the Doors at their best.

"When we listened to it in the studio, we found that it didn't really add up to a very good album," Morrison said. "It was a good evening, but on tape it didn't sound that good." (The "adults only" version of Them's 'Gloria' that the band ripped through during the sound check would later turn up on the 1983 live album *Alive, She Cried*.)

As they toured *The Soft Parade* and then the *Morrison Hotel* material, the band recorded several more shows. Entire concerts at the Felt Forum in New York, Cobo Hall in Detroit, the Spectrum in Philadelphia, the Civic Center in Pittsburgh and the Boston Arena were captured and, by May 1970, the band felt it had more than enough quality musical moments to put an album together. The Doors had done their part – now it fell to producer Paul Rothchild and engineer Bruce Botnick to turn a mountain of recordings into an acceptable album.

"You wouldn't believe what we had to do to make it," Rothchild told *BAM* in 1981. "How many centuries of tape we had to glean to make that fairly skinny double-record set. I couldn't get complete takes of a lot of songs, so I'd find myself suddenly cutting from Detroit to Philadelphia in mid-song. There must be 2000 edits on that album. Some of it was terrific though, and that's on there too."

There was no studio overdubbing or re-recording after the shows had been taped, but the heavy editing process made the title *Absolutely Live* something of a misnomer and in fact it was a title the band was unhappy with.

"Jim hated the name," says Patricia Kennealy Morrison. "He wanted to call it *Lions In The Streets* – from the first line of 'The Celebration Of The Lizard'. But the other guys in the band hated that. So Elektra went with *Absolutely Live*, which I think all four of them ended up hating."

The performances on *Absolutely Live* are generally strong, though there are lacklustre moments. Capturing the physical presence of Jim Morrison and the electrifying intensity of the band on record was always going to be a difficult task and some Doors insiders felt the album failed in that regard.

The Doors learned the craft of rock'n'roll performance during the summer of 1966 when they became the house band at the Whisky A Go Go. Some considered their talents to have dimmed after *The Soft Parade*, but the shows recorded across the U.S. for ***Absolutely Live*** proved that the band could bring some of the Whisky magic to larger venues.

"*Absolutely Live* was absolutely nothing like the band was live," says manager Bill Siddons. "Most of the time, when they were on stage, they were crazed, and they could transport you. Invariably, the bootleg recordings from that time are better than *Absolutely Live*."

What the double album did offer was some spirited fun. Instead of presenting the Doors as dark icons, *Absolutely Live* demystified the band and, in doing so, made some of what they achieved on stage even more exhilarating. Certainly a listener had to be amazed at just how much of the sound Ray was responsible for when the songs were brought to life in a concert setting – his playing on *Absolutely Live* is frequently astonishing. John and Robby's ability to produce a shifting, dynamic flow of music is also well showcased on the record – 'When The Music's Over' demonstrated some of their finest playing.

Most of all, the Jim Morrison one hears on *Absolutely Live* is neither a preening rock star nor a howling devil-man. And he's no drunken buffoon either (though admittedly he does sound rather loose on a tune or two).

On *Absolutely Live,* Jim is a vibrant, friendly, down-to-earth entertainer. If the audience gets over-excited during 'When The Music's Over', he doesn't scold angrily – instead he teases, "Is that any way to behave at a rock'n'roll concert?" and almost immediately regains control. He kids about picking his teeth with a "New York joint" that finds its way to the stage. And, most hilariously, he makes fun of his Miami reputation – at a Pittsburgh show, while introducing Ray's vocal turn on a cover of Willie Dixon's 'Close To You', Jim says, "Ladies and gentlemen, I don't know if you realize it, but tonight you're in for a special treat."

When the crowd breaks into wild cheers, he responds, "No, no, not that, not that… The last time that happened grown men were weeping. Policemen were turning in their badges." The crowd answers with howls of laughter.

Absolutely Live also featured material that was available on no other Doors record. In addition to 'Close To You', there's a stomp-along cover of Bo Diddley's 'Who Do You Love' and four Doors originals: 'Love Hides', 'Build Me A Woman', 'Universal Mind' and, finally on record, the full 'Celebration Of The Lizard'. The band also creates a 'Break On Through #2', which features some extended, and often hilarious, Morrison riffing.

For all its spotty charms, *Absolutely Live* effectively documents how the Doors connected with their audiences. The semi-mystical transport of the band's earlier days now sometimes slipped into a less-ephemeral party mood, but throughout their career the Doors communion with their audiences was as important a part of the music as keyboards, drums, guitar or vocals: the Doors often saw their bond with the audience as something that was even bigger than the music itself.

"You can take 10,000 people coming together and there's a sense of communion, a communal thing," Ray told Richard Goldstein on the band's public television special, just before the Aquarius shows. "A lot of energy is dissipated in the concert, but there's no reason that that same communal thing can't be taken out into the outside world and ideally, hopefully, that's what a good rock concert can do. People are together inside, and they get outside into the parking lot and start driving home, and get into their homes. I hope they still realize that they're together – you know, they were together in the concert and they're together in their homes. They're together in their schools – they're together on the street. And if the people can work that togetherness and keep that thing going… eventually everything's going to turn out all right."

love hides

On the first side of the *Absolutely Live* double album, the Doors perform a medley that includes 'Alabama Song', 'Back Door Man' and 'Five To One' – the band often enjoyed seamlessly segueing from one song to another, but it's hard to know on *Absolutely Live* whether this medley is a complete performance or the result of some careful editing.

After hitting a ferocious energy level during 'Back Door Man', Jim and the band ease back down and, as the song's pulsing riff continues at a subdued level, Jim launches in to a few lines of poetry entitled 'Love Hides'. In a bluesy croon, he announces that love can hide in the strangest of places, in familiar faces, in narrow corners, inside the rainbow and in molecular structures. He also adds that love comes when it is least expected and that it comes for those who seek it.

The final message of the short song (one minute, 49 seconds) is that "Love is the answer" and, on that note, the band instantly drops into the heavy opening riff of 'Five To One', as things get ferocious again.

'Love Hides' sounds like it may be some romantically inspired improvisation on Morrison's part, but in fact it was a poem he'd written for Patricia Kennealy Morrison. By the time *Absolutely Live* was released, the two were deeply involved and had been joined together in a Celtic handfasting ceremony. Their June 1970 marriage was not legally binding, but it was understood to be an exchange of solemn and lasting vows by practitioners of Celtic witchcraft (not to be confused with Satanism). Kennealy and Morrison exchanged traditional Irish wedding rings called *claddaghs*, which depicted hands holding a crowned heart. Hers was silver, his was gold.

Kennealy Morrison had heard 'Love Hides' well before the ceremony. While Jim was staying at her apartment in New York, just before the band left town for the Detroit concerts that were to become a part of *Absolutely Live*, Morrison read the poem to its inspiration. "Jim claimed he wrote 'Love Hides' for me," she says, "and at first I kind of doubted it. I thought it was something that Robby had written, or the kind of thing that Jim would write for Pam. But he always said he'd written it for me, so that's what I'd like to believe."

Metamorphosis blues: the writings of Franz Kafka were a great influence on Jim Morrison. Kafka once said, "A book must be an axe for the frozen sea inside us." Morrison hoped the Doors' performances could serve a similar function.

build me a woman

In a 1970 interview, Jim Morrison described his band this way: "The Doors are basically a blues-oriented band with heavy doses of rock'n'roll, a modicum of jazz, some popular elements and a minute quantity of classical influences… but, basically, (they are) a white blues band."

Morrison could work Nietzsche, Kafka, Celine, Kerouac and Blake into his music, but he also loved just belting out the blues. This was often enthusiastically supported by Ray Manzarek, who had found some of his earliest musical thrills in the electric blues of his hometown Chicago. 'Build Me A Woman' is constructed around the simplest blues pattern and its basic lyrical thrust is that Jim wants a large woman ("ten feet tall") that he can ball all night – he kicks the tune off by announcing that he needs a witness and he's got the "poontang blues". Not quite a work of literary depth, this is still a song the Doors could energetically dig into during a concert without any worry over verses, choruses, bridges or intricate musical cues – Ray, Robby and John simply cooked up the 3-chord groove and Jim bellowed to his heart's content.

The shaman's priestess. Patricia Kennealy (p.114) met Jim Morrison as a journalist and ended up becoming his wife in a pagan ceremony.

115

'Universal Mind' was a Morrison original that showed off some of his skills as a white interpreter of the blues. His contemporary Janis Joplin was an equally powerful interpreter, but was not a Jim fan. The first time they met, she ended up clubbing him with a bottle.

Rather than a crowd-pleaser, 'Build Me A Woman' can better be described as a Morrison-pleaser.

"There are songs I enjoy doing more in person than others," Jim told *Rolling Stone* in 1969. "I like singing the blues – these free, long blues trips where there's no specific beginning or end. It just gets into a groove, and I can just keep making up things. And everybody's soloing. I like that kind of song rather than just a 'song'. You know, just starting on a blues and just seeing where it takes us."

The Doors performed 'Build Me A Woman' along with some *Soft Parade* material on their 1969 public television special. In the wake of Miami, Jim and the band were particularly happy to be part of a programme which not only treated them respectfully, but also allowed them to work free of censorship worries.

That freedom was put to use during 'Build Me A Woman', when Jim included the lyrics "I'm a Sunday trucker Christian motherfucker."

In demure fashion, he slurred the words a bit (after all, who needed the spectacle of another Decency Rally?), but the meaning still came through. That verse was also capped with a humorous bit of blues for the nuclear age – "I'm a three-eyed boy, lookin' for a twelve-toed girl."

Naturally, those lines were kept in when the band performed the tune in concert, but, in order to excise the word "motherfucker", the trucker as well as the unusual boy and girl had to be clipped out of the version that appeared on *Absolutely Live.*

universal mind

'Runnin' Blue' on the *The Soft Parade* was the band's not-entirely-successful homage to Otis Redding – in fact, 'Universal Mind' was much closer to the spirit of the simmering, soulful blues ballads at which Redding excelled. (It's also the kind of tune at which Janis Joplin loved to take a full-throated rip.)

Beginning with the same sort of delicate Krieger strum and airy Morrison vocals used at the beginning of 'The Unknown Soldier', the song quickly swings into its groove. While most of the Doors' bluesy tracks had a rock'n'roll energy to them, the minor keys and 6/8 feel of 'Universal Mind' make it stand apart – it is an older, sadder, more anguished kind of blues tune.

The sadness is set aside for a moment mid-song when Ray, Robby and John jump into a fleeting bridge of pure, skipping jazz. With some great syncopated unison licks from Ray and Robby, this section cooks for a few bars – and provides clear evidence that Densmore wasn't kidding when he talked about loving to play jazz. But the melancholy groove soon locks in again and the band pounds it out to the end.

While 'Universal Mind' isn't remarkably substantial as far as Doors songs go, its lyrics do have an honest, personal tone that Morrison didn't often employ. "Doin' time in the universal mind" sounds like a very apt job description for Jim-as-rock star; success meant that Jim had watched himself become a figment of public imagination, desire and scorn.

He says he's "setting people free", he feels he's "doin' alright", but, after an encounter with someone who carries a "suitcase and a song", Jim's head is turned around and he finds himself alone, looking for a home in every face he sees. The chilling poignancy of the song comes through in the final line.

the celebration of the lizard

After telling his sad, cryptic tale, Morrison announces "I'm the freedom man" – and it doesn't sound like anything to be happy about. Is the "freedom man" the man who is truly free, the man who is supposed to be free, the man who is assumed to be free or the man who represents freedom to others?

Morrison does not make it clear what kind of "freedom man" he is, but that ambiguity is precisely what gives the song its sad soulfulness. 'Universal Mind' is valuable as yet another example of Morrison's ability to construct songs of simple words and infinite nuance.

break on through 2

One of the headiest moments on *Absolutely Live* comes when the band gets ready to tear into the opening of 'Break On Through'. John Densmore pounds around his drums before settling into the familiar beat, Ray toys about on the organ before hitting the bassline and Robby accentuates his riff with some slides down the neck of his guitar.

But Jim isn't quiet ready to head into the song proper and begins to sing of dead cats and dead rats wearing top hats and pretending to be aristocrats. After some spirited wordplay, he concludes, "That's crap."

The brief passage has some typically sombre Morrison imagery ("sucking on a young man's blood"), but rather than sounding fearsome, Morrison sounds like he's having a blast. Jim's sense of humour wasn't often taken into account when his music was analyzed, but this improvised intro makes clear the mischievous sense of fun (dark fun, to be sure) that Jim and the band often displayed on stage.

In a 1970 interview with Salli Stevenson of *Circus* magazine, Jim explained his sense of humour about himself succinctly, "I think of myself as an intelligent, sensitive human being with the soul of a clown, which always forces me to blow it at the most important moments."

If for no other reason, *Absolutely Live* is an important Doors album because it includes the only complete version of Jim Morrison's most ambitious work for the Doors, 'The Celebration Of The Lizard', recorded at the Aquarius shows in LA.

When Morrison's concentration wavered during the *Waiting For The Sun* sessions, he hadn't been able to see the development of the piece through with the band and the only section that was recorded was 'Not To Touch The Earth'.

The full 'Celebration' poem was printed on the inner sleeve of *Waiting For The Sun* and it was at first performed live as a kind of Morrison recitation with supporting music, before eventually being crafted by all four players into a full-grown, show-stopping epic. Morrison was glad to have the piece become a powerful part of Doors concerts, but he was always a bit regretful that it hadn't received the full studio treatment.

With reference to the version that appears on *Absolutely Live*, he told *Circus*, "I like 'The Celebration,' though it's not a great version of that piece, but I'm glad we went ahead and put it out, because I doubt if we would have ever put it on a record otherwise. If we hadn't put it on a live album, we would have just shelved it forever. I'm glad that we did it even in the imperfect form in which it exists."

In its complete form, 'The Celebration Of The Lizard' consists of seven sections: 'Lions In The Street', 'Wake Up', 'A Little Game', 'The Hill Dwellers', 'Not To Touch The Earth', 'Names Of The Kingdom' and 'The Palace of Exile'. Some of the lines and images of the poem were from Jim's Venice notebooks and, in fact, an early version of 'A Little Game', sometimes referred to as 'Go Insane', was one of the six tracks on the pre-Robby Doors' demo, recorded at World Pacific Studios in 1965. (In that version, Morrison delivers the song as a screaming rant – by the time 'A Little Game' was incorporated into 'The Celebration Of The Lizard', it was sung in a much more playful, teasing manner.)

Even fleshed out on *Absolutely Live*, 'Celebration' does not work particularly well as a coherent narrative – the story-telling is disjointed and difficult to follow. But there are many captivating moments in the piece – sex and terror mingle in 'Wake Up', innocents flee ancient terrors in 'The Hill Dwellers' and Jim announces a strangely triumphant homecoming for all of us in 'The Palace Of Exile'.

As performed on *Absolutely Live*, the piece had evolved quite a bit since its transcription on the sleeve of *Waiting For*

The minster's daughter is in love with a snake: *Absolutely Live* included the only complete recorded version of Jim Morrison's (p. 119) epic poem 'The Celebration of the Lizard'. His images of abundant reptiles and palaces of exile had the feel of ancient myth.

The Sun. 'Wake Up' now included a description of a woman with dark red hair and soft white skin – interestingly, a description that could fit both Pam Courson and Patricia Kennealy! There were some changes in the beginning of 'The Hill Dwellers' ("back where there's never any pain" becomes "back where there's never any rain").

Lines from 'The Hill Dwellers' and 'Not To Touch The Earth' were presented in a slightly different order. And, in its original written form, Jim's claim to being the Lizard King who could do anything was followed by another pair of lines – "I can make the earth stop in its tracks, I made the blue cars go away." Those lines never made it on to vinyl in 'Not To Touch The Earth' on *Waiting For The Sun* and they're not included in the *Absolutely Live* performance either.

The reptiles in 'Celebration' were familiar creatures to Morrison – as a small child in Albuquerque, New Mexico, he delighted in chasing and capturing horned toads and lizards. But Jim had been inspired to begin work on 'The Celebration Of The Lizard', logically enough, by a reference book on reptiles. "The first sentence of it struck me acutely – 'reptiles are the interesting descendants of magnificent ancestors'," he explained to the *Los Angeles Free Press* in 1971. "Another thing about them is that they are a complete anachronism. If every reptile in the world were to disappear tomorrow, it wouldn't really change the balance of nature one bit. They are a completely arbitrary species. I think maybe they might, if any creature could, survive another world war or some kind of total poisoning of the planet. I think that somehow reptiles could find a way to avoid it. Also, we must not forget that the lizard and the snake are identified with the unconscious and with the forces of evil. 'Celebration Of The Lizard' was kind of an invitation to the dark forces."

When that invitation was extended to the crowd at the Los Angeles Forum in December 1968, journalist and producer Harvey Kubernick was one of the teenagers in attendance and he was awe-struck. "The crowd was loud and crazy and people kept screaming for 'Light My Fire'," he remembers. "But Morrison actually managed to quiet the crowd down. He asked somebody down in front for a cigarette, and then he told us that he was going to read us some poetry. He had a notebook with him, and the band played behind him as he read 'The Celebration Of The Lizard.' It just felt very strange and very special – I'd been to rock concerts before and nothing like this had ever happened. And it felt like the audience really collaborated with the group on the piece – we were fully engaged. It wasn't the kind of thing that got a standing ovation, but I could tell it had an impact on everybody there. When I left the show that night, I didn't really want to be in a band, I didn't want to be Morrison, I didn't want to wear leather. But the world felt a little different. If we were ready to listen to 'The Celebration Of The Lizard', we weren't little kids anymore."

Patricia Kennealy Morrison had seen the Doors perform 'Celebration' at the Fillmore East in New York in March 1968 and had been equally impressed.

"I was completely blown away by it. I'd never heard such a quiet audience. It sounds hokey, but Jim had everybody completely in the palm of his hand. I have no idea how he learned to control a crowd like that with just his words and his presence. I saw some shows where it didn't work – where a crowd didn't want to be bothered. But when the crowd was into it and the band was into it and Jim was into it, 'Celebration' was phenomenal. It was magic."

The performance on *Absolutely Live* captures a good deal of that magic and there's a powerful empathy between Jim's words and the sometimes soothing, sometimes frantic work of the band.

Those who were not transported by 'The Celebration Of The Lizard' often criticized it as one of Morrison's more sophomoric, unfocused and pretentious works.

But shortly after the album's release, Morrison expressed surprise that so many listeners took the more ominous sections of his darkly intense epic at face value.

"It's all done tongue-in-cheek," he explained. "I don't think people realize that. It's not to be taken seriously. It's like if you play the villain in a Western, it doesn't mean that that's you. That's just an aspect that you keep for show. I don't really take that seriously. That's supposed to be ironic."

l.a. woman

woman

"See me change", the changeling hollered.
But before anyone could hear him, he was gone...

The summer and fall of 1970 were difficult times for the Doors. *Morrison Hotel* and *Absolutely Live* had won them back some of the musical respect they'd lost after *The Soft Parade*, but the band had more to worry about than album reviews – their lead singer was on trial. Literally!

The charges against Jim Morrison stemming from the Miami show on 1 March 1969, were finally due to be heard before a jury in August 1970. He was accused of lewd and lascivious behaviour, indecent exposure, open profanity and public drunkenness – if found guilty, Morrison faced three-and-a-half years in prison.

Before the trial began, Morrison was offered a plea bargain by the prosecution that would have had him paying a fine and serving 60 days in a minimum security stockade. But Jim's lawyers felt they had a strong First Amendment/freedom of speech case to make and announced that no plea would be put forward.

The trial stretched over a month, with the band at one point taking a weekend break to play in the UK at the third Isle of Wight festival, on a bill that included Jimi Hendrix, the Who, Sly & The Family Stone and the Moody Blues. Finally, on 20 September, the jury reached its decision – Jim was guilty of indecent exposure and profanity but the other charges were dismissed. The band returned to LA, where they marked time waiting to hear Jim's sentence.

Morrison himself was embittered and depressed by the trial experience and his gloom was deepened by the death of Jimi Hendrix on 18 September followed by Janis Joplin on 4 October.

At the end of October, Jim returned to Miami to be sentenced and Judge Murray Goodman hit him with the maximum punishment allowed: two six-month sentences to be served concurrently. Jim might be free after two months, and after that would be on probation for two-and-a-half years. Knowing that it might take years to be heard, his lawyers quickly filed an appeal and, in the meantime, Jim was free to return to Los Angeles after posting $50,000 bail.

Back in LA, Jim began to feel the strains of his personal turmoil: Miami wanted him in jail and Elektra wanted another studio album (the last the Doors were contracted for). He had lost his cachet as sexy rock icon, a fact which didn't particularly trouble him, but he felt that some of the more serious Doors supporters had abandoned him during the trial. He was irked that the press had used Miami to paint him as a clown, rather than using the trial as a rallying point for a defence of free speech in the

arts. And he was still not being taken entirely seriously as a poet.

As if Morrison didn't have enough of his past haunting him by way of the trial, to top things off Elektra decided to release the first Doors' greatest hits compilation in November, in time for Christmas shoppers. The cover of the album, *13*, was taken up mostly by a shot of Jim in his young lion/Lizard King prime.

It was as good a time as any for Jim Morrison to be singing the blues. "That's what I'm going to push for. That's the music I enjoy best," Morrison told the *Los Angeles Free Press* as sessions for *L.A. Woman* began. "That's what we do best...Just your basic blues."

The Doors gathered at the Doors Workshop to start working through some new ideas. The strongest pair of songs would come from some fresh Morrison lyrics: 'Riders On The Storm' and the song 'LA Woman'. He was also working on 'Been Down So Long' and 'Hyacinth House'. Robby's newest song would turn out to be the album's first single, 'Love Her Madly'.

The band decided they would record a cover of one of their old club standbys, John Lee Hooker's 'Crawling King Snake'. To fill out the album, the group updated some older material: 'Cars Hiss By My Window' from Jim's old Venice notebooks; 'The Changeling', which Jim had written a couple of years earlier; 'L'America', which had recently been worked up for a film soundtrack but never used; and 'The Wasp', a Morrison poem-to-music which the band had been developing for several years.

As the band began to get this material in shape for their "blues album", they called in Paul Rothchild to hear their work – and the blues that soon filled the air were not the kind they were expecting. Producer Rothchild had shepherded the band through their first five albums and was considered the "fifth Door", but he grew frustrated with the slow, dispiriting pace of the *L.A. Woman* rehearsals and decided not to produce the album.

Rothchild had just had a wonderful experience producing Janis Joplin's *Pearl* album and had a hard time adjusting to the downbeat mood settling in around the Doors.

"That music was full of heart, the way it's supposed to be in the studio," Rothchild told *BAM* in 1981. "You got 110 percent from everyone in the band and 150 percent from Janis. I went into rehearsals with the Doors for about a month... but it was a joke. They'd come straggling in. Jim wouldn't even show up half the time. They were drugged on their own boredom. Just totally bummed out."

The changeling: Jim Morrison's days as rock'n'roll's most beautiful frontman were over by the time *L.A. Woman* was being recorded, but the power of his writing was undiminished and he was still capable of some of his finest work with the Doors. He considered the band's sixth studio album to be the blues record that he'd always wanted to make.

Rothchild had moved the band into the Elektra studios to try and get some recording done, but was even less happy with the results there. Finally, he told the band that he wouldn't take part in the album and that they should produce themselves working with long-time Doors engineer Bruce Botnick (the final producer credit read "Bruce Botnick and the Doors").

Members of the band were taken aback at Rothchild's departure, but the shock gave them the jolt they needed to get serious about making some music. They decided that not only would the new material need to be more straightforward, but the entire recording process had to be streamlined as well. They got hold of recording equipment from Elektra, brought it into the Workshop and turned the place into their own private recording studio.

"The downstairs office had been the rehearsal hall, and now upstairs became a studio control room," remembers Bill Siddons. "The recording console was on my desk. When I went home from work they came in and recorded all night long, sometimes through the day as well."

By taking control of the recording process, and with Botnick allowing them to work at a much faster pace than usual, the Doors developed more of a band spirit than they'd had in quite some time.

"When I met them they had an us-against-the-world relationship," says Siddons. "But it slowly became more of a business relationship, because the guys just couldn't ever trust who Jim would be on a given day.

"They'd almost given up by the beginning of *L.A. Woman* and approached it on a purely pragmatic level – the last album of their contract. But when Paul Rothchild left, it became the first time in a couple of years that the Doors really had to work together. They composed a fair amount of the record in rehearsal at the studio, they collaborated on the production and Jim was a little more controlled than he'd been before. They functioned as a band, and that's what made the record successful."

Part of that unity was reflected in the song credits – the group had returned to a collective "Doors" credit on all the tunes. Unity was also evident in the forthright cover photo, in which the band appeared as four equals (if anything, Morrison actually seemed smaller than the rest).

Also contributing to the sound of *L.A. Woman* were Jerry Scheff, a bass player from Elvis Presley's backing band, and guitarist Marc Benno. Scheff and Densmore locked down together to become a formidable rhythm section throughout the record and Benno was particularly adept at providing Krieger with just the right rhythmic support when Robby soared off on a bottleneck run.

The extra guitar meant that most of the tracks could be recorded live without overdubs and Jim mostly sang live with the band as well – only a couple of tracks needed vocal overdubs. The album was completed quickly and released in April 1971.

In March, Jim Morrison had headed for Paris, where he hoped to clear his mind of anything to do with rock'n'roll and to apply all his creative energies to his poetry. Los Angeles, the "City of Night", had been a generous muse for Morrison's lyrics and music, but he hoped to find fresh inspiration in Paris – the City of Light. After all, this was the spiritual home of so many of the writers he'd been influenced by – Celine, Baudelaire, Rimbaud.

It was also the place where expatriates like Hemingway and Henry Miller had written some of their finest work. Jim hoped that the spirit of all their enduring words would help guide him towards a fresh start. "I ran into him in the elevator of the 9000 Sunset Boulevard building a few days before he left town," remembers Kim Fowley. "He was still a really strong guy – gave me a bone-crunching handshake. He said he was going to Paris to write poetry. I told him that sounded great, good luck and I told him I wished that I could write some poetry. He smiled and said, 'You'll become a poet when you fall in love.' And off he went."

There is some doubt as to whether or not Morrison officially quit the Doors before he left for Paris. He had expressed interest in doing another blues album with the band, but he also had the green light from Elektra to work on a spoken-word album. At any rate, the band was going to continue working on their own material in Los Angeles while Jim was out of town.

"By *LA Woman*, Jim was on his way out of the music business," says Bill Siddons. "It wasn't so much that the band broke up as it was that Jim was moving on. He became committed to

a different artistic vision at that point. He went to Paris saying, 'See you, guys, I'm out of here,' which was never acknowledged in the press, but it was true."

The last Door to speak to Jim Morrison was John Densmore, who in June 1971 got a call from Paris. Jim asked about how *L.A. Woman* was doing and got very excited when John told him it was a hit. (It made its way to Number 9 in the *Billboard* charts and gave the Doors an astonishing eight consecutive gold or platinum albums.) Morrison spoke with enthusiasm about Paris and also indicated to John that he was interested in recording with the Doors again.

At the time, Jim was also sending letters to Patricia Kennealy Morrison, hinting that he might end up with her in New York by the fall. "John was hearing that Jim was going to come back and record in September, and I was hearing that he was going to come back to New York to work on screenplays and do poetry readings," she says. "So who knows? He was also talking a lot about spoken-word albums and solo music albums – he liked what John and Yoko were doing."

The appropriate conclusion seems to be that Jim Morrison was at a crucial moment of change in his life and hadn't clearly decided which direction to head in. He envisaged a future in which he could be part of the Doors in some way and, at the same time, explore the various creative avenues that appealed to him.

Sadly for all of us, Jim Morrison never got the fresh start he was after in Paris. On 3 July, he was found dead in the bath tub at the apartment which he was sharing with Pam Courson; 17 rue Beautreillis, in the Marais on the Right Bank.

Morrison was 27 years old. The death certificate listed cause of death as heart failure and no autopsy was ever performed. Though no one will ever know exactly how Jim's life came to an end, it is fairly likely that he was the victim of an accidental overdose of heroin. The drug had never held much interest for him – he was a beer, wine and cocktails man – but,

by this time, Pam Courson was an addict and Jim may have decided to experiment with the drug that had such a strong hold on someone he was so close to.

There has been much controversy over who may have given Jim the drugs and how deeply implicated Pam may have been in his death. In addition, many sinister theories have been built up concerning the circumstances surrounding his death.

But those circumstances and controversies no longer seem particularly important – the fact is that Jim Morrison was too soon gone and we are simply fortunate to have the words and music that he left behind.

Ironically, when Jim Morrison was buried on 8 July at the Père-Lachaise cemetery in Paris, he achieved the status that had eluded him in life – he was among the poets. He was buried in a section of the graveyard known as "Poet's Corner" and nearby artistic souls keeping him company include Molière, Balzac, Chopin, Edith Piaf and Oscar Wilde.

'The Changeling' was a fairly old Morrison song that the band finally decided to record for *L.A. Woman*. It was written in 1968, about the time Jim was also coming up with things like 'Wild Child' and 'Shaman's Blues' and it has thematic ties to both of those songs. In folklore, the changeling was an otherworldly creature who would be switched with a human infant by evil or mischievous spirits. By all appearances, the changeling was identical to the stolen child, but would always remain connected to the spirit world.

When Morrison wrote the song, he was thinking of the change he was undergoing in the public eye – from sexy rock'n'roll icon to a less-easily understood singer of subtleties and contradictions. It was a way for him to let the audience know that he was not exactly who they thought or expected him to be.

In belting out the song on *L.A. Woman*, Morrison is pointing towards yet another kind of change. He is ready to move beyond being a rock singer altogether and wants to get away from the sensationalism of the rock'n'roll life (and the rock'n'roll press!).

In August 1970, before the *L.A. Woman* sessions had begun, the Doors took a break from Jim Morrison's trial on the Miami obscenity charges to take part in the last major rock event that they would perform at – the third Isle of Wight festival. Stress, alcohol and jet lag took their toll on Morrison and he delivered a notably lacklustre performance. Morrison later told the press that he thought this would be the last time the Doors appeared in concert.

the changeling

'The Changeling' became Jim's announcement that he was moving on to a new phase in his life, one in which the main goal would be to immerse himself in the creation of poetry. The line in the song about leaving town may once have been figurative, but he was getting ready to do just that as soon as the album was finished.

Jim Morrison was something of a broken spirit by the time he recorded 'The Changeling', but it is still an amazingly vibrant track. Jerry Scheff and John Densmore lay down an unstoppable groove, Ray works a great pulsing Hammond sound out of the organ and Robby manages to evoke the horn section of James Brown's band with his contribution on guitar. For his part, Jim shows that he is still capable of exhilarating vocals and 'The Changeling' crackles with energy.

"A lot of people had written Jim off by the summer of '68," says Patricia Kennealy Morrison. "People weren't really willing to let him grow – they wanted him to be this icon forever. When I heard 'The Changeling', I thought, 'That's it. He's out of here.' It's a very autobiographical song, and he was telling us that he's already gone. The whole album was like a good-bye."

Unfortunately, the album became a sad and final farewell. Jim left Los Angeles for Paris in March of 1971. *L.A. Woman* was released in April and was an immediate smash. 'The Changeling' was released in June as the B-side of 'Riders On The Storm', the last single of new material ever to come from the Doors.

But, by the first week of July, before many fans had even had a chance to get hold of the album or single and hear Jim shout "See me change," Jim Morrison was gone forever.

love her madly

Upon its release, *L.A. Woman* was heralded as a surprising return to form for the Doors by those who had begun to consider the band passé – the songs were tight and energetic, the production

was straightforward and Jim Morrison's voice was again a powerfully effective rock'n'roll instrument.

Once again, as had been the case so often before, it was Robby Krieger who calmly, quietly worked a bit of song writing magic that put the band back in the pop charts. 'Love Her Madly' was released in March a month before the album to become the first of the two *L.A. Woman* singles.

'Love Her Madly' was the first Doors single to be released in exactly a year – the last one, 'You Make Me Real'/'Roadhouse Blues', had been issued in March 1970 – and the band was immensely heartened when the song climbed the American charts to Number 11. The song's B-side was '(You Need Meat) Don't Go No Further', a Chicago-style blues tune sung by Ray Manzarek that did not get to appear on *L.A. Woman* but would later turn up on the 1972 compilation, *Weird Scenes Inside The Gold Mine*.

Robby Krieger's biggest songs for the Doors – 'Light My Fire', 'Love Me Two Times', 'Touch Me' – were written as pop capsules of intimate moments between lovers. In 'Love Her Madly',

Robby changed tactics. The lyrics were not words that would flow between lovers, but words that Robby offers to an ostensibly sympathetic ear as his love relationship is falling apart.

The concept behind the 'Love Her Madly' lyrics gives the song an interesting hook. Rather than offering a lament of love gone wrong, an angry dismissal of an ex-lover or a "baby come back" plea, Krieger seems to shrug it all off – he loves his departing lover all the more irrationally precisely because she's headed for the door.

'Love Her Madly' was an easy choice as first single – its musically upbeat mood and subtly layered sound make it a perfect radio track. But as the song was readied in rehearsals for *L.A. Woman*, it was not held in very high esteem by long-time producer Paul Rothchild. Doors lore holds that Rothchild refused to become involved with *L.A. Woman* because he was put off by 'Riders On The Storm', which he dismissed as "cocktail music".

But in a 1981 interview with *BAM*, Rothchild said that 'Love Her Madly' was actually the song that had bothered him most when rehearsals for *L.A. Woman* began at the Doors' Workshop.

The music the Doors created for *L.A. Woman* rejuvenated them as a band (above), and they were further bolstered by a positive response from listeners. (Opposite) Old for his age: Jim Morrison was still capable of some fine pop crooning on tracks like 'Love Her Madly', but throughout most of L.A. Woman he sounded wearied and weathered far beyond his 27 years.

"They only had four or five songs that were even defined enough to play as songs by this point. The most complete were 'LA Woman' and 'Riders On The Storm', both of which I thought were great, great songs. My problem was I couldn't get them to play either of them decently. It was like watching an 80-year-old man trying to run the marathon…

"We went into the studio and it was dreadful. Wall to wall boredom. I worked my ass off for a week, but it was still fucking awful. I'd go into them and tell them that, hoping it would make them angry enough to do something good: 'This isn't rock'n'roll! It's cocktail lounge music!' But they just didn't have the heart any more. I did not say that about 'Riders On The Storm' though. 'Love Her Madly' is exactly the song I was talking about. That's the song that drove me out of the studio. That it sold a million copies means nothing to me."

'Love Her Madly' serves as a symbol of just how mixed the Doors' fortunes had become by 1971 – the very song that drove off their trusted producer and collaborator became the biggest hit single off their final album.

The song would have also probably served as a concert opener if the Doors had been able to tour for *L.A. Woman* – that's the role it served in the band's final pair of concert appearances, 11 and 12 December 1970, at the Dallas Music Hall and the Warehouse in New Orleans respectively.

been down so long

The grittiest, hardest-edged blues track on *L.A. Woman*, 'Been Down So Long' again demonstrates that Jim Morrison wasn't often caught without a book in his hand.

The title, and main lyric, came from a familiar, well-travelled blues phrase but it was also the name of a novel Jim had enjoyed deeply – Richard Farina's *Been Down So Long It Looks Like Up To Me*.

After its publication in 1966, the book was widely read and celebrated as a kind of countercultural testimonial. The novel's

protagonist, Gnossos Papodoupolis, is a restless, wandering soul who tries to hang on to his cool through a series of difficult circumstances (often failing to realize the degree to which his own actions seal his fate). Gnossos rages against his impending loss of youth and believes quite fiercely in his "immunity" and "exemption" from the mediocrity of the society around him as well as the responsibilities that society expects him to shoulder.

Author Richard Farina was also an accomplished folk singer. His wife, Mimi, was Joan Baez's younger sister and together the Farinas released a pair of albums in 1965 and 1966, *Celebrations For A Grey Day* and *Reflections In A Crystal Wind*.

The Farinas' song writing was both personal and socially conscious and tended to avoid pop conventions in favour of a traditional folk approach. They also began to experiment with a combination of straight poetry and musical soundscapes – a blend Morrison himself later displayed great interest in.

Richard Farina's career as a singer/songwriter and novelist was cut sadly short – he died in a motorcycle accident just a few days after the publication of *Been Down So Long It Looks Like Up To Me*. (A third album of previously unreleased music by the Farinas, *Memories*, was released posthumously in 1968.)

Morrison was a fan of the novel – it was on his unofficial "Recommended List" when friends asked for reading tips – but the lyrics of 'Been Down So Long' don't specifically detail the story of Gnossos Papodoupolis. Instead, Morrison offers a kind of primer on how to build the basic, bone-rattling blues tune: the first verse is a hollerin' statement of the blues in general; the second verse is a plea to a warden for freedom; the third verse a plea for some oral satisfaction (When Jim asks a little darlin' to get down on her knees and give her "love" to him, it's not a request for flowers and chocolates); and finally Jim hollers out a final re-statement of those general blues.

Like most of *L.A. Woman*, the track was mostly cut live in the studio and, alongside Jim's full-throated vocals, it also showcases some of the great guitar-interplay between Robby and rhythm guitarist Marc Benno.

This is also one of the few Doors' tracks where there is no keyboard presence. (Manzarek may not have sat the track out though – by the third verse of the song there's an extra rhythm guitar under all the action that seems to be chunking along in a Ray-like fashion.)

Some Doors-watchers saw the band's return to the blues as

something of a retreat from significance – a surrender of the Lizard King's crown. But on a song like 'Been Down So Long', as simple in form as it is, one could still hear all the dread, drama and confusion that had once been packed into 'The End'.

Five years had gone by, but the band was still there and so was the music – by now though, the message had been stripped down to its essentials.

cars hiss by my window

The Doors are mostly remembered as a band with their own big sound – there is a certain dark grandeur in the music and formidable scope to the ideas being expressed in the lyrics. One doesn't often get the sense that the Doors were the kind of band given to back-porch jams, but that is exactly the feel of 'Cars Hiss By My Window'.

A pair of lazy guitars, Jerry Scheff's muddy-bottomed bass and John Densmore's expert brush work create a swampy, Howlin' Wolf-style mess o' blues and it's all capped off with Morrison delivering a playful, fake harmonica solo.

The warm sound of the music is a reflection of the friendliness and unity of purpose that the band managed to recapture as the album sessions progressed. Drummer Bruce Gary, who went on to become a member of the Knack and later worked extensively with Robby Krieger on the guitarist's solo projects, was a guest at the Doors' Workshop as 'Cars Hiss' began to take shape.

"I remember walking in and John and Ray and Robby were playing for a while, and then Jim showed up, big and unkempt and probably a little drunk. They jammed on some old blues, very loose, and it was exciting just to watch them work. When the four of them were into the music, they could still do some amazing work. They were still a great band. And I was in a great mood when I left that session, because John had given me a pair of his signature drumsticks."

While 'Cars Hiss By My Window' has a ramshackle, good-time vibe to it, the lyrics are packed with classic Morrison night-terrors. The song is possibly the creepiest, post-coital lament ever recorded. Jim's got a girl beside him but she's "out of reach".

Love seems to have come and gone and there's no longer any connection between the two lovers. Instead of sweet words and whispers, the only noise in the room is the sound of passing cars – which sound like surf – and planes which rattle the windows. The song ends with Jim announcing, rather complacently, that this "cold girl" may kill him as soon as darkness falls.

'Cars Hiss By My Window' was the last Doors song to be developed from lyrics Jim had written in his Venice notebooks.

The decision to record *L.A. Woman* at the Doors' office on Santa Monica Blvd. had a great deal to do with the loose, relaxed feel of much of the music on the album. Bruce Gary, pictured here with the Knack, was one of the band's old Sunset Strip acquaintances who dropped in during a session.

Motel, money, murder, madness: Jim Morrison perfectly captured the sun'n'psychosis vibe of Los Angeles in *L.A. Woman*. The song served as the singer's bittersweet farewell to the town that he drew much artistic inspiration from.

l.a. woman

Los Angeles is a welcoming paradise built out of an unforgiving desert: a palace of hopeful dreams as well as a repository of soul-sapping nightmares. LA seems to promise that anything can happen, but there's no telling whether it will be delightful, dreary or demented. There are no guarantees: inspiration and demoralization may swoop upon a resident at one and the same moment.

Perhaps no other rock'n'roller has captured the tantalizing contradictions of this sun-drenched, quake-shaken city as well as Jim Morrison. The music he created with the Doors is filled with the dread, the wonder, the exultant uplift and curious weight of life in Southern California. It's fitting that on his last album of songs, the strongest song — the one that will be blasting through car stereos as long as there are such things as cars and stereos — is a remarkable celebration and indictment of Morrison's adopted hometown. And 'LA Woman' also functions as a deeply felt musical good-bye.

The song is not really addressed to a person but to the city itself and it is Morrison's somewhat saddened summary of the sprawling town he has loved so well. The woman's hair — the

city's hills — are burning. There is nothing but blues in the suburbs. All those freeways and alleys just lead to loneliness. And in four beautifully concise words, Jim sums up the underbelly vibe of all of LA: motel, money, murder and madness.

This wasn't a wholly original take on LA — writers such as Raymond Chandler, James Cain and Nathaniel West had also presented engagingly bleak *noir* visions of Los Angeles. In fact, Morrison borrowed one of his key phrases from 'LA Woman' — "City of Night" — from the title of a 1963 novel by John Rechy. The book detailed the grim misadventures of young gay hustlers in Hollywood and, in describing them, Rechy used the phrase "lost angels", which was also adapted by Morrison for use in 'LA Woman'.

The most gripping section of the song is in the middle, where the tempo slows to half-time and Jim begins to sing about "Mr Mojo Risin'". That stretch is the Doors at their best, with the band playing off each other all in support of Morrison. It was John Densmore's idea to slowly increase the tempo — symbolic of Jim's rising mojo — until the song exploded back into its original tempo with one of Robby's wonderful screaming butterfly solos.

This was a blues album, so the band was not surprised to hear Jim make reference to his "mojo". It was only after the track was cut that Jim explained to the others that "Mr Mojo Risin'" was an anagram of "Jim Morrison". He later joked that, if he ever disappeared into Africa the way his hero Rimbaud had, he would use that phrase as identification if he wanted to contact anybody.

Morrison may have originally intended the album to offer his reflections on his old home, LA, and his new one, Paris. His feelings for the former were made clear in 'LA Woman'. His thoughts on the latter came in a song called 'Paris Blues', which was cut at the album sessions but was not included on the record. 'Paris Blues' also uses the conceit of viewing that city as a woman and it makes clear Jim's eagerness to "start my life all over again".

The Doors did provide a specific image of the 'LA Woman' – she was illustrated on the inner sleeve of the album: a young girl crucified on a telephone pole.

This image created an interesting book-end to the Doors' career: Their faces had filled the first-ever rock'n'roll billboard on Sunset Boulevard and now, five years later, when Sunset was nearly choked with out-sized pop advertisements, the image of the LA Woman gave the Doors their second and final billboard on the Strip.

As John Densmore points out in *Riders On The Storm*, the first billboard faced east, towards sunrise and a new day. The *L.A. Woman* billboard faced west, towards the sunset. Sadly, the Doors days with Jim Morrison had drawn to a close.

before the *L.A. Woman* sessions and was intended to have a home elsewhere – on the soundtrack of director Michael Antonioni's 1969 film *Zabriskie Point*.

Antonioni found himself at the cutting edge of hip after writing and directing *Blow Up* – his first English language feature – in 1966. The film was an odd mix of think piece, murder mystery and fashion revue and it attracted a wide audience at least partly because it offered glimpses of nudity and an insider's peek at some of London's most swinging hot-spots (the music of the Yardbirds was featured in one club scene).

In *L.A. Woman*, Jim Morrison offered an update of the noir visions of Los Angeles that writers like Raymond Chandler had established.

The Doors grew out of the UCLA film school, and their music would seem perfect for arty film soundtracks, but director Michelangelo Antonioni didn't like what he heard when the Doors auditioned 'L'America' for him.

l'america

With a dripping, molten guitar note (that sounds for a moment like it might kick off a Doors cover of 'Wild Thing'), Robby Krieger begins the oddest track on *L.A. Woman*, 'L'America'.

Rather than following any kind of blues progression, the song is built on a lurching, descending bass and guitar riff that supports some haunting sing-song vocals from Morrison. There are a couple of sections of bluesy free-for-all in the song, but 'L'America' sounds a bit out of place on *L.A. Woman* – like it could have been a missing section from 'The Celebration Of The Lizard'. In fact, the song sprang from band rehearsals two years

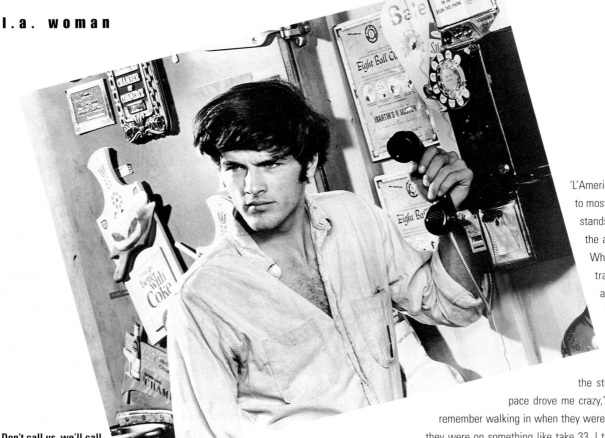

‘L'America' has a different feel to most of *L.A. Woman* and it stands apart from the rest of the album in another way. While many of the other tracks were cut fresh and live, often in a few takes, ‘L'America' was the result of some gruelling studio sessions. "I hated the studio just because the pace drove me crazy," says Bill Siddons. "I remember walking in when they were doing ‘L'America' and they were on something like take 33. I think that squeezed all the emotion out of the song."

The song may have had extra resonance for members of the band, who took a trip to ‘L'America' themselves in July 1969. The Doors had planned to give a concert at the largest bull-ring in Mexico City, the Plaza Monumental, in June and the band were looking forward to the show – it would have been the first rock concert in the giant stadium and they intended to scale down ticket prices so that poor fans would have access to the show.

But the June date of the concert happened to fall on the first anniversary of an organized student rebellion in Mexico City and city officials grew anxious that the Doors show would become a flash point for further demonstrations. After much wrangling over dates and venues, the Mexican promoters working on the show booked the Doors into the Forum Club, an

Don't call us, we'll call you: ‘L'America' was written specifically for *Zabriskie Point*, but rejected. Interestingly enough, a major revival of interest in the Doors was sparked later by a movie soundtrack, when Francis Ford Coppola used ‘The End' in *Apocalypse Now*.

For *Zabriskie Point*, Antonioni turned his gaze on America and he attempted to explore the churning tides of social change through the sometimes aimless wanderings of a Los Angeles student. The student escapes from some violent student demonstrations, steals a plane and eventually has a series of highly-stylized moments of epiphany in the middle of Death Valley.

Revolution, American decline, desert revelations – the images of *Zabriskie Point* seemed to be a natural match for the music of the Doors. When Antonioni expressed interest in using a Doors song on the soundtrack, Morrison turned to some images he had collected in his notebooks and composed ‘L'America'.

Morrison said the title was an abbreviation of "Latin America" and the song describes a strange trip south of the border. Morrison speaks of friendly strangers who sweep into a town where they are generally not eyed in a friendly manner, but "the women loved their ways". Jim also engages in some enjoyably adolescent wordplay, rhyming "change your luck" with "how to – find yourself".

I ain't got you – the Yardbirds had made the cut into director Antonioni's *Blow Up*, but the Doors didn't even make it to the cutting room floor. ‘L'America' was never used in *Zabriskie Point*, finding a home on *L.A. Woman* instead.

The song has an interesting mix of menace and release to it, but apparently it was not what Antonioni was looking for. After listening to a run-through at the Doors' Workshop, he declined to use it in *Zabriskie Point*. (The Doors would not have gained much by being associated with the film – it was a box-office dud and critically savaged.)

upmarket 1000-seat supper club.

With pricey tickets and an exclusive crowd, the Forum Club was the antithesis of the kind of venue the Doors had wanted to use, but gigs were hard to come by in the wake of Miami and they went ahead and played four nights at the officially sanctioned venue. The band was very well-received and Jim Morrison drew wild applause when he introduced his band as Ramon Manzarek, Roberto Krieger and Juan Densmore.

hyacinth house

Distinguished by some unusually pretty keyboard and guitar sounds from Ray and Robby, 'Hyacinth House' is a flowing ballad with a sad heart. On a basic level, the phrase 'Hyacinth House' is a possible take off on "Hyatt House", the hotel on Sunset Boulevard famous as a stop for touring rock'n'roll bands. Once again, Jim's words are packed with several levels of meaning and it's clear that he had the actual myth of Hyacinthus in mind as well when 'Hyacinth House' was written.

The myth is one of youthful death and resurrection through beauty. Hyacinthus was a beautiful young boy and a cherished friend of Apollo, the god of sunlight, prophecy, music and poetry. The two were engaged in a friendly discus-throwing contest, until Apollo forgot his strength and made a throw that sped further than he meant and hit Hyacinthus in the forehead. The boy began to bleed profusely and collapsed. The god then cradled the boy in his arms and began to weep. As Hyacinthus died, the god promised to immortalize him and the blood-stained ground promptly blossomed with the flower that would make the boy's name known forever.

By the time 'Hyacinth House' was written, Jim Morrison was no longer a "beautiful boy" – he was a hulking, shaggy man. But the tale of Hyacinthus, a story of a youthful spirit being cut down, to be remembered by the beauty it created, had a definite appeal for Jim. He could sing 'Hyacinth House' with a sense of

Growing up in the home of Navy man George S. Morrison meant that Jim was moved from town to town as his father's assignments changed. One of the few happy constants in Jim's young life was the radio, and he celebrated some of the sounds he heard as a child in 'The Wasp'.

personal sadness for himself, the Doors and, on a grander scale, the nation. The singer, the band and the country were no longer young, innocent and beautiful and they all could use a "brand new friend" that didn't make any demands in return.

One peculiar line in 'Hyacinth House' has Jim almost wistfully announcing that "the bathroom is clear". The line may have had a more cryptic meaning for Jim, but the bathroom at the Doors Workshop did actually play an important part in the making of L.A. Woman.

"For those sessions the bathroom was our echo chamber," says Bill Siddons. "So it wasn't unusual at all to see Jim singing away in the bathroom. I also remember Jim drinking 36 beers in one day during the L.A. Woman sessions – that was a new record for him. And, needless to say, that was a day when the bathroom got a lot of use."

the wasp (texas radio & the big beat)

'Texas Radio & the Big Beat' was one of the first "straight" Morrison poems to become a piece of Doors work. The poem was originally included in the Doors' first souvenir tour book compiled in 1968: during performances it was frequently used as a spoken intro before a song kicked in (it often led into 'Love Me Two Times').

On L.A. Woman, the poem was extended and the backing

L.A. Woman was a struggle but the band realised they'd created a great album. New tracks were potent and older pieces like 'The Wasp' had come to life at the Workshop. They could still make great music – but was Jim Morrison interested in making it with them? He was gone before the answer was clear.

music the band had come up with was fully developed to create a moving, atmospheric tribute to the mysterious Texas beat.

The song/poem grew out of some of Jim's powerful childhood memories of the radio sounds he heard while growing up. As his father's Naval assignments changed and the family moved between Florida, California and New Mexico, one of the constants in Jim's young life was the border radio stations he could pick up on a multi-band radio.

Powerful signals from Mexico and Texas could be heard as far away as Chicago and, as the signal faded in and out, Jim was exposed to blues shows, R&B programmes, strange rock'n'roll songs, ethnic music and many other exotic sounds that would never be made available on commercial pop stations.

The odd mix of compelling music had a greater effect on Jim than all the Top 40 stations ever would and 'The Wasp' was the eventual result.

"I remember sitting in the outside room listening to him sing 'The Wasp'," says Patricia Kennealy Morrison. "It was pretty amazing. I'd seen a lot of bands in the studio, but those sessions were special. Jim told me he always knew when he wrote something whether it would be a song or a poem. There was never any doubt about that from the moment it came to him. I know for 'The Wasp' he was concerned for the words and music to work together and that's what he got. It was very exciting to listen to it happen."

Portions of 'The Wasp' would turn up again in the 'Stoned Immaculate' section of *An American Prayer*.

riders on the storm

'Riders On The Storm' was the final track cut for *L.A. Woman*, which makes it the last track on Jim Morrison's last album with the Doors.

For all the finality, the song has the very strong feel of a new beginning – it points toward a brand new approach to sound that the Doors might have explored. The Doors had created music in the past that had a hypnotic effect, but 'Riders On The Storm' was actually mesmerizing. It gently soothed at the same time as it calmly proceeded to terrify ("killer on the road").

The upfront, jazzy sound of Ray Manzarek's electric piano actually does have a smooth, lounge-muzak feel to it (hence the confusion when Paul Rothchild dismissed 'Love Her Madly' as cocktail lounge music), but the pulsing drone that underlies the track created the kind of moody tension that enlivened the best of vintage Doors music.

And where early Doors songs such as 'Horse Latitudes' and 'Five To One' employed sometimes jarring sound effects, the subtle undertone of thunder heard during several of 'Riders' quieter moments are effectively and tastefully restrained. Morrison's vocals are – it seems the only word to use – "ghostly": as if he's already had a glimpse of what lies beyond the storm!

Morrison, who wanted so much to be heard as a poet, adapted the phrase "riders on the storm" from the poem of another troubled American writer – Hart Crane.

Crane was born in Ohio and his short life stretched from 1899 to 1932. Throughout these years, he was hounded by a sense of personal failure and, in the end, he committed suicide by jumping off a ship in Mexico. Crane's poetry was delicately crafted, but also complex in its vision.

Crane wrote many short works, but was best known in his lifetime for *The Bridge*, an epic poem published in 1930. Using the Brooklyn Bridge as a unifying symbol, Crane's poem explores the psyche and myths of America through the life of its cities. In his short work, *Praise For An Urn*, Crane composed a beautiful memoriam for a friend, and he described the insights he received from the friend on his death bed as "inheritances – delicate riders of the storm".

In its quiet, creepy, steadfast way, 'Riders On The Storm' touched upon many of the themes that had dominated many of its singer's previous lyrics and poems. Love, death, murder, family and fate are all intoned against the easy-loping, ever-forward groove of 'Riders'.

The song also contained a singular bit of drama that Morrison presented in various forms – the "killer on the road" verse seems to be directly inspired by *HWY*, the arty, road-rambling film that Morrison had written, directed and produced. And Morrison tapped the same macabre scene again with 'The Hitchhiker', a thematically similar spoken-word piece that emerged on 1978's posthumous *An American Prayer* album. There, listeners get a first-person view of the strange events, when a hitchhiker speaks to someone over the phone and nonchalantly admits that he has just killed – meanwhile 'Riders On The Storm' rolls on in the background.

The song was released as a single in June 1971 and climbed to Number 14 in the *Billboard* charts. It was the last hit for the Doors (its B-side was 'The Changeling'). As had been the case with 'Light My Fire' it took an expert edit to get the seven-minute-plus song played heavily on the radio and Bruce Botnick, with some assistance from John Densmore, came up with a radio version that the band, Elektra and the stations were all happy with.

Today, the song lives on as a staple of FM radio and it remains capable of eliciting the kind of responses the Doors were famous for: some fans love the song, others hate it – but it still gets heard. The riders ride on.

Poet Hart Crane used the Brooklyn Bridge as a central image in an epic poem that explored the inner life of New York, 'The Bridge'. *L.A. Woman* can be listened to as Jim Morrison's extended analysis of life out West, with highways and freeways serving the same purpose as Crane's bridge. Morrison borrowed a phrase from Crane, "riders of the storm", for a song that set a mysterious killer out on those roads.

Jim Morrison left the *L.A. Woman* sessions, and Los Angeles altogether, looking ahead to a life less strange. He talked of writing books, poetry, screenplays, and making music with and without the Doors, but would not be with us long enough to get any of it done. Doors music would live on, but for Jim, this was the end.

other voices

And then there were three: the music continued but the shaman was sorely missed.

Without their singer behind the microphone, the Doors couldn't possibly work the same magic in their music. Ray, Robby and John produced some solid sounds on *Other Voices*, but the work was haunted by the one thing the band could no longer give its fans – Jim Morrison.

Many times Ray Manzarek, Robby Krieger and John Densmore had asked themselves, "What do we do about Jim?" After 3 July 1971, they had to ask themselves a much more harrowing question: "What do we do *without* Jim?"

For six years, the Doors had been a singular entity – four souls entwined in one sound. Perhaps more than any other rock'n'roll band, the Doors were a group of irreplaceable parts. The talents of the members were idiosyncratic and unique, so finely tuned to the talents of the others, that no one Door could ever have been replaced without doing a great deal of damage to the music being made.

And all those talents had been hitched to the unsteady genius of Jim Morrison – he was the frontman, the face, the voice, the forward attack. The band had at times bristled to see and hear themselves being treated as Jim Morrison's back-up band: but Ray, Robby and John – plus Jim too! – understood that the magic did not come simply from Jim Morrison and a back-up band: it came from the Doors.

When Jim was gone, the members of the Doors were deeply saddened and deeply confused. They agonized over what should happen next for them. Had the Doors lost Jim at some earlier point in their history, perhaps it would have been easier to end the band. But the notion of going on without Jim had already been discussed – no one was positive that Jim wanted to remain a member of the Doors after *LA Woman*, or how central his role would be if he did decide to record again with them.

While Jim was in Paris, the group had been working on new material at the Doors Workshop and, after a great deal of soul-searching, they decided to continue to do so after his death. "It was difficult to do," remembers Bill Siddons, "but the guys were determined to keep moving. They knew they could never replace Jim, so they decided to just be themselves and do it. Jac Holzman at Elektra gave them enough money to say 'thank you' for the last few years."

Ray had toyed with the idea of changing the band's name to "And the Doors" – a playful way of acknowledging that Jim was gone. Robby thought that a new name was needed for the trio. But they stuck with the original and forged ahead. They signed up again with Elektra and in August began work on what was to become *Other Voices*, the first post-Jim Morrison Doors album. (They did of course have one past experience playing as a Doors

trio – at the 1968 concert in Amsterdam, when Jim had collapsed during the Jefferson Airplane's opening set and Ray, Robby and John put on a well-received show with Ray handling vocals.)

The band adopted a hit or miss approach to putting vocals on top of the music they recorded, with each band member taking turns on the same song to see whose voice, or what combination of voices, worked best. Ray wound up handling most of the lead vocals on the album and Robby, when not handling lead, was given a chance to develop his skills as a harmony singer.

The album was released in November 1971 and made it to Number 31 in the US album charts. In November, the trio began an 11-date tour of some smaller concert venues across the US. Reviews, and audience responses, were generally warm and supportive – but the feeling persisted that some of that good will was just for Jim's sake. He was so freshly gone that he couldn't help but still be a presence at Doors' shows.

"I remember going to the party for *Other Voices* after the band played at the Hollywood Palladium," remembers Kim Fowley. "It really wasn't a bad show, but everybody just seemed to be walking away saying, 'It's not the same'. The party was very quiet."

The loss of Jim Morrison shook the other Doors terribly, but they felt they had no choice but to go on making music, and audiences supported them warmly for a while. While in London towards the end of 1972, while looking for a new lead singer, the band finally grew dispirited enough to call it quits.

in the eye of the sun

An innovator to the end: even as the Doors' material became weaker and less focused, John Densmore found ways to keep the rhythms interesting. On 'Variety is the Spice of Love', he bashed out straight ahead rock'n'roll, while on 'Ships w/ Sails' he did some of his nicest jazz-rock work.

Other Voices was recorded quickly and efficiently, just as *LA Woman* had been. The band used the same recording set-up they'd created for the previous album as well – namely, their personal recording space at the Doors Workshop. Bruce Botnick stayed on to produce the record with Ray, Robby and John – this time the credit read "the Doors and Bruce Botnick".

Swelling out of an odd rush of noise, 'In The Eye Of The Sun', a Manzarek composition, kicks off *Other Voices* in fairly promising fashion. Ray's trademark electric piano sound and Robby's gentle touch on guitar are both intact and Densmore lets loose with a heavy floor-tom beat that powers the song along. Handling the bottom end is bassist Jack Conrad.

The tune has the groove feel of an old swamp-rocker and features some impressive Ray and Robby instrumental interplay in a slightly jazzier middle section. Ray handles the vocals, giving a rough, energetic performance. The lyrics are somewhat enigmatic, but Ray seems to be looking back at the perils and pleasures of the time he has spent at the centre of the Doors' crazy universe. The "eye of the sun" is a dangerous place to be, but it's ultimately the only place he wants to be.

In the final verse, Ray makes it clear that he's not happy with "nothin' to do". He needs to get back to the eye of the sun. It may be that Ray was beginning *Other Voices* with his own personal explanation of why he needed to keep making music with the Doors.

variety is the spice of love

Robby Krieger took to the mike on this surprisingly rollicking tune. He also double-tracked his vocals to get some tight and effective rock'n'roll harmonies.

With Jack Conrad on bass again locking into a steady groove with John Densmore, the song has a kind of rolling momentum that's reminiscent of the Lovin' Spoonful's 'Did You Ever Have To Make Up Your Mind' and even Elvis' 'Burning Love'. The lyrics

are basically a randy joke — the title phrase is what Krieger expects a less-than-sympathetic judge to tell his wife when he goes on trial as a philandering lover. Krieger shrugs that "you've gotta try everything once" and he can't resist trying something new. (He also points out that you need both insurance and endurance if you're going to pursue this philosophy.)

Musically the song has some strong moments — Ray's wild and woolly boogie-woogie piano is a real kick throughout the tune and Robby has a quick double tracked guitar solo in which he shows off some interesting new guitar sounds.

ships w/sails

If 'Riders On The Storm' had been extended into an album-length work, 'Ships W/ Sails' might have been a part of it. The same soothing tones the Doors experimented with to excellent effect on 'Riders' show up on 'Ships', but the groove is entirely new.

Instead of the steady pulse of 'Riders', 'Ships W/Sails' is a jazzy waltz that seems to be constantly surging forward. Part of that propulsive feel comes from the use of two basses — the Doors brought in Ray Neapolitan, whom they'd used on *Morrison Hotel*, to play electric bass and they also invited Willie

Ruff to play some punchy, syncopated figures on stand-up bass.

John Densmore, who'd demonstrated a flair for Latin rhythms as far back as 'Break On Through', adds a bit of Latin feel to the groove here and is aided by percussionist Francisco Aguabella on congas. The wildly playful middle section is one of the instrumental highlights of the entire album.

Ray's demonstrates on this song that, while his voice isn't the most elegant of instruments, it has power. He belts out this slightly off-kilter love song without any bashfulness. The song is directed to a questioning lover and Ray is in the role of the Wandering Soul, who expects to return to his love but can't make any promises. The lover is told not to ask what direction Ray is heading in — just to have faith that the love is strong.

When asked how much he loves whoever it is he's singing to, Ray's answer comes in cryptic form, "Why do ships with sails love the wind?"

tightrope ride

'Tightrope Ride' is the most engaging track on *Other Voices*, the hardest rocking track and the angriest track.

Ray Manzarek was several years older than his bandmates — four years older than Jim — and he always served as something of a father figure within the group dynamic of the Doors. As such, Ray must have felt some obligation to be the coolest of heads when the life of the Doors, and the life of Jim Morrison in particular, became chaotic.

While the rest of the band grew tired of Jim's unreliability and unresponsiveness, Ray was the one who continued to offer him compassion and guidance. But, to some extent, after July 1971, Ray must have felt a sense of betrayal — despite all his support and empathy, one of his best friends had insisted on walking a tightrope alone and proceeded to plummet right off the planet. Ray lets his anger and pain loose on this track, a song that is clearly sung to Jim.

Jim Morrison had been the big Elvis Presley fan in the Doors, and had been the most excited about moving the band towards blues and a classic rock 'n'roll feel. Without Jim around, the band were free to explore more fully the jazzier side of their sound, but they also came up with old-style rockers like 'Tightrope Ride'.

down on the farm

If Ray, Robby and John had had the choice between going 'Down On The Farm' and getting Jim Morrison back, they no doubt would have opted to see Jim again.

But as it was, Jim was gone and the band was free to develop some of the song ideas that Jim had previously rejected. Morrison hadn't been thrilled about singing some of Robby's songs, like 'Tell All The People' and 'Touch Me', but if he felt absolutely no connection with a song – if he could not under any circumstances "feel it" – he would refuse to sing it.

'Down On The Farm' was one of those songs and the Doors decided to return to it when they were collecting material for *Other Voices*.

Compositionally, the song is an odd mix of hippie-pop, jazzy breaks and some down home country-rock. Ray and Robby sang it together and the lyrics are an encouragement for "city boys" to get back to an earthier way of living – sort of the Doors version of Canned Heat's 'Goin' Up The Country'. (And as the band swings along during the "run a rainbow ragged" section, they even sound a bit like the Grateful Dead, a band with which the Doors never got along particularly well.)

The Doors had some fun with the instrumentation on 'Down On The Farm'. They brought Jerry Scheff, bassist from *LA Woman*, back into the studio to lay down some bottom and they got multi-instrumentalist Emil Richards to cut loose on what are credited as "marimbas, kickshaws, and whimwhams."

Ray Manzarek had earned a reputation as the Doors' cool-headed, impeccably capable voice of reason, but on 'Tightrope Ride' he vented his powerfully conflicting emotions over the loss of his friend and colleague Jim Morrison.

Ray sings of Jim's need to be alone and his desire to find a new home. He offers the kind of advice he must have thought a 1000 times for Jim's sake: be careful, don't slip, keep your balance.

Ray's ragged voice makes clear the combination of fury, sadness and, ultimately, understanding that must have been tearing him up inside. In the pulsing bridge section of the song, Ray asks Jim if he had ever considered the fact that he could have got help from his bandmates if he'd wanted it. Couldn't Ray have helped Jim remember his name, "remember the game?"

Towards the end of the song, Ray sounds choked with emotion as he lets Jim know that the band is still by Jim's side, but he acknowledges that clearly Jim is all alone. Like a Rolling Stone, Ray says, "like Brian Jones".

This is a particularly pointed reference because Jim had been moved to write a memorial poem to Brian Jones after the guitarist and founding member of the Rolling Stones was found drowned in his swimming pool in 1969. Morrison's poem was called, 'Ode To LA While Thinking Of Brian Jones, Deceased'. (And, through some ugly cosmic coincidence, both Jones and Morrison died on 3 July.)

A sad chain of words: Jim Morrison had memorialised Brian Jones after the Stones' guitarist died on July 3, 1969. Ray Manzarek made reference to that work when he bid a musical farewell to Jim after the singer's death July 3, 1971.

The emotion of the lyrics is matched by the music – the track rages along with the Doors sounding like the rawest of garage bands. 'Tightrope Ride' came out as the single from *Other Voices* shortly after the album's release. It peaked at Number 71 in the *Billboard* singles charts.

i'm horny
i'm stoned

Robby Krieger's playful, mischievous sense of humour is given free rein on this tune, which, to a perky, boogie-woogie groove, sets forth the various miseries of bachelor life (though the lyrics could also apply to any young person who's just moved out of their parents' house).

His list of complaints, along with those enumerated in the title, includes being tired, bored, nervous, lonely, ugly and cold. He's also been ripped off, he's been wiped out and he's been burned. Robby's conclusion: "Life ain't so easy when you're on your own."

There's an odd little break in the song that seems to borrow a melodic line from 'Puttin On The Ritz' and that's followed by some great piano and bottleneck work. At the end of the tune, the Doors and Bruce Botnick indulge in some "Beatlesque" studio-play — the track swells and crescendoes until it sounds like there are dozens of Robbys and Rays singing, mumbling and making nonsense noises.

wandering
musician

Other Voices gave Ray a chance to play some keyboard parts that weren't as resolutely "Doors-like " as the stuff he'd played with the band previously. Ray had developed a trademark sound and a unique approach to the keys with the Doors, but that approach only showed off a portion of his skills.

On 'Wandering Musician', Ray plays some beautiful, nearly majestic piano parts unlike anything on any other Doors track. But the song itself does not shoot for a "majestic vibe" — it is another one of the tracks with a loose, down home feel to it. It is basically Robby and Ray's chance to tell the world that, as musicians who love to make music, they aren't going to change their ways no matter who tells them they're wrong-headed or wasting their time.

The song insists that the band and their fans must

accept the fact that the insights and intensities of the past are just that — of the past. The surviving, "wandering musicians" must go on humbly putting their heart into their music, as they do on this track.

hang on
to your life

Ray and John's love of jazz certainly gave some heart to the final track on *Other Voices*. With masterful bassist Wolfgang Meltz letting rip on all manner of bass runs and Francisco Aguabella again adding congas and percussion, the song is an engaging suite of bouncy, funky, Latinesque grooves that build to a wild, climactic end section marked by sonic frenzy.

For a band in the position of the Doors during the making of *Other Voices*, it is not at all surprising that one of the songs they came up with turned out to be a stirring meditation on mortality. They'd been witnesses too close, too long, to a life lived as an act of self-destruction. Their advice to listeners at large — advice born of hard-earned, soul-wrenching experience — couldn't be any clearer than the title of this song.

For those who wondered why Ray, Robby, and John would even attempt to carry on as the Doors after Jim Morrison's death, the survivor's sentiments were made clear in 'Wandering Musician'.

full circle

With their second trio album, Ray, Robby and John gently closed the strange story of the Doors. For a while...

Hoping for a new beginning: the Doors knew it was going to take a lot of fresh musical energy to make up for the loss of Jim Morrison. On *Full Circle* they tried to create that energy by moving to a new studio at A&M to record, by working for the first time without Bruce Botnick and by touring with some additional players – bassist Jack Conrad and guitarist Bobby Ray.

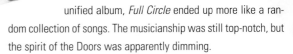

The Doors as a trio received a good deal of praise for their concerts in support of *Other Voices* – Ray Manzarek, John Densmore and Robby Krieger had spent six years becoming a sublimely integrated performing unit and they could still certainly deliver a good show.

They played to sell-out crowds and got huge ovations whenever they dug into an older Doors tune. But it was clear to many fans and reviewers, if not to the band itself, that Jim Morrison still dominated any stage the band was on – it's just that by this time he was dominating through his absence rather than his presence. The Doors without Morrison weren't seen as a wholly new entity: instead fans flocked to the trio's shows almost as if they were taking part in a ritual tribute to Jim. Even a bit of reflected magic from the departed shaman was better than nothing.

But Ray, Robby and John still wanted to make good music. In January 1972, only six months after Jim's death, they began work on their second album without him. In retrospect, perhaps the three would have been better off giving themselves more time to decide what to do after losing Morrison. But in their grief, anger and desire for some uplift, it seemed right to stick together and to continue doing what they were best at – writing, recording and performing.

A few changes were made for *Full Circle* however. Most notably, the band decided not to work again with Bruce Botnick, the engineer/producer who had played a part in every other Doors album. On top of that decision, they moved out of the Doors Workshop and recorded instead at the A&M Studios in Hollywood.

On the whole, the song writing for *Other Voices* had taken place rather freely and naturally – in addition to the stuff they were already working on when Jim died, the band also had lots of material that he hadn't wanted to do. Things were quite different during the making of *Full Circle* and tensions began to arise over whose songs should be recorded and what treatment each track should receive.

Ray, Robby and John each had their own ideas about the kind of music the band should be playing and it wasn't always easy to work out differences of opinion. One result of these tensions was that individual song writing credits were again used. And, consequently, while *Other Voices* had still come out sounding like a

unified album, *Full Circle* ended up more like a random collection of songs. The musicianship was still top-notch, but the spirit of the Doors was apparently dimming.

The most energetic highlight of *Full Circle* was not even an original tune, but a Ray-sung cover of Roy Brown's 'Good Rockin Tonight' which ripped along just like 'Roadhouse Blues' had in the past. (The song was simply called 'Good Rockin'' in the credits.)

In March, the trio took a break from recording in order to tour for a couple of weeks in the southern United States (this included a non-controversial, pants-up return to Miami and a show at Florida State University, the college Jim Morrison had attended before transferring to UCLA).

The Doors still played to enthusiastic crowds, partly because Elektra had kept interest in the Doors alive with the release of *Weird Scenes Inside The Goldmine* in January 1972. This double album compilation (taking its title from a line in 'The End') was less a greatest hits package than a selective track-by-track history of the Doors and it included two B-sides that had never appeared on albums, 'Who Scared You' and '(You Need Meat) Don't Go No Further'.

Towards the end of March, the band went back to making *Full Circle* and then took off again to tour Europe throughout April and May. The Doors were beginning to have conflicting feelings about their future as a trio, but both the US and European tours offered the band a chance to enjoy the simple satisfaction of performing for fans.

"It wasn't as bad as you might think," Robby Krieger told *Creem* magazine in 1981. "The crowds were real good and everything. We had a couple of extra people with us – a rhythm guitarist and a bass player and they did some singing. Jack Conrad and Bobby Ray. It was kind of fun really. And then we did a European tour with the same set-up and that was real fun."

The band returned to the States to finish recording and *Full Circle* was released in August. Fans, who were unsure what to

expect from this second Doors trio album, may not have been encouraged by *Full Circle*'s cover art. Where *Other Voices* had simply used very plain, black and white photos of the trio, the somewhat crudely rendered full-colour wraparound illustration for *Full Circle* looked like it was trying to be cosmic, but was instead mostly dopey. Circus refugees on horseback, man evolving and devolving into rings of fire, a sphinx, a tiger and a flower-encircled foetus – one could almost hear Jim Morrison barking "No" from wherever he was.

Inside, the fold-out album featured a photograph that actually was rather poignant – the three survivors, in silhouette, were staring out at a Pacific Ocean sunset. After *Full Circle*, the band and the fans would agree that there wasn't much point in waiting for the sun. The album only made it to Number 68 in the American charts.

"You missed that voice," remembers drummer Bruce Gary. "Without that voice it really wasn't the same thing. They had the same band chemistry, but they were missing a major part of the machinery."

The band's last concert as a trio was at the Hollywood Bowl on 10 September 1972. The Doors played the middle of a triple bill between opener Tim Buckley and headliner Frank Zappa &

The Mothers Of Invention. At this show, the crowd did not offer the same good will and support that the trio had experienced elsewhere and Ray grew particularly frustrated. After dedicating a version of 'Light My Fire' to Jim, he told the crowd, "Next time we'll be sure and bring Jim Morrison" and promptly walked off the stage. The end was near.

"I thought *Other Voices* was a pretty good record, and *Full Circle* wasn't," says Bill Siddons. "When that one failed, they thought about starting a new band with a new singer. They wanted to try not to be 'the Doors'. They went to London for a while and talked it over, but nothing came of it."

"We were in England looking for a new singer, a new bass player, an additional guitar player, whatever," Ray told *Creem* magazine. "Something to give some new life and change the Doors. But it just got old. It got boring. We'd been together too long. Without Jim, the Doors just weren't the Doors anymore. It wasn't the same band… I thought it was just time to put the Doors to bed, to close the Doors. So I said to John and Robby, 'Listen you guys, let's just pass on this and end it.' And we did."

Said Robby, "I think the main reason we broke up was not because the fans missed Jim, but because we as a group missed him."

Turn out the light: the Doors returned to the Hollywood Bowl without Jim Morrison for their second appearance there in September 1972. The show did not go well, and turned out to be the Doors' final concert.

get up and dance

This Manzarek/Krieger composition didn't get *Full Circle* off to a very promising start. It was understandable that the band might want to lose themselves in some simple, feel-good, rock'n'roll music, but still, even at this late date, fans expected to hear something more from the Doors than a call to the dance floor.

The title of 'Get Up And Dance' pretty much summed up all the tune had to say. The song wasn't helped much by its semi-funky, pre-disco groove and an insistent clap-track. Ray turned in serviceable vocals on this one and was in fact backed rather nicely by "The Other Voices" (as they were credited on the record) featuring back-up singers Clydie King, Venetta Fields and Melissa McKay. Chris Ethridge, then a member of the Flying Burrito Brothers, handled bass duties on this track, but didn't appear elsewhere on the album.

The surviving Doors counted on many of their musician friends to help them pull together the songs on *Other Voices* and *Full Circle*, including Chris Etheridge of the Flying Burrito Brothers.

4 billion souls

Krieger had long toiled as second-billed songwriter for the Doors behind Morrison. But perhaps creative tension between the writers fueled their best work. Compositions like '4 Billion Souls' were interesting but not inspired.

Musically, '4 Billion Souls' is a fairly strong Robby Krieger tune. It chugs along with a kind of neo-vaudeville shuffle and has some nicely layered piano and organ, as well as acoustic and electric guitars. There's also a touch of country twang in Robby's vocals that fits well with the lyrics.

'4 Billion Souls' basically explains that there are too many people on the planet and we're all going to come to an early end if we don't work together. Robby asks the listener to take a long view of the future and to help clean up the planet and "make it shine".

In a couple of breaks, the song shifts into a funk beat that only works to break the mood of the tune, but at the end of the song Robby uses that beat to unleash an impressive flurry of guitar work, very unlike anything he'd done previously with the Doors. Throughout the *Full Circle* sessions, the band was working with guitarist/bassist Jack Conrad in the studio and he went with them on the US and European tours. He's the one playing bass on '4 Billion Souls'.

verdilac

This sprawling, playful tune has a mysterious, unexplained title (although there are a few hints at what exactly a "verdilac" may be).

The nearly 6-minute track begins with a few random noises – almost as if the band is tuning up – and then kicks into a dead-on, straight-ahead funk groove. When the trio only hinted at funk in their music, the results were often weak, but on 'Verdilac' the groove is deep and easy and the band sounds great. Densmore locks in with bassist Charles Larkey, Ray comes up with some sly, bubbling organ parts and Robby finally gets to

hardwood floor

Robby Krieger wrote this bouncy, good-time tune for Ray to sing. It's basically a celebration of a pair of lovers who've got no material wealth other than what's under their feet: "all we got to live on is a hardwood floor."

The message is that love is enough to get by on, although there is a funny middle section where Ray sings about going to his lover's father to ask for money, at which point he is told that he should be out "fighting the war" rather than sponging off the in-laws.

Robby pumps up this section musically with some heavy fuzz tones on guitar, while Densmore and bassist Leland Sklar pump a steady groove. Robby also used this track to show off his now estimable harmonica skills — there are some very impressive harp lines towards the end of the tune.

The Doors worked a bit of creepy conjuring in the mysterious 'Verdilac', a tune that made pointed reference to the act of hanging off a lover's neck. Was the band in fact conjuring up a tribute to Transylvania's most famous count, or perhaps his predecessor, Vlad the Impaler.

cut loose with a wah-wah pedal. (On the first Doors album, Paul Rothchild insisted Krieger didn't use wah-wah so that his guitar, and the band's overall sound, would remain unique and never sound dated.) Some of Ray's organ parts are doubled by Charles Lloyd on tenor sax.

The song, a Krieger/Manzarek composition, is a kind of boastful come-on, albeit one that is stylishly enigmatic. Ray sings that he's going to hang on his woman's neck "like a verdilac" and take her for a ride in his Cadillac. If she doesn't bring him coffee in his favourite cup, he's going to take the rather drastic step of conjuring up spirits.

At that point in the song, the music shifts into a jazzy "conjure" mode — Lloyd begins to take a wailing solo, percussionist Bobbi Hall pumps up the beat and Krieger soon joins in with some stinging guitar notes. The section ends with Ray intoning some strange, unintelligible oaths and then the funk kicks back in. At the end of the song, there is a sudden burst of energy that sounds like the Doors have chewed up a piece of '7 and 7 Is', a tune by their old Sunset Strip comrades Love.

So what is a "verdilac"? Given that Ray talks about hanging "off your neck," and that he also claims in the song "I'm more than just a man", it's possible that the band may have composed a vampire love song. "Verdilac" is an anagram of "Evil Drac"? Or "Drac Live"? Possibly. This interpretation is strengthened by a bit of gothic humour Ray chips in at the end of the song, when he solemnly announces "You know too much, Van Helsing." The fictional Dr Abraham Van Helsing was the specialist in obscure diseases who did battle with that most famous of neck-hangers, Dracula.

the mosquito

'The Mosquito' was released as the *Full Circle* single in September 1972. It is the only song on the album that is credited to Krieger, Densmore and Manzarek as a song writing team — it's also the only bilingual track on the album (if one doesn't count the semi-Satanic conjuring of 'Verdilac').

Robby begins the tune, strumming an acoustic guitar and singing "No me moleste, mosquito" — basically, "don't bug me, bug." In the pre-"politically correct" climate of 1972, Robby's rhyming line, "Let me eat my burrito", may not have drawn ire, but it sounds a little ill-advised today. Robby's verses are backed by Leland Sklar's thumping bass and some nice work from Densmore, first on brushes and then with sticks, to add a touch of *bossa nova* vibe.

Between Robby's verses is a kind of "sounds of fiesta" montage, in which Ray employs a rather rude sounding electronic keyboard. Later the tune breaks into a syncopated go-go groove that picks up steam until the band is engaged in one of its old-fashioned jams. The pulsing rhythms behind Robby's fiery guitar

The strangest life they'd ever known: in the space of a few short years, Ray Manzarek, Robby Krieger and John Densmore had moved from the tiny stage of London Fog to become rock 'n' roll survivors, fallen heroes, heroes revived, and, finally and sadly, surviving witnesses to a perhaps unavoidable rock 'n' roll tragedy - the death of Jim Morrison. The three would bring the Doors to a close shortly after their two trio albums were released.

licks call to mind older rockers like 'My Eyes Have Seen You'. Krieger and Densmore are in particularly good form in this section, proving that, even in bleak circumstances, they can still make some pretty wild noise.

beautiful flute work. However, the general conceit of the song is weakened by some lyrics that don't quite sparkle ("I played real good, I played what I could").

the piano bird

The drummer's bird – Doors were looking for new ways to push their music forward until the end, and John Densmore proved his musical talent stretched beyond a sense of rhythm when he brought the band 'The Piano Bird', a song he'd co-written with Jack Conrad.

'The Piano Bird' sees the band working a gentle jazz-funk groove, with Ray singing about a semi-magical little bird who sings along with a piano player as he practises at home.

Curiously, the song was not written by the Doors' piano player, but by its drummer. John Densmore came up with the number while working with Jack Conrad, who also gained a song writing credit here. 'The Piano Bird' has a pleasant enough feel to it and Charles Lloyd brings the song bird to life with some

Ran's Ornamental Bird-cage and Flower-stand.

it slipped my mind

Robby Krieger never does make clear what exactly slipped his mind on this tune, but he does suggest a way to calm his mind down – meditation.

Robby, Ray and John had first met through the Maharishi's Meditation Center on Third Street in Los Angeles, back in 1965. In 1972, Robby was still devoted to the pursuit of inner peace through meditation.

This song isn't a serious attempt to get transcendental though. It's a comic song, built on a loping, shuffling, party-blues beat. Ray and Robby team up their voices for this one and their droll phrasing makes this one of the most effective vocal performances on *Full Circle*.

Referring to a mind and body sadly out of tune, Krieger hopes that they "run into each other real soon". He also adds some impressively bluesy finger-picking on guitar and the jazzy break which the band launches into in the middle of the song throws off some of the sparks of classic Doors work.

the peking king and the new york queen

Fittingly, the final track on the final Doors album is a six-and-a-half minute epic drama. But this Manzarek composition falls well short of 'The End' or 'When The Music's Over' and ends up being a little more embarrassing than it is entertaining.

Musically, the song is skilful and it flows along with a groove similar to that of 'LA Woman'. There are some very interesting keyboard sounds and parts from Ray and Robby does double duty, playing wah-wah rhythm patterns as well as some screaming butterfly solo licks.

Unfortunately, the story that unfolds in the lyrics isn't particularly captivating. Ray sings a tale of the Sun and the Moon falling in love, and of how they become frustrated that they pass each other every day but cannot touch. They decide to take human forms and meet on the earth, where they can consummate their romance. They become a pair of strikingly attractive people, the Sun a handsome man and the Moon a beautiful woman. But, down on Earth, they find themselves separated by geography and culture – he's landed in China as the Peking King and she's in the States, a New York Queen.

To demonstrate the gulf between east and west, the music slows down, almost to a reggae pulse and a pair of voices are heard comparing Asian and American habits. (The Asian voice is a cartoonish stereotype and the American, presumably a New Yorker, actually sounds more like JFK.) The voices argue over whether a book should be read right-to-left or left-to-right, whether one can see a rabbit on the moon or a man and whether raw fish is tasty or disgusting.

Things grow more heated when the voices disagree on whether Buddha or Jesus shows the one true way and whether communism or democracy is the best political ideology. All of this turns out not to matter much. With disregard for "Passports, visas, and government quotas", the Peking King and the New York Queen get together in the Philippines and make the satisfying whoopee they came down to earth to make in the first place.

The Doors may have intended this fulfilment of solar and lunar lusts to serve as a heart-warming example of how unimportant cultural and social differences should be between humans, but the song is unwieldy, unfocused and, in short, a misfire.

There was a certain amount of truth behind the strange story though – 'The Peking King And The New York Queen' is a sort of gender flip of Ray's enduring real life romance – a romance that, as in the song, led to an East Meets West marriage (or, as in the song, "an alchemical wedding").

When Ray first met Jim at UCLA, Ray's girlfriend was Dorothy Fujikawa. (Ray became something of a *cause celebre* on campus when he refused to edit nude shots of Dorothy out of his student film.) Ray and Dorothy were together throughout the early days of the Doors – Jim briefly shared a Venice apartment with the two of them – and, in December 1967, after the Doors had received their first substantial royalty checks, Ray figured there was now enough money for him and Dorothy to live happily as man and wife. (Or, perhaps to Ray's way of thinking, they'd live happily as "the Japanese Queen and the LA King".)

They were married at the Los Angeles City Hall that month, with Jim Morrison serving as Ray's best man and Pam Courson as Dorothy's bridesmaid.

an american
prayer

Well preserved reel-to-reel tape brought the shaman back to the studio, and the reunited Doors created the poetry album he had longed for.

Down and out? The work of the Doors didn't seem to be held in particularly high regard in the years after Jim Morrison's death. Ironically, and perhaps fittingly, it took an album of Jim's poetry to inspire a resurgence of interest in the Doors.

With the death of Jim Morrison in 1971, the poetic soul of the Doors was lost and, as *Other Voices* and *Full Circle* proved, the group's work could never be the same. Fans respected Ray, Robby and John's attempt to carry on, but without Jim's words, voice and presence, it seemed to many that the music was indeed over.

For those who had been particularly close to the Doors, Morrison's death was a sad event but not a shock – it was sometimes hard to imagine that Morrison's life could have ended in any other way.

"I hated his dying," remembers Bruce Gary, "but I wasn't surprised. I saw how he'd gone from being a vital virile presence on stage – a perfect-looking rock'n'roll star – to a man caught in a cycle of deterioration. It's amazing that a person who is that bright a light can't help but burn out so soon."

There was also the feeling that Jim's inevitable demise simply made him one more casualty on a grim, growing list that had already claimed Janis Joplin and Jimi Hendrix, with many more to come. "By the time Miami had happened, some of us felt that there was already a downward slide taking place," says Paul Body. "That was the beginning of a two-year farewell from Jim that lasted from 1969-1971. And Jim wasn't the only one sliding – it felt like the whole scene was burning out."

Unfortunately, Morrison's youthful death was the perfect finale to elevate his personal myth above the Doors' music and, in the mid-Seventies, some very curious things began to happen to the Doors' legacy. A kind of death-cult coalesced around Morrison's memory, celebrating in perversely romantic fashion the early demise of a dark fallen hero.

Ironically, this was the kind of idolatry that Morrison had been struggling to break free of in the final years of the Doors – the kind of attention that had driven him to Paris – but his early demise and the unclear circumstances surrounding his death seemed to seal a cruel fate for Jim. He would be remembered by many as that omnipotent creature that had come to overshadow the man and the artist: namely the Lizard King.

Oddly, as Morrison's legend began to creep towards "rock deity" proportions, the Doors' music was actually heard less and less frequently. Morrison's death did not seem to bring forth from the rock world at large any immediate re-evaluation of the Doors' best work – instead, it seemed that many critics and listeners felt Morrison's fall from grace needed to be followed up with a period of posthumous banishment.

At the time, rock was entering a period of stylish self-consciousness, when glitter and glam would define the boundaries of hipdom, and Jim Morrison's earnest explorations of the shadows, and his belief that rock'n'roll could be both an extension of literature and an uplifting communal adventure, were seen by many as an embarrassment.

Additionally, on the Doors' home turf in Los Angeles, new sounds were steadily gaining in popularity – the soft-edged country-rock sound of such performers as the Eagles, Jackson Browne and the mellow, pleasant-dream pop of British LA-transplants Fleetwood Mac. This was music that was more concerned with being laid back than "breaking on through" and, so the fierce intensity of the Doors sounded hopelessly crude and overblown.

As if to punish Morrison and the Doors for their artistic *hubris* and to penalise the fans who took their music too seriously, the taste makers of the time deemed the Doors "uncool".

The Beatles' career was over, but they were a group that continued to have a strong presence on radio, in the bins of record stores and in the minds of their fans. There was always a new way to listen to Beatles music. The same did not seem to hold true for the Doors. Morrison had managed to turn off as many people as he had turned on – part of any shaman's predicament, perhaps – and now, even in death, many were not ready to forgive the man his excesses and return to a fair hearing of the music and the writing. It was over. Morrison was gone: the Doors were closed.

"I think the Doors were already on their way out when Jim Morrison died," says Dallas Taylor. "A lot of people felt that they were passé and nobody really seemed to care about the band the same way that they had just a couple of years earlier. People now tend to forget about that period when the Doors didn't get talked about and didn't get listened to, because of the resurgence."

By the end of the Seventies, the music of the Doors and the words of Jim Morrison did indeed enjoy a phenomenal revival in popularity and the band was finally given its full measure of critical respect. That resurgence began, fittingly, with an album of poetry: *An American Prayer*.

On 8 December 1970, Jim Morrison's 27th and final birthday,

Jim treated himself to a special present. Though many friends had offered to take him out to celebrate, he preferred instead to rent some studio time at Village Recorders in Los Angeles and record his poetry.

LA Woman was near completion and Morrison now had a contract with Elektra to do a solo album of poetry. This session was intended to capture most of the major pieces that Jim wanted to present on that album. He'd done an earlier poetry session in March 1969, when the band was forced to lay low after the Miami controversy. Jim had gone into Elektra Studios with engineer John Haeny and recorded several full-length pieces.

The singer asked Haeny to engineer the 8 December session and also invited some friends to come along to the studio: Florentine Pabst and Frank and Kathy Lisciandro – Frank was an old UCLA buddy who'd become an integral part of the Doors' team. His wife Kathy worked as the Doors' secretary.

As Frank Lisciandro describes in his photojournal and remembrance *An Hour for Magic*, the session was loose, with the small group in very high spirits – Morrison was particularly thrilled that he was finally making a record as a poet. Kathy Lisciandro had neatly typed up page after page of Jim's hand-written work and, as soon as John Haeny was ready, Jim began his readings with what would become the 'Stoned Immaculate' section of 'To Come Of Age'.

The house the Doors built: the former headquarters of Elektra Records at 962 North La Cienega Boulevard, in West Hollywood. (p156) Jim's grave in Paris.

Jim re-recorded much of the material from his earlier session – pieces that he had since edited and reworked. He only paused when Haeny needed time to change reels of tape and, after two had been filled, the small group took a break at the Lucky U – the homey Mexican restaurant where Jim had spent a lot of time back in his student days.

Upon returning to the studio, John Haeny presented Jim with another birthday present – a bottle of Irish whiskey – and, as the bottle was passed around, the studio atmosphere became even looser. Jim began using a tambourine to accompany his words and broke into a few impromptu blues songs. He also got his friends up to the microphone to pitch in and read some of his work. Hours later, with many reels of tape filled, Jim was in the best mood he'd been in for a long time. "Brilliant, brilliant," he told Florentine, Kathy, Frank and John. "Oh my god, I couldn't believe it. This was incredible."

Unfortunately, Jim didn't live long enough to see his poetry album through and for several years his recorded words languished unheard.

After *Full Circle,* the remaining Doors took divergent paths. There had been some talk of finding a replacement singer – Iggy Pop was briefly considered – but the band called it quits while in England in early 1973.

In 1974, John Densmore and Robby Krieger teamed up again as the Butts Band and recorded an album. Though that record was not a commercial success, it did further Densmore and Krieger's reputations as musical pioneers: both had developed a strong interest in the pulsing rhythms of the Jamaican music scene and, as founders of the Butts Band, they numbered among the first white Americans to perform reggae.

Ray Manzarek went on to put together a pair of solo records in 1974. The first was *The Golden Scarab* followed by *The Whole Thing Started With Rock & Roll, Now It's Out Of Control.* The latter included a track called "I Wake Up Screaming" which featured punk poetess and staunch Morrison defender Patti Smith reciting some of Jim's words from *The New Creatures.*

Manzarek and Iggy Pop brought Jim Morrison back to the stage of the Whisky A Go Go for a night on July 3 1974, three years to the day after his death. Ray helped organise a 'Jim Morrison Memorial Disappearance Party' at the Doors' old homestead, and when his band cranked out 'L.A. Woman', Pop hopped up on stage wearing a t-shirt that bore Jim's face and belted out the tune. Manzarek and Pop also took part in a 'Death of Glitter Rock' concert at the Hollywood Palladium in 1975, playing with a band that included guitarist James Williamson, drummer Gary Malabar and bassist Nigel Harrison (who later joined Blondie). Manzarek and Harrison attempted to put a permanent band together, and started a potent but short-lived group called Nite City, which dissolved amid furious internal squabbles.

Clearly, it was not going to be easy for Krieger, Densmore or Manzarek to move ahead to any musical projects that would serve their talents as well as the Doors had. And though they felt the need to move forward musically and to move beyond the limitations of their past work together, they also needed to reconcile themselves to the fact that their work with Jim Morrison, their work as the Doors, was going to endure as the most important music they would ever make.

By the end of 1976, Robby Krieger had decided that the Doors could create important new music by looking to the past for inspiration. Krieger called up John Haeny to ask where the tapes of Jim's poetry sessions were. Haeny still had the originals and suggested that Robby, Ray and John get together with him to listen to them.

Upon hearing the strength of Jim's work and the quality of his readings, the surviving Doors were inspired to complete a poetry album for their departed friend. Frank Lisciandro was brought in to help in the production of the album and Pam Courson's father Corky also lent support to the project. (When Pam died in 1974, allegedly of a heroin overdose, control of Jim's estate had passed to Pam's parents.)

The album was to take its title from the closing poem – the first work that Morrison had performed as a solo spoken word piece, and one that he had worked hard to perfect, 'An American Prayer'.

After combing through over 20 hours of tape to find the best album's worth of material, the Doors set to work. None of the recorded poetry had previously been published, though Jim had self-published a pamphlet version of the title poem, 'An American Prayer'. Once the group knew which poems they were going to use, they worked on presenting them in an order that made sense conceptually.

The main idea behind *An American Prayer* was that Jim's poetry would be layered over extracts of old Doors material as well as new music created by Ray, Robby and John. It was a way for the Doors to reclaim their past and pay tribute to Morrison at the same time.

Jim's individual poems were grouped into five thematic sections: 'Awake', 'To Come Of Age', 'The Poet's Dreams', 'World On Fire' and 'An American Prayer'. Next, the group began to find music that fitted the mood and words of each poem. Sometimes it was snippets of Doors tracks that Jim's words seemed to naturally work with ('Riders On The Storm', 'Peace Frog'), but they also came up with new material in the studio – their first time recording together in five years. Jim's rhythmic, musical reading style made his poems fit well generally with the music tracks, but quite often his words had to be spliced and edited to fit specific arrangements.

The three survivors were relying on their departed comrade to supply the creative sparks that they needed to get some music started – just like old times. But they were also hoping to move the Doors' legacy forward by creating a work that reflected a future denied to the band by Morrison's death.

"I think the Doors would have been making music very much like *An American Prayer* ," Ray told Robert Matheu in a *Creem* interview in 1983. "An album would have been a 45-minute presentation of a body of ideas, a series of pieces. We'd probably have done two more albums in the vein of *LA Woman* and then moved on to *An American Prayer*. Because Jim actually recorded 'An American Prayer' just before he left for Paris, and he had the idea to do an extended poem piece of some sort or another working with sound effects, music, whatever."

Not everyone from the old Doors' camp was thrilled with the concept behind *An American Prayer*. Morrison had originally planned to record his poetry with only minimal accompaniment – some sound effects and percussion – and had occasionally talked about backing his words with orchestral arrangements.

Knowing this, producer Paul Rothchild was adamantly opposed to setting Morrison's poetry atop the music of his bandmates. "Jim never intended this kind of approach to be done with his poetry," he told Blair Jackson in a 1981 *BAM* interview. "When he went to the studio to record it, it was to get away from the Doors. In a way, it was his signal to the other Doors that he was moving away from them. He definitely wouldn't have used Doors music. He was talking to people as diverse as Lalo Schifrin, whom he wanted to write some very avant-garde classical music. He wanted it to be sparsely orchestrated. I think *An American Prayer* is rude."

But *An American Prayer* became a labour of love for the surviving Doors. They wanted to honour Jim's memory, give him the gift he had so badly wanted and, for themselves, enjoy a few more moments of sublime chemistry with him, even if that was only possible through some carefully preserved reels of tape.

"It really was the Doors getting back together," Manzarek told *BAM* shortly after the album's release in 1978. "As it happened, it was three musicians and a tape recorder. But when the Doors get together there's no way they can play except like the Doors. We didn't talk about how to play at all. We just sat down and said 'Okay what's best for Jim's poetry?' We made this album because we wanted the public to realize that Jim Morrison was a brilliant poet as well as a shaman, superstar and an incredible rock'n'roll entertainer. We did it because Jim never got his poetry album. Jim Morrison was the greatest rock'n'roll poet, bar none."

Those who had been close to Morrison were generally glad his words would be receiving a new focus of attention, but found it a little troubling that what would have been a Morrison solo album was now coming together as a Doors album. But for Jim's sake, some differences were put aside.

"I was opposed to it at first," says Bill Siddons, "because Jim had started that record thinking it was going to be a project without them. But when the Doors started working on it, I called John and

Echoes of Jim Morrison's stage presence and sense of shock theatre could be found in a performer like Iggy Pop, who regularly rolled bare-chested in broken glass on stage and harangued the audience as he flung himself at them.

Jim vs. Them:
Morrison never had
an easy relationship
with authority fig-
ures, from his father
the Admiral to the
judge in Miami, and
he often came out on
the losing end of the
struggle to be free of
authority's con-
straints. At the time
of his death the
appeal of the Miami
verdict was still
hanging over him.
Some of his most
eloquent calls for
rebellion against the
powers-that-be can
be found in *An
American Prayer*.

said that, if they were doing a poetry album for Jim, they could count me in. I owed Jim that, because the one thing he wanted was recognition as a poet. When they played it for me from beginning to end, I sat there like a limp rag. Unbelievable. I thought people had to experience it the way I did, so I suggested to Elektra that we start doing playback parties for press people."

These listening parties turned out to be one of the wisest business decisions of the Doors career. The buzz that was created around Jim Morrison and *An American Prayer* eventually sent sales of the Doors' back catalogue skyrocketing.

Kim Fowley was invited to one of the first parties and felt the impact of hearing Morrison anew. "All the Doors' songs are conceived in pain and written in blood and delivered in desperation. At the same time, they made those songs enlightening and entertaining and educational. I was surprised to hear all that coming out of the speaker again. It was Jim doing his thing and the band making that music. It sounded like a Doors album. And it was very nice to have Jim back for a while."

In November 1978, nearly a year after the Doors began the project, and almost eight years after his final poetry sessions, *An American Prayer* was released. Fittingly, it was released as a Jim Morrison album, with "Music by the Doors". It reached Number 54 in the *Billboard* charts and became the first and only Doors album to be nominated for a Grammy award. And – this must have delighted Jim wherever he was – *An American Prayer* became the largest selling album of spoken-word verse in history.

An American Prayer is not quite the solo album that Jim Morrison intended nor is it truly an album of new Doors music. But, in many ways, it caps off the Doors' career as their most challenging album and it also holds up as an amazing document of Morrison's work: because of the nature of its conception, the album takes on life as a kind of behind-the-scenes examination of both the Doors music and the life of Morrison. And it is the Doors and Morrison who are conducting that examination.

The first half of the album, including 'Awake', 'To Come Of Age' and 'The Poet's Dreams', roughly sketch out an autobiography of Morrison's early years, with the Doors' background use of bits of 'The Unknown Soldier' 'The End', 'Peace Frog' and other songs creating a kind of time-warp commentary on Jim's life.

The second half of the record functions as a dissection of

"Jim Morrison", the fictional icon, by Jim Morrison the writer. It is as much a work of autobiography as imagination, and it is a more revealing glimpse into Morrison than his song writing ever provided. Perhaps the most striking thing about *An American Prayer* is the Morrison that is revealed. His voice is so soft and gentle, his manner so open and his language so perfectly simple – it comes as a fresh shock that this is the man so many mistook for the "Lizard King".

"I think people are going to be really surprised," Ray Manzarek told Harvey Kubernick in a *Goldmine* interview, "because they think of Jim Morrison as this hell-bent-for-leather screaming maniac, wild lizard king. When they hear him read his poetry, they're going to know the side of Jim Morrison that I knew when I first started the Doors. A sensitive person. A very quiet guy. Softspoken. You can hear the vulnerability. I think that's what people are going to be just shocked at. Jim is a vulnerable human being, a poet putting his words out in complete nakedness for you to hear, to judge. And opening himself like a flower."

An American Prayer began a resurgence of interest in the Doors that has continued unabated ever since. The album received a great deal of attention and began some of the classic enduring "meaning of Morrison/Doors" debates all over again. And just when it seemed like interest in the Doors might have peaked once more, that interest was kicked up another notch by the cinematic rebirth of that headiest of Doors' head trips – that ugliest of nightmares – 'The End', which was heard during a particularly riveting scene as part of the soundtrack of Francis Ford Coppola's 1979 Vietnam epic, *Apocalypse Now.*

The song was re-mixed to accentuate Morrison chanting "Fuck, fuck, fuck" during the instrumental section (originally Paul Rothchild had buried this outburst so that it just sounded like some rhythmic yelling on the original record). With a few twiddles of the sound board, Jim Morrison was able to shock a whole new audience.

The music of the Doors and the wild life of Morrison were further promoted by the publication in 1980 of *No One Here Gets Out Alive,* by Jerry Hopkins and Danny Sugerman. Hopkins had been working as a journalist when he got the opportunity to meet, interview and become close to Jim Morrison; Sugerman, who currently manages the affairs of the Doors, became associated with the band when he was a teenager who was befriended by Morrison and made a part of the staff at the Doors

Workshop. Their provocative biography of Morrison, hard on the heels of *An American Prayer*, convinced countless new fans to accord Morrison and the Doors their proper place in the rock-'n'roll pantheon. And more to the point, the album and book got radio interested in cranking Doors tunes all over again, which in turn made hot sellers of all the old Doors albums and the many compilations available.

Despite the renewed Doors commotion it set in motion, *An American Prayer* had always been intended as something of a special interest release – an album not just for average Doors fans but for keen Doors *aficionados*. After its initial run of success, it went out of print and became hard to get hold of. Manzarek, Krieger and Densmore eventually decided that this was an unacceptable situation and in 1994 began work on updating the record for re-release on CD in the summer of 1995. The Doors worked with their old winning team – producer Paul Rothchild (who by this time had come to think more charitably of *An American Prayer*) and engineer Bruce Botnick. Together, they created two new pieces from Morrison's original poetry recordings 'Babylon Fading' and 'Bird of Prey', and also came up with a new version of 'Ghost Song'.

"This was the first time the three Doors had been in the studio together since the first *American Prayer* recordings," Ray Manzarek told the *Los Angeles Times*. "What was amazing is it really was like taking up where we left off. The only change is everyone plays a little better now."

After the most recent *American Prayer* sessions, Manzarek also dropped a cryptic hint to *Rolling Stone* that the Doors may continue to record. "We've just had the appetizer, and we're thinking a little more seriously about the *entrée* now. You never know what the future holds, and the end is always infinite."

awake
('ghost song',
'dawn's highway,
'newborn awakening')

An American Prayer begins with a familiar question; Jim gently, almost timidly asks if everybody's in. He follows that

query with an insistent, far-from-timid "Wake up!" call. These lines, from the second section of 'The Celebration Of The Lizard', are taken from a live performance. Then the band, with Bob Glaub on bass, cuts in with some of their newly recorded material adding coolly funky support to Jim's 'Ghost Song'.

The piece is an exploration of innocence and a celebration of vibrant new life. In a perfectly controlled, calm, captivating voice, Morrison speaks of a timeless, natural paradise available to lovers of carefree spirit. Some of the words and images, as well as the intensity of the piece, support the concept of "mythic Morrison", but Jim's delivery works entirely against that. He has never sounded more human – he is the artist speaking straightforwardly to his audience, simply wanting his words to be heard.

Drummer Bruce Gary was a guest at several of the *American Prayer* sessions (Gary had his own turn in the spotlight as a member of the Knack, and became a close associate of Robby Krieger's, recording and performing as part of Robby's various solo projects).

"I remember watching them piece together the poetry," he says. "I thought the new music they were coming up with was very *apropos*. And once I heard the finished album, I thought it was brilliant. It was eerie though, standing in the studio and hearing Jim speak, having that voice come over the speakers. It was like he was there all night with us."

'Ghost Song' segues into 'Dawn's Highway', in which Jim, in very conversational fashion, expands on the incident he had made veiled reference to with the "Indians scattered" lines of 'Peace Frog'. Jim recounts seeing a terrible highway accident when he was very small, riding in the family car. A truckload of Indians had crashed and their broken bodies lying bleeding on the highway gave him his first look at death and his first taste of true fear. That vision affected Jim so much throughout his life that he wondered whether a couple of dying Indian souls might have latched on to him. Again, it is the striking simplicity of the words and the easy, open fashion in which Morrison tells his story that lend the reading its power.

As Jim completes his story, the band kicks in with 'Peace Frog' and he repeats the "dawn's highway bleeding" lines. An interesting connection is then made to the "blood in the streets" images that Morrison belts out in 'Peace Frog'. But in this context, what jumps out of the 'Peace Frog' lyrics is not

By December 1970, Jim Morrison was a tired soul. But some of the poetry he recorded then is remarkably hopeful. 'Newborn Awakening' demonstrates that Morrison believed a resurrection of the spirit was possible, even when the future was uncertain and the end was near.

An American Prayer packs the strange history of the Doors – from lazy days in Venice to hard times in the City of Night – into an albums worth of words, sounds and music.

blood as an indicator of carnage, but blood as a means of catharsis and renewal, as in the blood that accompanies a birth.

The band shifts suddenly from 'Peace Frog' to 'Blue Sunday', just like on *Morrison Hotel*, but this time the music comes from a lone, haunting piano. In fact, the chords from 'Blue Sunday' seem to have opened up into what Morrison refers to as "the Ghost Song", a number which in his poem is being practised by a young woman on a baby grand piano. Jim then tenderly intones the lines of 'Newborn Awakening', a short piece about resurrection and re-invention of the self.

"Jim was obsessed with sex and death," Ray told *BAM* in 1978. "After all, sex starts it and death ends it. In between is your life. But Jim was also obsessed with birth and rebirth. Look at the beginning of the album – it's saying 'to be born again'."

to come of age
('black polished chrome/latino chrome', 'angels and sailors', 'stoned immaculate')

The second section of *An American Prayer* begins with a bit of the execution sequence from 'The Unknown Soldier'. The grim, military tie-in is appropriate, as Jim begins recounting his sometimes grim upbringing with the line "A military station in the desert".

'To Come Of Age' deals with scenarios of adolescence and, in the 'Black Polished Chrome/Latino Chrome' section, Jim unleashes some quick Kerouac-style images of dance parties and teen hijinks. Morrison was a creature of the Sixties, but he had a deep affection for Fifties pop culture and in these phrases looks back fondly, but without the rosy glow of nostalgia, at the big cars, summer suns and record-playing parties of his youth.

(The bubbly pop music of those parties stayed with Morrison to the end. "The last time I saw Jim Morrison was at The Experience on Sunset," recalls Len Fagan, former member of Spontaneous Combustion. "It was the summer of 1970. He seemed overweight and had the long beard. We all came out of the club late. Jim was quite drunk, but he made a point of saying good night to everybody. Then he calmly strolled off down the street and – I'll never forget this – he was singing 'Rockin' Robin'.")

As 'To Come Of Age' progresses, the mood grows more menacing. The Doors jam out on a stylized Fifties rocker tune and then slide into a snaky salsa beat for the startling, profane 'Latino Chrome' lines. (The band is aided here by percussionist Reinol Andino, who appeared on *The Soft Parade* and in fact the groove here is very similar to the groove of that album's title track.)

The innocent sensuality of puberty starts to become corrupted in Morrison's words – there are rapes

the poet's dreams
('the movie'; 'curses, invocations')

and fights taking place across a dusty, decrepit landscape. The dawning awareness of this world of corruption leads to the street sounds that open the next section, 'Angels And Sailors', which sets sharp, disturbing images of sex and violence against some of the blues singing that Jim had improvised during his reading sessions. Robby Krieger beautifully matches Jim's blues with some especially sweet and tasty guitar work.

'To Come Of Age' ends with 'Stoned Immaculate', which begins with the familiar pulse of 'The Wasp (Texas Radio & the Big Beat)' newly revamped by the band. Jim repeats some lines from that song, but adds the haunting image of a pair of girls, one named Freedom and one named Enterprise. The result is particularly effective when Jim reads the "Texas radio" lines at the same time we hear him singing them.

Poet Michael C Ford feels that the repetition of phrases and images in many of Morrison's poems is an indication that Jim was striving to craft his words into their most effective form.

"Even with the appeal of rock'n'roll music, Morrison still had more critics than he had people praising him as an artist," Ford explains. "People were hard on him, but he was young. He was emerging. There are moments of very unique voicings in his word clusters. The sad thing is that he dropped off the planet before he had a chance to really edit himself. He was searching for the right way to say things. That's why you have certain lines showing up four or five times in his work. He was fine-tuning."

There are two parts to 'The Poet's Dreams' – 'The Movie' and 'Curses, Invocations'. The first is a short series of other-worldly announcements and a strange conversation between two Jims. The second is a deadpan comic rant that functions as an ugly recapitulation of what was once "the Soft Parade". This time the procession of oddities that Morrison describes includes "garden hogs and cunt veterans" as well as "shit hoarders and individualists". The Doors set the distasteful list to a jazzy waltz. The section ends with the unforgettable couplet, "I'll always be a word man, Better than a bird man."

Keyboardist Arthur Barrow had met Robby Krieger through Mothers of Invention alumnus Don Preston, and mixed the sound for one of Robby's bands at a Whisky show. When the Doors needed a synthesist for 'The Movie', Robby brought in Barrow.

"It was my first real recording session at a real recording studio in LA," remembers Barrow. "It was a thrill. I had a pile of weird equipment, analogue synths, and I created the background noises for 'The Movie'. John and Ray and Robby were there, along with John Haeny, who was full of ideas and very intent. I remember looking at the two-inch multi-track tape as it was rolling – and there were many, many edits going by. They had edited Morrison's talking pretty drastically to give it some musical spacing.

It was the editing and rearrangement of Morrison's words that most infuriated the album's critics – most notably Paul Rothchild. In the 1981 *BAM* interview, he was quite blunt about it.

"That album is a rape of Jim Morrison," he said. "It was heavily edited. I have a tape of Jim reading most of that poetry in the style and meter he intended. Jim and I discussed poetry a great deal. I got him to listen to poets like Dylan Thomas reading his own works and Jim definitely got things out of it. Jim was always talking to me about the progress of words, their sequence, their flow. He was very concerned about how he presented his poetry. When I listen to the original tape, I hear something compelling.

"To me, what was done on *American Prayer* is the same as taking a Picasso and cutting it into postage stamp-sized pieces, spreading it across a supermarket wall."

Morrison felt his lyric-writing and poetry were separate creative acts, but in works like 'Stoned Immaculate', the Doors gave Jim's lyrics and poetry added power by having them play off each other.

Such negativity did not find its way into the studio as *An American Prayer* was being assembled. "There was a really good vibe in the studio", says Arthur Barrow. "I remember getting into a discussion with John, trying to convince him that the song 'Waiting For The Sun' wasn't on the album *Waiting For The Sun*. I kept saying, 'I know you were there, but I'm pretty sure about this.' I finally convinced him. The guys have an odd assortment of personalities. I'd always thought of them as such heavy guys, but Ray is very friendly, and Robby's a nice soft-spoken guy, and John's just a real nice regular guy. I asked Robby about Jim, and he said, 'No, Jim wasn't like us – he was always cosmic. He was always a poet. He was always being Jim Morrison'."

world on fire
('american night', 'roadhouse blues', 'lament', 'the hitchhiker')

The 'World On Fire' section probably has the most integrated moments of poetry and music on *An American Prayer*. Jim begins with his short salute to the 'American Night' and a pounding piano note stands in for the sounds of guns and/or thunder. Then crowd noises swell and we are back in the realm of rock'n'roll and the madness that Jim and the Doors often found themselves confronting.

The simple, rockin' strains of a live 'Roadhouse Blues' might seem like a very odd choice for inclusion on a poetry album, but it beautifully sums up the other half of the Morrison equation – he was the poet who could rock, the philosopher who could swig beer for breakfast with the best of them.

Jim's speech at the end of the concert track is particularly enlightening, funny and a little scary. When he mentions that he's a Sagittarius, a young girl yells back "So am I" but, when Jim follows up by saying he doesn't believe in astrology, she quickly says "Neither do I". The crowd roars when Jim says, "I want to have my kicks before the whole shithouse goes up in flames."

Then we hear crowd sounds that give a sense of the fan-hunger that focused on Jim, a beckoning need that Jim politely put up with all through his career. The montage of crowd sounds fades as Jim recites a few lines about autobiographical fatigue. 'Roadhouse Blues' shows him to be, still, a consummate performer, but the lines of poetry that follow reveal that the thrill is gone – the rock star now even gets sick of his own "stinky boots".

'Lament' follows and it could be more accurately named 'Lament For My Cock'. This is the poem largely responsible for the sticker on copies of *An American Prayer* that read "Caution: This album contains material that may not be suitable for broadcast." Jim isn't just talking dirty, though. The piece is a comedic phallic eulogy, as Jim ponders the curses and blessings of his young lion/sex god image. One of the lines in the poem refers to a "Guitar player" and, when Jim says it, Robby enters the piece with some very pretty instrumental work.

The poem has all the candour and self-amused resignation of Henry Miller's work, which Jim admired greatly. (Miller's first completed novel, which went unpublished for many years, was titled *Crazy Cock*.)

Soon after its release, Harvey Kubernick played *An American Prayer* at a college radio convention and found that 'Lament' had all the power to shock, outrage and delight that Morrison had embodied while alive.

"The graphic content absolutely divided the room," he remembers. "But I loved hearing raw, naked poetry like that from Jim. And I think, one more time, his timing as a local poet was impeccable. He was breaking down language barriers, goring sacred cows and getting people either inspired or upset, right at the time when punk rock was taking off locally in LA with the same kind of energy."

"It was the first full-length rock'n'roll poetry record that's been released," Ray Manzarek told *Goldmine*. "Back in the Fifties we used to get spoken word albums by everybody – Dylan Thomas, E.E. Cummings, Kenneth Patchen. This is entirely

Jim Morrison no doubt felt some connection to another hard-drinking poet of Celtic descent – Dylan Thomas. Thomas's spoken-word recordings of his work provided Morrison with an example of how effective, and affecting a poetry album could be.

Jim Morrison had a good deal of respect and admiration for Henry Miller's simple, earthy, deeply personal writing. A Miller influence can be detected in 'Lament'.

One of the more comic moments of *An American Prayer* is a live recording of Morrison giving a crowd a brief discourse on astrology. The Sagittarian concludes that he simply wants to get his kicks "before the whole shithouse goes up in flames".

different. I don't think anybody has been actually ready for this record. I think the record was 15 years ahead of its time. The subject matter was very different, very difficult. Dirty words. I would advise anybody under 21 not to buy this record – certainly not to let your parents see you in possession of this record."

The 'World On Fire' section ends very creepily with 'The Hitchhiker'. This spoken piece is a reverse angle view of the "killer on the road" verse in 'Riders On The Storm'. We hear that song quietly drift along as Jim, the hitchhiker, relays in a phone conservation that he has "wasted" a guy who gave him a ride and gave him trouble. He is completely without remorse, or any emotion at all for that matter.

The flatness of his voice chills to the bone. This scenario comes directly from Jim's film *HWY*, in which he played the same role and has a similar roadside phone booth conversation with Michael McClure.

him – he talked, he sang, he acted it out. I've always thought that 'An American Prayer' could have been a play. It could have easily been a one-man show – a real theatre piece."

The poem, in edited form, became the centre-piece and finale of the album that took its title. The Doors accompany Jim with more of the same funk music that flows beneath 'Awake', but when Jim asks the sorrowful question, "Where are the feasts we were promised?", the Doors move into some raga-riffing reminiscent of 'The End'. As Morrison works his way towards the conclusion of the poem, the music swells in a rock *Adagio* (which features Jerry Scheff on bass).

'An American Prayer' serves as an alternately persuasive and cryptic concluding statement to the chain of images and ideas that have been laid out on the album. The piece deals with power – the powers that individuals find themselves up against (doubt, death, the authorities), as well as the powers that enable individuals to make the necessary changes in the world around them.

For all the crude and cruel images in the poems throughout the album, 'An American Prayer' stands out as the most disturbing, because it is the one poem in which a listener can hear real sadness and frustration in Morrison, unalloyed by any of his usual sly humour. There is pain and a recognition of real loss in the words of this prayer and Morrison makes it endurable only with his sense of relief in being able to express some deeply held truths.

'An American Prayer' ends with one of Jim's most pointedly powerful lines, "Prefer a Feast of Friends to the Giant Family ... "

"It worked," says Bill Siddons referring to both the poem and the album. "And it worked because, when you experienced Jim Morrison face to face without being able to avoid him, you were changed by Jim. That's what happened to me from 'Horse Latitudes' all the way through to *An American Prayer*. When you spend time with someone of that power, it's going to change you."

an american prayer

Bigger than ever. Musically and otherwise, Jim Morrison and the Doors are still a vital presence in Los Angeles, the West, the rock'n'roll world at large. The moonlight drive continues.

As Jim became more serious about his poetry, he became increasingly interested in publishing it himself. When his trial began in Miami in August 1970, Jim made his latest work available to the newsmen covering the event. This was 'An American Prayer' presented in small, bound editions. Thematically, his timing couldn't have been better – the poem was both an indictment of America's decay of the spirit and a call for a rediscovery of a higher human consciousness.

Jim had performed 'An American Prayer' in its entirety at the Norman Mailer mayoral campaign benefit in June 1969. "He even went beyond what was in the booklet," says Michael C Ford, who read that night as well. "It was an inspired reading for

chronology

1939
FEBRUARY 12: Ray Manzarek is born Raymond Daniel Manczarek in Chicago, Illinois.

1943
DECEMBER 8: Jim Morrison is born James Douglas Morrison in Pensacola, Florida.

1944
DECEMBER 1: John Densmore is born John Paul Densmore in Santa Monica, California.

1946
JANUARY 8: Robby Krieger is born Robert Alan Krieger in Los Angeles, California.

1964
FEBRUARY: Jim Morrison transfers from Florida State University to the theatre arts department at UCLA, where Ray Manzarek is a film student.

FALL: Morrison is filling notebooks. The writings he puts together on film aesthetics will later be published as *The Lords: Notes On Vision*.

1965
APRIL: John Densmore and Robby Krieger begin playing together in a short-lived group called the Psychedelic Rangers. The first song they write together is called 'Paranoia'.

SPRING: Screamin' Ray Daniels, aka Ray Manzarek, leads Rick & the Ravens during their frequent gigs at the Turkey Joint West in Santa Monica. Occasionally Jim Morrison steps up on stage with the band to holler out a chorus of 'Louie, Louie'. Rick & the Ravens will release one mostly unheard single on Aura Records.

JUNE: Jim Morrison receives a bachelor's degree in cinematography from UCLA. He gets his first paid gig as a musician when Ray Manzarek asks him to hold an unplugged electric guitar as a member of Rick & the Ravens at a high school graduation dance. The band backs a singing duo who had formerly recorded as Caesar and Cleo, but have just renamed themselves Sonny and Cher.

SUMMER: Jim Morrison is living on the rooftop of a building at the corner of Speedway and Westminster in Venice. He spends a great deal of time there filling notebooks with lyrics and poems. That work will turn into most of the Doors' first two albums.

AUGUST: Jim encounters his school chum Ray Manzarek on Venice Beach. When he sings Ray the lyrics to 'Moonlight Drive', Ray insists they get a band together. Jim suggests they call themselves "the Doors" after a line of William Blake poetry.

SEPTEMBER: Ray asks John Densmore, an acquaintance from the Third Street Meditation Center, to drum in the band which he, his brothers and Morrison are putting together. Densmore accepts. After two weeks of rehearsals, the Ravens/Doors line-up (Jim Morrison, Ray, Rick and Jim Manzarek, John Densmore and a female bassist fated to anonymity) go to World Pacific Studios to make a demo tape. In approximately three hours, the band records six songs: 'Moonlight Drive', 'End Of The Night', 'Hello, I Love You', 'Summer's Almost Gone', 'My Eyes Have Seen You' and 'Go Insane' (later known as 'A Little Game').

OCTOBER: The band makes of point of getting its tape to Billy James at Columbia Records, because Morrison has seen a picture of him in the trades and thinks that James' beard is a good omen. He's right. James is the only record exec in LA who hears something special in the Doors' demo and signs them to a five-and-a-half year contract, contingent on the release of a single in the first six-month period.

NOVEMBER: The Columbia single is not forthcoming. Rick and Jim Manzarek decide to leave the band. John Densmore brings in his old friend, Robby Krieger. The guitarist is asked to become a member of the Doors. He agrees to do so, and drops out of the band he is currently in, the Clouds.

DECEMBER: The finalized Doors line-up begins rigorous rehearsals. When no bass player seems right for the band's sound, Ray begins to use a Fender Piano Bass.

1966
JANUARY: The Doors get their first steady gig, at the dingiest of Sunset Strip clubs, the London Fog. During a performance there, Jim Morrison meets Pamela Courson.

APRIL: Columbia has not released a Doors' single and drops the band from their roster.

MAY: The managers of the London Fog blame the Doors for inciting brawls and give them a week's notice. On their final night, they are seen by Ronnie Haran, talent booker for the Strip's premier club, the Whisky A Go Go. She promptly wrangles the Doors a job as house band at the Whisky without further audition.

SUMMER: The Doors begin to build a reputation for wild, unpredictable shows as they open for headlining acts such as Them, Love, the Mothers Of Invention, Captain Beefheart, Buffalo Springfield, the Byrds, the Rascals, the Animals and the Paul Butterfield Blues Band.

JUNE: Ronnie Haran and Arthur Lee of Love convince Elektra Records' founder and president Jac Holzman to see the Doors at the Whisky. He dislikes them at first, but comes back four nights in a row and is eventually won over. So is Elektra ace staff producer Paul Rothchild, who first feels the band is awful, then hears brilliance in their music. Elektra offers the band a contract, and, after cautious consideration, the band accepts.

JULY: Jim Morrison first creates the Oedipal section of 'The End' on-stage at the Whisky. Owner Elmer Valentine is outraged by the profanity and fires the band. They begin to work regularly down the Strip at Gazzari's.

SEPTEMBER: The Doors spend two weeks at Sunset Sound Recording Studios recording their debut album with producer Paul Rothchild and engineer Bruce Botnick.

NOVEMBER: The Doors travel to New York for their first gigs outside LA. They play a week at the Ondine.

While in New York, the band agrees to edit the "She gets high" line in 'Break On Through' to "She gets … ".

DECEMBER: Jim moves in with Pam Courson at 1812 Rothdell Trail, just off of Laurel Canyon Boulevard in Hollywood.

1967
JANUARY: *The Doors* is released. The 'Break On Through'/'End Of The Night' single is released. Elektra creates rock hype history by making the Doors the first rock band to promote their album on a Sunset Strip billboard.

JANUARY 6-8: The Doors play Bill Graham's Fillmore Auditorium in San Francisco on a bill with the Young Rascals and Sopwith Camel.

JANUARY 13-14: The Doors return to the Fillmore to open a bill with the Grateful Dead and the Junior Wells Blues Band.

FEBRUARY: The band plays a week of gigs in San Francisco with the Peanut Butter Conspiracy. In LA, they headline at Gazzari's.

FEBRUARY 22: The Doors play a benefit concert at the Valley Music Theater in Woodland Hills, CA, on a bill that includes the Byrds, Buffalo Springfield, Hugh Masakela and Peter, Paul & Mary.

MARCH 3,4: The Doors headline the Avalon Ballroom in San Francisco on a bill with Country Joe & the Fish and the Sparrow (who would later become Steppenwolf).

MARCH 7-11: The Doors play the Matrix in San Francisco.

MID-MARCH: The band returns to New York for a successful three-week run at the Ondine.

APRIL: The 'Light My Fire'/'Crystal Ship' single is released. In LA, the Doors headline at Ciro's and Bido Lito's.

APRIL 9: The Doors headline a bill with the Jefferson Airplane at the Cheetah on the Santa Monica Pier.

APRIL 14-15: The Doors headline at the Avalon in San Francisco on a bill with the Steve Miller Blues Band.

MAY 12-13: The Doors play the Avalon again, this time with the Sparrow.

MAY 16-21: The Doors play a week's return engagement at the Whisky.

MAY 20: The Doors play Birmingham High School football stadium in Van Nuys, CA, opening for the Jefferson Airplane.

JUNE 3-4: The Doors play the Avalon with the Steve Miller Blues Band, then headline the Fillmore on the 9th and 10th, the Hullabaloo in LA on the 11th, finally returning to New York on the 12th for a three-week stand at the Scene, one of the city's hippest night-clubs.

JULY 3: The Doors play the Santa Monica Civic Center; the Anaheim Convention Center with the Jefferson Airplane on the 15th; and, from July 28-30, three nights at the Fillmore with the James Cotton Blues Band and Richie Havens.

JULY 29: 'Light My Fire' becomes the Number 1 song in US charts.

AUGUST: The band returns to Sunset Sound to begin three months of recording sessions for *Strange Days*.

AUGUST 12: The Doors open for Simon & Garfunkel at the Forest Hills Tennis Stadium in New York.

AUGUST 27: The Doors headline the Cheetah on a bill with the Nazz and the 103rd Street Rhythm Band.

SEPTEMBER: 'People Are Strange'/'Unhappy Girl' single released.

SEPTEMBER 9: The Doors play the Village Theater in New York with the Chambers Brothers, followed by the band's first mid-West appearance at the Musicarnival in Cleveland, Ohio on September 15.

SEPTEMBER 17: In New York, the Doors appear on *The Ed Sullivan Show*. The band is asked to drop the word "higher" from 'Light My Fire' by the show's producer. The band agrees, but during the live broadcast Morrison leaves it in. The Doors do not appear on the show again.

LATE-SEPTEMBER: While the Doors are in New York, photographer Joel Brodsky takes the "young lion" shots of Jim Morrison. The day of a show in Washington DC, Morrison's mother shows up at the hotel the band is staying at and asks to see Jim. He declines to meet her.

OCTOBER: *Strange Days* is released.

OCTOBER 15: The Doors play at the Berkeley Community Theatre.

NOVEMBER: 'Love Me Two Times'/'Moonlight Drive' single released.

NOVEMBER 16: The Doors play the Fillmore in San Francisco and the Winterland in San Francisco the following two nights.

NOVEMBER 24: Play Hunter College in New York.

DECEMBER 1: Play Cal State Long Beach with Canned Heat.

DECEMBER 8: Play the Rensselaer Polytechnic Institute in Troy, New York.

DECEMBER 9: Play the New Haven Arena. Morrison is maced backstage by a policeman who doesn't know who he is. During the performance of 'Back Door Man', Morrison recounts what happened to him complete with obscenities. The show is halted and Jim Morrison becomes the first rock star to be arrested on stage during a concert. He is charged with indecent exhibition, breach of the peace and resisting arrest.

DECEMBER 21: Ray Manzarek and Dorothy Fujikawa are married at City Hall in Los Angeles. Jim Morrison is best man and Pam Courson is the bridesmaid.

DECEMBER 22-23: The Doors play the Shrine Auditorium in Los Angeles on a bill with the Bluesberry Jam, Sweetwater and Iron Butterfly.

DECEMBER 26-28: Play the Winterland with Chuck Berry.

DECEMBER 29-31: Play three nights in Denver, Colorado with Allmen Joy (soon to be the Allman Brothers Band).

1968
JANUARY: The Doors return to Sunset Sound and begin sessions for *Waiting For the Sun*.

JANUARY 19-20: The Doors play the Carousel Theater in West Covina, CA.

JANUARY 28: In the parking lot of a Las Vegas, Nevada adult theatre, Jim taunts a security guard by pretending to smoke a joint. Guards rush Morrison and his friends and beat them. When Las Vegas police arrive, they arrest Morrison and charge him with vagrancy and public drunkenness.

FEBRUARY: The Doors open their own offices at 8512 Santa Monica Boulevard in West Hollywood.

MARCH: 'The Unknown Soldier'/'We Could Be So Good Together' released.

MARCH 22-23: The Doors headline the Fillmore East in New York.

APRIL 11: Play a benefit at the Kaleidoscope in Los Angeles on a bill with Love, Bo Diddley and Pacific Gas and Electric.

APRIL 19: Play the Westbury Music Fair in Long Island.

MAY 10: Morrison gets his audience so roused at a Chicago concert that the crowd riots.

MAY 19: The Doors perform at the Northern California Folk-Rock Festival, which also includes performances by the Jefferson Airplane, the Animals, Big Brother, the Electric Flag, Country Joe & the Fish and Taj Mahal.

JUNE: 'Hello, I Love You'/'Love Street' single is released.

JULY: *Waiting For The Sun* is released.

JULY 5: The Doors headline the Hollywood Bowl, on a bill with Steppenwolf and the Chambers Brothers.

JULY 13: The Doors perform in Houston.

JULY 14: Perform in Dallas.

JULY 20: Perform in Honolulu.

AUGUST 2: Play the Singer Bowl in New York, headlining a bill with the Who and the Kangaroo. At the end of the Doors' set, the crowd rushes the stage and a riot erupts.

AUGUST 3: 'Hello, I Love You' becomes the Number 1 song in the US. The Doors perform at the Musicarnival in Cleveland, where another riot nearly breaks out.

SEPTEMBER 2: The Doors embark on a 17-day tour of Europe, with the Jefferson Airplane. There are concerts in London, Frankfurt, Copenhagen, Amsterdam and Stockholm. At the Amsterdam show, Morrison passes out while dancing on stage during the Airplane's opening set – Manzarek, Krieger and Densmore perform as a trio.

OCTOBER: The Doors begin rehearsals for *The Soft Parade*.

NOVEMBER: The Doors tour the US with concerts in Milwaukee, Columbus, Chicago, Phoenix, Madison, St Louis and Minneapolis. At the November 7 show at Veterans Coliseum in Phoenix, Morrison incites the crowd to riot.

LATE-NOVEMBER: The Doors begin recording *The Soft Parade* at Elektra Studios.

DECEMBER: The 'Touch Me'/'Wild Child' single is released.

DECEMBER 14: The Doors play the Forum in Los Angeles, on a bill with Sweetwater, Jerry Lee Lewis and a Japanese *koto* player.

DECEMBER 15: The Doors appear on *The Smothers Brothers Show* performing 'Wild Child' and 'Touch Me'.

1969

JANUARY 24: The Doors play to a sell-out crowd at Madison Square Garden in New York.

JANUARY 25: Jim Morrison meets Patricia Kennealy when she interviews him for *Jazz & Pop* magazine.

FEBRUARY: The 'Wishful Sinful'/ 'Who Scared You' single is released.

FEBRUARY 7: Jim Morrison is arrested in Los Angeles for drunk driving and driving without a licence.

FEBRUARY 24-28: Jim Morrison attends a week of performances by Julian Beck's Living Theater at the USC's Bouvard Auditorium.

MARCH 1: The Doors play the Dinner Key Auditorium in Miami. Jim heckles the crowd relentlessly and possibly exposes himself.

MARCH 5: The city of Miami issues a warrant for Jim Morrison's arrest. He is charged with lewd and lascivious behaviour, indecent exposure, public profanity and public drunkenness.

MARCH 23: In response to the Doors' performance at the Dinner Key, a Rally for Decency is held at the Orange Bowl. Entertainment is provided by Jackie Gleason, Kate Smith, Anita Bryant, the Lettermen and the Miami Drum & Bugle Corps.

LATE-MARCH: Jim Morrison records several of his poems, without musical accompaniment, at Elektra Studios.

APRIL 3: Jim Morrison turns himself in to the FBI in Los Angeles in order to stand trial on the Miami charges.

MID-APRIL: Jim Morrison and friends film *HWY*.

MAY: 'Tell All The People'/'Easy Ride' single is released. The Atlanta Film Festival bestows a first prize documentary award on *Feast Of Friends*, a chronicle of the Doors road trips throughout 1968. Credits list photography by Paul Ferrara, sound by Babe Hill, editing by Frank Lisciandro, with the Doors down as producers.

MID-MAY: The Doors tape a public television special for WNET in New York. They perform material from the forthcoming *Soft Parade* and are interviewed by Richard Goldstein. This is followed by a panel of journalists, including Patricia Kennealy, discussing the band's merits.

LATE MAY: Jim Morrison makes his debut as a solo spoken word performer, reading 'An American Prayer' at a benefit for Norman Mailer's New York mayoral campaign at the Cinematheque Theater in Los Angeles.

JUNE 14: After a spell of cancelled dates in the wake of Miami, the Doors play a concert in Chicago on a bill with the Staple Singers.

JUNE 28-JULY 1: The Doors perform four nights at the upmarket Forum Club in Mexico City.

JULY: *The Soft Parade* is released.

JULY 3: Brian Jones of the Rolling Stones is found dead in his swimming pool, and Jim Morrison memorialises him in a poem, 'Ode to LA While Thinking of Brian Jones, Deceased'.

JULY 21: The Doors play two shows at the Aquarius Theater, LA. The shows are taped for a planned live album.

JULY 27: The Doors play the Seattle Pop Festival, where Led Zeppelin, Santana, Ike & Tina Turner, Chuck Berry and Vanilla Fudge also perform.

AUGUST: 'Runnin' Blue'/'Do It' single released.

SEPTEMBER 13: The Doors headline the Rock & Roll Revival Show at Toronto's Varsity Stadium. On the bill are Chuck Berry, Jerry Lee Lewis, Gene Vincent, Little Richard, Fats Domino and, making their debut, John Lennon and the Plastic Ono Band.

SEPTEMBER 19: Play two shows in Philadelphia.

SEPTEMBER 20: Play Pittsburgh.

NOVEMBER 9: Jim Morrison returns to Miami to enter a plea of not guilty.

NOVEMBER 11: Morrison and drinking buddy decide to attend a Rolling Stones concert in Phoenix. On the flight from LA, they engage in drunken horseplay that gets them arrested before they can get off the plane in Phoenix. Morrison is charged with interference with the flight of an aircraft.

LATE-NOVEMBER: The Doors begin sessions for *Morrison Hotel* at Sunset Sound.

1970

JANUARY 17,18: The Doors play the Felt Forum at Madison Square Garden in New York.

FEBRUARY: *Morrison Hotel* is released.

FEBRUARY 5,6: The Doors play two concerts at the Winterland in San Francisco.

MARCH: 'You Make Me Real'/'Roadhouse Blues' single is released.

MARCH 28: Jim Morrison is found guilty of the Phoenix charges, and faces three months in jail. He will be acquitted the following month when a testifying stewardess realizes that she had confused Morrison with the more troublesome Tom Baker.

APRIL: Simon & Schuster publish *The Lords and the New Creatures* by James Douglas Morrison.

APRIL 10: The Doors have their power cut off when a concert at the Boston Arena runs long.

MAY 2: The Doors play the Civic Arena in Pittsburgh.

MAY 8: The Doors play a very well-received show at Cobo Hall in Detroit.

JUNE: Jim Morrison has poetry published in *Mt Alverno Review*.

JUNE 5: The Doors play a disastrously sloppy show in Seattle.

JUNE 24: Midsummer Day; Jim Morrison and Patricia Kennealy are unofficially married in a Celtic handfasting ceremony.

JULY: *Absolutely Live* is released. It comprises concert recordings from July 1969 to May 1970. When the album comes out, Jim Morrison is vacationing in Paris, Spain and North Africa.

AUGUST 6: After a night of drinking in Los Angeles, Morrison can't find his way home and curls up in a doorway to sleep. The home owner calls the police and Jim is arrested for public drunkenness. The next day he flies to Miami to stand trial.

AUGUST 10: The Miami trial begins.

AUGUST 21,22: The Doors take a break from the trial to perform concerts in Bakersfield and San Diego.

AUGUST 29: The Doors again break from the trial to perform at the Isle of Wight Festival, England. Also performing at the festival are Jimi Hendrix, the Who, Sly & the Family Stone, the Moody Blues and Emerson, Lake & Palmer. The Doors performance is notably lacklustre; afterwards

Morrison tells the press that it may have been his last live performance.

SEPTEMBER 20: Jim Morrison is found guilty of misdemeanour charges of indecent exposure and public profanity. He faces six months in jail. The decision is immediately appealed by Morrison's lawyers.

NOVEMBER: The Doors begin recording sessions for *LA Woman* at the Doors' Workshop. Producer Paul Rothchild is unhappy with the mood of the sessions and the material being created – he declines to produce the album. Engineer Bruce Botnick takes over production duties.

DECEMBER 8: Jim Morrison arranges for an extensive recording session of his poetry at Village Recorders in LA. The tapes from these recordings will later be used on *An American Prayer*.

DECEMBER 12: Jim Morrison's last performance with the Doors at the Warehouse in New Orleans.

1971

MARCH: 'Love Her Madly'/'(You Need Meat) Don't Go No Further' single released. Jim Morrison leaves LA for Paris.

APRIL: *LA Woman* is released.

JUNE: 'Riders On The Storm'/'The Changeling' single is released.

JULY 3: Jim Morrison is found dead in the bathtub of the apartment in Paris he is sharing with Pam Courson.

JULY 8: Jim Morrison is buried at the Père-Lachaise cemetery in Paris.

AUGUST: The surviving Doors begin recording new material at the Doors Workshop, working with Bruce Botnick as producer.

OCTOBER: *Other Voices* is released.

NOVEMBER: The Doors play an 11-date tour of smaller venues across the US.

1972

JANUARY: The Doors begin recording new material at A&M Studios in Hollywood. For the first time in their career, they decide not to work with Bruce Botnick.

MARCH 2-12: The Doors embark on a short US tour, including dates in Miami and at Jim Morrison's alma mater, Florida State University.

APRIL-MAY: The Doors tour Europe.

JULY: *Full Circle* is released.

SEPTEMBER 10: The Doors' final performance is a return engagement at the Hollywood Bowl, on a bill with opener Tim Buckley and headliner Frank Zappa and the Mothers Of Invention.

FALL: The Doors travel to London and consider finding a replacement singer. By early 1973, they decide that it's time to call it quits.

1974

APRIL 25: Pamela Courson dies in her Hollywood apartment, apparently of a heroin overdose.

1977

FALL: The Doors begin work assembling Jim Morrison's recorded poetry for an album.

1978

November: *An American Prayer* is released.

discography

Catalogue numbers are given for the country of release. If released in the UK and US then both numbers are given.

SINGLES

'Break On Through'/'End Of The Night' (January, 1967), Elektra 45611; UK: Elektra EKSN 45009

'Light My Fire'/'Crystal Ship' (April, 1967) Elektra 45615; UK: Elektra EKSN 45014

'People Are Strange'/'Unhappy Girl' (September, 1967), Elektra 45621; UK: Elektra EKSN 45017

'Love Me Two Times'/'Moonlight Drive' (November, 1967), Elektra 45624; UK: Elektra EKSN 45022

'The Unknown Soldier'/'We Could Be So Good Together' (March, 1968) Elektra 45628; UK: Elektra EKSN 45030

'Hello, I Love You'/'Love Street' (June, 1968) Elektra 45635; UK: Elektra EKSN 45037

'Touch Me'/'Wild Child' (December, 1968) Elektra 45646; UK: Elektra EKSN 45050

'Wishful Sinful'/'Who Scared You' (February, 1969), Elektra 45656; UK: Elektra EKSN 45059

'Tell All The People'/'Easy Ride' (May, 1969) Elektra 45663; UK: Elektra EKSN 45065

'Running Blue'/'Do It' (August, 1969) Elektra 45675

'You Make Me Real'/'Roadhouse Blues' (March, 1970), Elektra 45685

'Love Her Madly'/'(You Need Meat) Don't Go No Further' (March, 1971), Elektra 45726; UK: Elektra EK 45726

'Riders On The Storm'/'The Changeling' (June, 1971), Elektra 45738; UK: Elektra K 12021

'Tightrope Ride' (October, 1971) Elektra 45757; UK: Elektra K 12036

'The Mosquito' (August, 1972) Elektra 45807

'Roadhouse Blues'/'Albinoni Adagio' (January, 1979), Elektra E-46005

'Gloria (Clean Edit)'/'Gloria (Dirty Version)' (November, 1983), Elektra 69770

SPUN GOLD SERIES SINGLES

'Light My Fire'/'Love Me Two Times' (April, 1971), Elektra 45051

'Touch Me'/'Hello, I Love You' (April, 1971) Elektra 45052

'Riders On The Storm'/'Love Her Madly' (September, 1972), Elektra 45059

SINGLES IN UK ONLY

'Alabama Song'/'Take It As It Comes' Elektra EKSN 45012

'You Make Me Real'/'The Spy' Elektra 210 004

'Ship W/Sails'/'In The Eye Of The Sun' Elektra K 12048

'Get Up And Dance'/ 'Tree Trunks' Elektra K 12059

'Love Me Two Times'/'Hello, I love You'/'Ghost House'/'Roadhouse Blues', Elektra K12215/SAM 94

'Gloria'/'Love Me Two Times' Elektra E 9974T

'Light My Fire'/'People Are Strange'/'Soul Kitchen', Elektra EKR 125TW

ALBUMS

THE DOORS January, 1967
(Elektra 74007; UK: Elektra EKS 74007/EKR 4007) – 'Break On Through'; 'Soul Kitchen'; 'Crystal Ship'; 'Twentieth Century Fox'; 'Alabama Song'; 'Light My Fire'; 'Back Door Man'; 'I Looked At You'; 'End Of The Night'; 'Take It As It Comes'; 'The End'.

STRANGE DAYS October, 1967
(Elektra 74014; UK: Elektra EKS 74014/EKL 4014) – 'Strange Days'; 'You're Lost Little Girl'; 'Love Me Two Times'; 'Unhappy Girl'; 'Horse Latitudes'; 'Moonlight Drive'; 'People Are Strange'; 'My Eyes Have Seen You'; 'I Can't See Your Face in My Mind'; 'When The Music's Over'.

WAITING FOR THE SUN July, 1968
(Elektra 74024; UK: Elektra EKS 74024/EKL 4024) – 'Hello, I Love You'; 'Love Street'; 'Not To Touch The Earth'; 'Summer's Almost Gone'; 'Wintertime Love'; 'The Unknown Soldier'; 'Spanish Caravan'; 'My Wild Love'; 'We Could Be So Good Together'; 'Yes, The River Knows'; 'Five To One'.

THE SOFT PARADE July 1969
(Elektra 75005; UK: Elektra EKS 75005) 'Tell All The People'; 'Touch Me'; 'Shaman's Blues'; 'Do It'; 'Easy Ride'; 'Wild Child'; 'Runnin' Blue'; 'Wishful Sinful'; 'The Soft Parade'.

MORRISON HOTEL February, 1970
(Elektra 75007; UK: Elektra EKS 75007) 'Roadhouse Blues'; 'Waiting For The Sun'; 'You Make Me Real'; 'Peace Frog'; 'Blue Sunday'; 'Ship Of Fools'; 'Land Ho!'; 'The Spy'; 'Queen Of The Highway'; 'Indian Summer'; 'Maggie M'Gill'.

LA WOMAN April 1971
(Elektra 75011; UK: Elektra K 42090/HMV C8816 [CD Box Set]) – 'The Changeling'; 'Love Her Madly'; 'Been Down So Long'; 'Cars Hiss By My Window'; 'LA Woman'; 'L'America'; 'Hyacinth House'; 'Crawling King Snake'; 'The Wasp (Texas Radio And The Big Beat)'; 'Riders On The Storm'.

OTHER VOICES October, 1971
(Elektra 75017) – 'In The Eye Of The Sun'; 'Variety Is The Spice Of Life'; 'Ships W/Sails'; 'Tightrope Ride'; 'Down On The Farm'; 'I'm Horny, I'm Stoned'; 'Wandering Musician'; 'Hang On To Your Life'.

FULL CIRCLE July, 1972
(Elektra 75038) – 'Get Up And Dance'; '4 Billion Souls'; 'Verdilac'; 'Hardwood Floor'; 'Good Rockin'; 'The Mosquito'; 'The Piano Bird'; 'It Slipped My Mind'; 'The Peking King And The New York Queen'.

JIM MORRISON, MUSIC BY THE DOORS

AN AMERICAN PRAYER November, 1978
(Elektra 5E-502; UK: Elektra K52111)
'Awake'; 'The Ghost Song'; 'Dawn's
Highway'; 'Newborn Awakening'; 'To Come
Of Age'; 'Black Polished Chrome/Latino
Chrome'; 'Angels And Sailors'; 'Stoned
Immaculate'; 'The Movie'; 'Curses,
Invocations'; 'American Night'; 'Roadhouse
Blues'; 'The World On Fire'; 'Lament'; 'The
Hitchhiker'; 'An American Prayer'.

Released on CD June, 1995
(Elektra 61812-2). All the above plus addi-
tional material: 'Babylon Fading'; 'Bird Of
Prey'; 'The Ghost Song'.

LIVE ALBUMS

ABSOLUTELY LIVE July, 1970
(Elektra 9002 (double album); UK: Elektra
2665 002/K262005) – 'Who Do You Love';
'Medley: Alabama Song, Back Door Man,
Love Hides, Five To One'; 'Build Me A
Woman'; 'When The Music's Over'; 'Close To
You'; 'Universal Mind'; 'Break On Thru, #2';
'The Celebration Of The Lizard'; 'Soul
Kitchen'.

ALIVE, SHE CRIED October, 1983
(Elektra 9 60269-1) – 'Gloria'; 'Light My Fire';
'You Make Me Real'; 'Texas Radio & The Big
Beat'; 'Love Me Two Times'; 'Little Red
Rooster'; 'Moonlight Drive'.

LIVE AT THE HOLLYWOOD BOWL June, 1987
(Elektra 9 60741-1) – 'Wake Up'; 'Light My
Fire'; 'Unknown Soldier'; 'A Little Game';
'The Hill Dwellers'; 'Spanish Caravan'.

IN CONCERT May, 1991
(Elektra 9 61082-2 [double CD]) – 'Who Do
You Love'; 'Medley: Alabama Song, Back
Door Man, Love Hides, Five To One'; 'Build
Me A Woman'; 'When The Music's Over';

'Universal Mind'; 'Petition The Lord With
Prayer'; 'Dead Cats, Dead Rats'; 'Break On
Through #2'; 'The Celebration Of The Lizard:
Lions In The Street, Wake Up, A Little Game,
The Hill Dwellers, Not To Touch The Earth,
Names Of The Kingdom, The Palace Of
Exile'; 'Soul Kitchen'; 'Roadhouse Blues';
'Gloria'; 'Light My Fire (Including 'Graveyard
Poem')'; 'You Make Me Real'; 'Texas Radio &
The Big Beat'; 'Love Me Two Times'; 'Little
Red Rooster'; 'Moonlight Drive'; 'Close To
You'; 'Unknown Soldier'; 'The End'.

COMPILATIONS

13 November, 1970, (Elektra 74079; UK: Elektra
K 42062) – 'Light My Fire'; 'People Are
Strange'; 'Back Door Man'; 'Moonlight
Drive'; 'Crystal Ship'; 'Roadhouse Blues';
'Touch Me'; 'Love Me Two Times'; 'You're
Lost Little Girl'; 'Hello, I Love You'; 'Wild
Child'; 'Unknown Soldier'; 'Land Ho!'.

WEIRD SCENES INSIDE THE GOLD MINE
January, 1972, (Elektra 2-6001 (double
album); UK Elektra K 62009) – 'Break On
Through'; 'Strange Days'; 'Blue Sunday';
'Shaman's Blues'; 'Love Street'; 'Peace Frog';
'The Wasp'; 'End Of The Night'; 'Love Her
Madly'; 'Spanish Caravan'; 'Ship Of Fools';
'The Spy'; 'The End'; 'Take It As It Comes';
'Runnin' Blue'; 'LA Woman'; 'Five To One';
'Who Scared You'; '(You Need Meat) Don't
Go No Further'; 'Riders On The Storm';
'Maggie M'Gill'; 'Horse Latitudes'; 'When
The Music's Over'.

THE BEST OF THE DOORS August, 1973
(Elektra EQ-5035 (quadrophonic); UK: Elektra
K2 42143) – 'Who Do You Love'; 'Soul
Kitchen'; 'Hello, I Love You'; 'People Are
Strange'; 'Riders On The Storm'; 'Touch Me';
'Love Her Madly'; 'Love Me Two Times';

'Take It As It Comes'; 'Moonlight Drive';
'Light My Fire'.

THE DOORS GREATEST HITS October, 1980
(Elektra 515) – 'Hello, I Love You'; 'Light My
Fire'; 'People Are Strange'; 'Love Me Two
Times'; 'Riders On The Storm'; Break On
Through'; 'Roadhouse Blues'; 'Not To Touch
The Earth'; 'Touch Me'; 'LA Woman'.

CLASSICS May, 1985
(Elektra 60417) – 'Crystal Ship'; 'Five To
One'; 'I Can't See Your Face In My Mind';
'Land Ho!'; 'Love Her Madly'; 'My Eyes Have
Seen You'; 'Peace Frog'; 'Roadhouse Blues';
'Strange Days'; 'Unknown Soldier'; 'Waiting
For The Sun'; 'The Wasp (Texas Radio & The
Big Beat)'; 'Wild Child'.

THE BEST OF THE DOORS July, 1987
(Elektra 60345-2 [double CD]) – 'Break On
Through'; 'Light My Fire'; 'The Crystal Ship';
'People Are Strange'; 'Strange Days'; 'Love
Me Two Times'; 'Alabama Song'; 'Five To
One'; 'Waiting For The Sun'; 'Spanish
Caravan'; 'When The Music's Over'; 'Hello, I
Love You'; 'Roadhouse Blues'; 'LA Woman';
'Riders On The Storm'; 'Touch Me'; 'Love Her
Madly'; 'The Unknown Soldier'; 'The End'.

index

Absolutely Live 111-19

Alabama Song 25, 41, 115

Albertano, Linda 29, 56, 57

Alive She Cried 54

All Day and All of the Night 61, 62

America, L' 121, 131-3

American Night 167-8

American Prayer, An (album) 9, 87, 103, 134, 135, 154-69

American Prayer, An (poem) 168

Amy, Curtis 80

Angels and Sailors 164-5

Antonioni, Michael 131-2

Apocalypse Now 132

Awake 163-4

Back Door Man 25, 106, 115

Baker, Tom 91

Barrow, Arthur 87, 165

Beach Boys, The 21, 64

Beatles, The 36-7, 157

Beaver, Paul 44, 46, 51

Beck, Julian 88

Been Down So Long 128-9

Been Down So Long It Looks Like Up to Me (Farina) 128

Benno, Marc 122

Berry, Chuck 69, 70, 96

Beyond Good and Evil (Nietzsche) 51

Bingenheimer, Rodney 15, 21

Birth of Tragedy (Out of the Spirit of Music) (Nietzsche) 50

Black Polished Chrome/Latino Chrome 164-5

Blake, William 16

Blakey, Art 24

Blue Sunday 104

Body, Paul 17, 38, 42, 73, 156

Booker T and the MGs 85

Botnick, Bruce 25, 42, 122, 135

Break on Through 26-7

Break on Through 2 117

Brecht, Bertolt 25

Bridge, The (Crane) 135

Buckley, Tim 151

Build Me a Woman 114-15

Byrds, The 47

Carpenter, John 42, 82

Cars Hiss By My Window 121, 129

Celebration of the Lizard, The 58, 61, 63, 112, 117-18

Celine, Louis Ferdinand 32-3

Changeling, The 121, 126

City of Night 130

Clear Light 42, 58, 60

Columbia Records 18-19, 41

Conrad, Jack 144

Cooper, Alice 96

Coppola, Francis Ford 132

Courson, Corky 158

Courson, Pamela: 155; and Jim Morrison 123; and *Morrison Hotel* 96, 100, 102, 106-7; and *Strange Days* 47; 73; and *The Doors* 31; and *Waiting for the Sun* 62, 71

Crane, Hart 135

Crawling King Snake 121

Crosby, Stills, Nash & Young 58

Crystal Ship, The 28

Curses/Invocations 165, 167

Darrow, Chris 21, 46, 47

Davies, Ray 61

Dawn's Highway 103, 163-4

Densmore, John: creation of *The Doors* 17-18, 19; early life 12; and Jim Morrison 123; and *Morrison Hotel* 109; musical influences 24; and *Strange Days* 53; and *The Doors* 37; and *The Soft Parade* 86; and *Waiting for the Sun* 72

Diddley, Bo 112, 113

Didion, Joan 60

Diltz, Henry 21, 68-9, 78, 93

Dixon, Willy 25, 106

Do it 82

Dolenz, Micky 46

Doors, The 24-39

Doors of Perception, The (Huxley) 26

Domino, Fats 12

Down on the Farm 146

Easy Ride 83-4

Elektra 21, 25, 26, 92, 121, 142, 157

End, The 37-9, 41

End of the Night 32-3

Fagan, Len 26

Farina, Richard 128

Farrow, Mia 47

Feast of Friends 51, 101

Feliciano, Jose 31

Ferrara, Paul 101

Five to One 58, 72-3, 115

Fong-Terres, Ben 31

Ford, Michael C. 14, 15, 92, 165, 168

Fornatale, Pete 49

4 Billion Souls 152

Fowley, Kim: 12, 13, 16, 18, 20; and *An American Prayer* 162; and *Morrison Hotel* 96; and *Other Voices* 142; and *Strange Days* 51; and *The Doors* 27, 28; and *Waiting for the Sun* 62

Fowlie, Wallace 85

Franklin, Aretha 85

Frazer J.G. 64

Fujikawa, Dorothy 17, 155

Full Circle 149-55

Gary, Bruce 18, 20, 28, 129, 151, 156, 163

Gazzari's 56-7

Get Up and Dance 152

Ghost Song 103-4

Glimpses (Shiner) 60

Golden Bough, The (Frazer) 63-4

Goldman, Albert 27

Goldstein, Richard 69, 80, 113

Good Rockin Tonight 150

Greenspoon, Jimmy 12, 13, 19, 32, 63, 73

Haeny, John 157, 158, 165

Hang on to Your Life 147
Haran, Ronnie 21, 37
Hardwood Floor 153
Harris, Heather 16
Hello, I Love You 61-2
Hendrix, Jimi 25, 86, 121
Hill, Babe 103
Hitchhiker, The 167-8
Hoffman, Abbie 46
Holzman, Adam 61-2
Holzman, Jac 21, 23, and *The Doors* 25, 29, 37; and *Other Voices* 142
Hooker, John Lee 121
Hopkins, Jerry 25, 51, 58, 162-3
Horse Latitudes 50-1, 54
Huxley, Aldous 16, 26
HWY 78, 135, 168
Hyacinth House 133

I Can't See Your Face 56, 71
I Looked at You 32
I'm Horny I'm Stoned 147
In the Eye of the Sun 144
Indian Summer 107
It Slipped My Mind 155
Isle of Wight festival 125

Jackson, Blair 25, 37, 49, 159
James, Billy 18-19, 25, 41
James, Lizze 80, 106
Jefferson Airplane 68, 69
Jones, Brian 146
Jones, Elvin 24
Joplin, Janis 121
Journey to the End of the Night (Celine) 32-3

Kafka, Franz 14, 51, 115
Kerouac, Jack 51
Kinks, The 62
Klein, Bobby 30, 83
Knack, The 18, 129
Knechtel, Larry 25
Krieger, Lynn 79

Krieger, Robby: and *An American Prayer* 158, 165; creation of *The Doors* 19; early life 12; and *Full Circle* 150, 155; and *L.A. Woman* 127; and *Morrison Hotel* 92, 104, 109; musical influences 24, 36-7, 86; and *Other Voices* 144, 147; as song writer 18, 30, 66, 69-70, 78-80, 82, 87-8, 118; and *Strange Days* 41, 53, 54; and *The Doors* 30; and *The Soft Parade* 78-80, 82, 86, 87-8; and *Waiting for the Sun* 58, 66, 69-71, 72
Kubernick, Harvey 12, 16, 39, 62-3, 118, 162, 167

L.A. Woman (album) 120-37, 157
L.A. Woman (song) 130-1
Lament 167-8
Land Ho! 104
Laurel Canyon Boulevard 62, 63
Laurence, Paul 51
Lee, Arthur 17
Lennon, John 96
Light My Fire 25, 28, 30-1, 72
Lisciandro, Frank 157
Little Red Rooster 106
London Fog 20-1, 56
Lords, The: Notes on Vision (Morrison) 78, 92
Love 17
Love Her Madly 126-8
Love Hides 115
Love Me Two Times 41, 48-9
Love Street 63
Lovin' Spoonful 100
Lubahn, Doug 42

MacClure, Michael 91, 168
Mack, Lonnie 100, 109
Maggie M'Gill 106, 109
Maharisi Mahesh Yogi 17, 35, 37, 155
Mailer, Norman 91-2
Manzarek, Ray: and *Absolutely Live* 113; and *An American Prayer* 159, 162, 163, 164, 167-8; creation of *The Doors* 17-18, 19; early life 12; and *Full Circle*

151, 155; and *Morrison Hotel* 109; musical influences 24; and *Other Voices* 144, 145-6; as soloist 158; and *Strange Days* 46, 49, 51, 53-4; and *The Doors* 25, 26, 27, 30, 32, 37; and *The Soft Parade* 77; at UCLA 15-18
Matheu, Robert 72, 159
Miller, Henry 105, 167
Monkees, The 46
Monterey Pop Festival 86
Moonlight Drive 18, 19, 41, 51, 53-4
Morrison, Clara 13, 38
Morrison, Jim: and *Absolutely Live* 112-19; and *An American Prayer* 155-69; arrested 48-9; character 10; creation of *The Doors* 17-21; death 123, 156; early life 12-15, 67, 84, 103, 133-4; and *L.A. Woman* 121-37; literary influences 14, 16, 24, 26, 28, 32-3, 50-1, 63-4, 84-5, 104, 105-7, 115, 122, 135; and *Morrison Hotel* 91-109; musical influences 12, 14 47; in Paris 122-3; poetry 58, 61, 78, 92, 133-4, 155-69; as song writer 10, 12; and *Strange Days* 41-57; and *The Doors* 24-39; trial 121; at UCLA 15-17; and *The Soft Parade* 76-89; and *Waiting for the Sun* 58-73
Morrison, Patricia Kennealy: and *Absolutely Live* 112, 118; and Jim Morrison 17, 28, 92, 114-15, 123; and *L.A. Woman* 126, 134; and *Morrison Hotel* 100; and *Strange Days* 56, 57; and *The Soft Parade* 76; and *Waiting for the Sun* 64
Morrison, Steve 13, 38
Morrison Hotel 90-109
Mosquito, The 154-5
Movies, The 165, 167
My Eyes Have Seen You 41, 55
My Wild Love 58, 71

Neapolitan, Ray 100, 103, 145
Neuwirth, Bobby 64

index

New Creatures (Morrison) 78, 92

Newborn Awakening 163-4

Nietzsche, Friedrich 14, 50, 51

Nin, Anais 104, 105-7

No One Here Gets Out Alive (Hopkins & Sugerman) 162-3

Not to Touch the Earth 63-4, 117

On the Road (Kerouac) 51

Other Voices 141-7

Pabst, Florentine 157

Peace Frog 102-3

Peckinpah, Sam 8

Peking King and the New York Queen, The 155

People are Strange 41, 54

Piano Bird, The 154

Poet's Drams, The 165, 167

Praise for an Urn (Crane) 135

Presley, Elvis 12, 14

Queen of the Highway 106-7

Raphael, Judy 15-16, 20, 38-9, 53

Rechy, John 130

Redding, Otis 85-6

Rick & The Ravens 16, 17

Riders on the Storm (book) (Densmore) 37, 72

Riders on the Storm (song) 135

Rimbaud, Arthur 84-5

Rimbaud and Morrison: The Rebel as Poet (Fowlie) 85

Rise and Fall of the City of Mahogany, The (Weill & Brecht) 25

Roadhouse Blues 96, 100, 109, 167-8

Rothchild, Paul 21, and *Absolutely Live* 112; and *An American Prayer* 159, 165, 167; and *L.A. Woman* 121-2, 127-8; and *Morrison Hotel* 100, 103; and *Strange Days* 42, 47, 49; and *The Doors* 25, 29, 30-1, 37-8, 39; and *The Soft Parade* 76, 78, 89; and *Waiting for the Sun* 58

Ruff, Willie 145

Runnin' Blue 79, 85-6

Season in Hell, A (Rimbaud) 85

Sebastian, John 100

Shaman's Blues 80, 82

Shankar, Ravi 36-7

Shiner, Lew 60

Ship of Fools 104

Ships W/Sails 145

Siddons, Bill 13, 14, 18; and *Absolutely Live* 113; and *An American Prayer* 159, 162; and *Full Circle* 151; and *L.A. Woman* 122-3, 132, 133; and *Other Voices* 142; and *Strange Days* 48, 50, 51, 54; and *The Doors* 31, 35; and *The Soft Parade* 76, 77, 78, 80, 82, 83

Sinatra, Frank 47

Smothers Brothers' Comedy Hour 79-80

Soft Parade, The (album) 18, 75-89

Soft Parade, The (song) 88-9

Soul Kitchen 27, 41

Spanish Caravan 69-70

Spy, The 105-6

Stavers, Gloria 64

Stevenson, Salli 93, 117

Stoned Immaculate 134, 157, 164-5

Strange Days (album) 41-57

Strange Days (book) (Morrison) 100

Strange Days (song) 44, 46

Sugerman, Danny 162-3

Summer's Almost Gone 64-5

Take it as it Comes 36-7

Taylor, Dallas 58, 60, 157

Tell All the People 78, 79, 82, 83

Three Dog Night 13, 63

Tightrope Ride 145-6

To Come of Age 164-5

Touch Me 78-80

Trip, The 27

Tropic of Cancer (Miller) 105

Twentieth Century Fox 29

Unhappy Girl 49-50

Universal Mind 116-17

Unknown Soldier, The 58, 66-9

Valentine, Elmer 38

Variety is the Spice of Life 144-5

Verdilac 152-3

Waiting for the Sun (album) 58-73

Waiting for the Sun (song) 101

Warhol, Andy 31, 86

Weill, Kurt 25

Wandering Musician 147

Wasp, The 133-4

We Could be so Good Together 71

Weird Scenes Inside the Goldmine 88, 127, 150

When the Music's Over 41, 56-7, 58

Whiskey a Go Go 17, 21, 37, 56

White Trash Quintet, The 15

Who Do You Love 112, 113

Who Scared You 88

Wild Child 84-5

Wilson, Brian 64

Wintertime Love 66

Wishful Sinful 79, 87-8

Woodstock Festival 96

World on Fire 167-8

Yardbirds, The 131

Yes, the River Knows 72

You Make Me Real 102

(You Need Meat) Don't Go No Further 127

You're Lost Little Girl 47

Zabrieskie Point 131-2

Zappa, Frank 62, 151